LMS
ENGINE SHEDS

Derby, heart of the Midland Empire.

LMS
ENGINE SHEDS

Their History and Development

VOLUME TWO

THE MIDLAND RAILWAY

by

Chris Hawkins & George Reeve

WILD SWAN PUBLICATIONS LTD.

ISBN No. 0 906867 05 3

FOR
ELSIE, DENNIS, MAY and GEORGE

Designed by Paul Karau
Typesetting by Berkshire Publishing Services
Photo reproduction and offset plates by Oxford Litho Plates Ltd.
Printed by Didcot Press, Didcot, Oxon

Published by
WILD SWAN PUBLICATIONS LTD.,
Hopgoods Farm Cottage, Upper Bucklebury, Berks.

Contents

DRAWING SCALES

Most of the track plans have been reproduced at a uniform scale of approximately two chains to one inch in order to show the comparative sizes of various locations. However, where this has not been possible these appear at a scale of approximately four chains to one inch. Drawings of structures have mainly been reproduced at recognised modelling scales of 2, 3 and 4 mm to one foot as space permits.

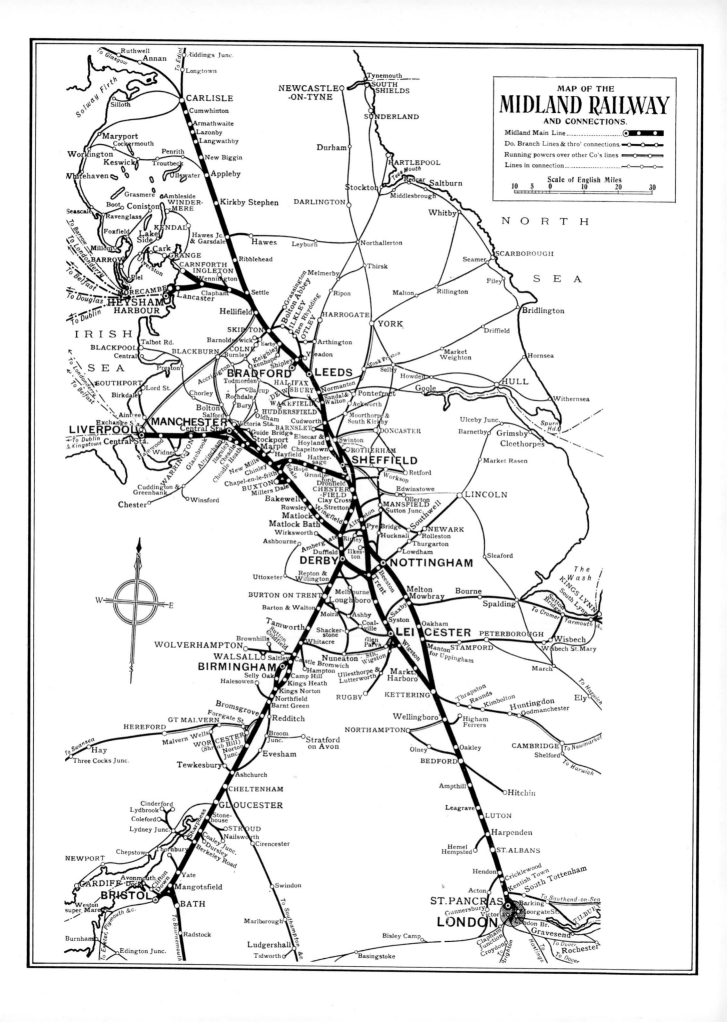

Introduction

THIS second volume of *LMS Engine Sheds* recounts the history of those sheds inherited from the Midland Railway. The sheds concerned are once more those which operated throughout the LMS period to 1947, the very eve of Nationalisation, and again a separate section deals briefly with those closed prior to 1947.

Great changes were wrought during the relatively short heyday of the 'Big Four' years. The forced partnership of great companies, widely at variance in their basic practices and concepts, meant that agreed, coherent and long term policies took crucial years to emerge. The developments which finally forged the London Midland and Scottish Railway were thus effectively concentrated into the 1930s, and were cut short by the storm of war.

Changes concerning the LMS Locomotive Department were described in detail in Volume One; they affected the sheds of all the pre-Grouping companies and the principal features were embodied in two main projects. The first was a far-reaching programme inaugurated in 1933 which saw many of the most important depots equipped with mechanical coal and ash handling apparatus and improved layouts. Many of the depots were rebuilt with modern roofs in various standard styles, though these particular benefits applied in the main to the great 'steam sheds' of London North Western and Lancashire and Yorkshire origin. The high, airy Midland roundhouses resisted the corrosive effects of their inhabitants to a greater degree than engine sheds elsewhere on the system and so, apparently, did the straight sheds of Midland origin. (The ubiquitous re-roofing on the Western Division was hardly known on the former Midland lines). The first proposals for rebuilding the roundhouses appeared shortly after the war, in 1946, for new roofs at Belle Vue and Saltley, but BR eventually undertook the bulk of the work. Two main styles were used, one involving the replacement of the great pitched roofs by an unattractive squat design using tubular, asbestos-cement smoke funnels, the other a more satisfactory steel and glass arrangement.

Divisional independence was not allowed to stand in the way of mechanical and layout improvements, however, and many of the larger ex-MR depots had their distinctive coaling stages replaced by a variety of concrete plants, erected by various private contractors. Water treatment

Victorian Industrial Pride. Two immaculate Midland engines pose with various attendant staff from 'the artisan classes' around 1895. The backdrop is the fine frontage of Bournville roundhouse, only recently opened. The building was amongst the last of its type and the level of decorative adornment can be seen to have waned markedly since the 1870s.

Courtesy Leicester Museum

1

plants and vacuum operated turntables were also applied to ex-Midland sheds, but these general developments, including drawings and diagrams, are dealt with in Volume One.

Accompanying all this was an organisational revolution inaugurated in 1935 and entitled the 'Motive Power Area Locomotive Supply, Repair, Concentration and Garage Scheme'. Its main feature was the rearrangement of the sheds into a series of districts. Based on former Midland practice, the system became familiar through its adoption by British Railways. Once again details can be found in Volume One, but briefly, districts were divided into a number of 'garage' sheds, grouped under a main 'concentration' depot, where improved mechanical facilities were in many cases provided and where repair work was concentrated. The most significant outcome of all this was that a number of sheds either closed completely or had their accommodation reduced. The old Midland circular shed at Normanton was demolished, leaving only the straight shed (erected by the MR for the L & Y), the four road straight shed at Manningham was demolished and many ex-MR depots closed completely, some of them formerly of great importance. There were a number of reasons for this. Firstly, by 1936 the total number of locomotives in use had been reduced by over a quarter, to 7,691, and the hours spent in traffic together with the daily mileage of individual engines had also greatly increased. All this was due in the main to increased mechanisation at the sheds. The Depression was the second factor, leading to the storage of many engines and thirdly, the increasing number of modern designs, requiring less maintenance than their predecessors, meant that less accommodation was necessary.

CODING

The Midland had an engine shed code numbered from 1 to 33 but the familiar smokebox door plates were a relatively late development. They were introduced in 1898 and were initially fitted inside the cab on the back of the spectacle plate. Subsequently a few engines carried them on the outside of the spectacle plate and one is known to have carried a shed plate on the front buffer beam. The practice of fitting them on the lower part of the smokebox door was begun in 1908-9 and this position became standard, with only a few exceptions on non-MR engines in LMS and BR days.

In 1905 the railway press reported that "up to now Midland Railway locomotives have carried just MR on their buffer beams but now they will carry thus:

$$M \begin{smallmatrix} NOTTM \\ 453 \end{smallmatrix} R \text{ ''}$$

This practice was not apparently adopted on any great scale and only seven examples are known, all but one Nottingham engines.

In 1911 the code was as follows:

1	DERBY, W.E.	3	SALTLEY
2	BURTON		3a Bournville
	2a Overseal		3b Walsall
	2b Stoke		3c Redditch

4	WORCESTER	19	LIVERPOOL
	4a Bromsgrove		19a Walton
	4b Malvern		19b Sandhills
5	BRECON		19c Widnes
	5a Hereford	20	BUXTON
6	UPPER BANK		20a Rowsley
	6a Gurnos	21	BELLE VUE
7	GLOUCESTER		21a Trafford Park
	7a Tewkesbury		21b Heaton Mersey
	7b Evesham		21c Northwich
	7c Dursley		21d Lower Darwen
8	BRISTOL		21e Ancoats, Hyde *
	8a Bath	22	WESTHOUSES
	8b Thornbury	23	HASLAND
9	PETERBOROUGH	24	STAVELEY
	9a Bourne		24a Sheepbridge
10	LEICESTER	25	SHEFFIELD
	10a Stockingford		25a Millhouses
	10b Coalville		25b Canklow
	10c West Bridge		25c Doncaster
11	WIGSTON	26	NORMANTON
12	KETTERING		26a Wakefield
	12a Cambridge	27	YORK
13	WELLINGBOROUGH	28	LEEDS
	13a Northampton		28a Stourton
14	BEDFORD	29	MANNINGHAM
	14a Hitchin		29a Keighley
15	CRICKLEWOOD		29b Ilkley
	15a St. Albans	30	SKIPTON
16	LONDON		30a Hellifield
	16a Poplar		30b Colne
17	TOTON		30c Barnoldswick
18	NOTTINGHAM	31	CARNFORTH
	18a Mansfield	32	LANCASTER
	18b Kirkby	33	CARLISLE
	18c Lincoln		33a Appleby
	18d Southwell		

See notes on page 236.

The list bore the signature of Sandham John Symes, soon to become Chief Draughtsman at Derby and is reproduced by courtesy of Mr. J. B. Radford. The exact date, noted by Symes, is 26th June 1911.

Engines were allocated to districts only and sub-shed codes were not carried, but in early LMS days four subsheds were provided with plates, the suffix letter appearing beside the number and not beneath as in the later 1935 scheme. The sheds involved were Heaton Mersey 21B, Canklow 25B, Royston 26A (built by the LMS but part of the Midland Division) and Stourton 28A.

The first attempt by the LMS to sort out its engine sheds into some sensible order came in August 1925 when the office of the 'Chief General Superintendent, Derby' compiled the list given in Volume 1.

It was a somewhat chaotic list with numerous subsequent alterations and gave way to a divisional system based on each pre-Grouping company, the Midland emerging as opposite. Brecon and Upper Bank had formerly been shed Nos. 5 and 6 but with the final absorption of the S & DJR in that year these numbers were given to Templecombe and Highbridge. The LTSR sheds had not hitherto had codes and from the same date were given Nos. 34, 35, 36 and 37. Carnforth MR (shed No. 31) although remaining in use had come under the control of the LNW shed in 1926, its engines carrying Western Division No. 36 plates.

1	DERBY	9	PETERBOROUGH
2	BURTON		Bourne
	Overseal	10	LEICESTER
3	SALTLEY		Coalville
	Bournville		Stockingford
	Redditch	11	WIGSTON
	Stratford on Avon	12	KETTERING
	Blisworth		Cambridge
4	WORCESTER	13	WELLINGBOROUGH
	Bromsgrove	14	BEDFORD
	Malvern	15	CRICKLEWOOD
5	TEMPLECOMBE		St. Albans
6	HIGHBRIDGE	16	KENTISH TOWN
	Wells	17	TOTON
7	GLOUCESTER	18	NOTTINGHAM
	Evesham		Mansfield
	Tewkesbury		Kirkby
	Dursley		Lincoln
	Ashchurch		Southwell
8	BRISTOL	19	LIVERPOOL
	Bath		Walton
	Thornbury	20	BUXTON
	Radstock		Rowsley
	Bournemouth		

21	BELLE VUE
	Trafford Park
	Heaton Mersey
	Northwich
22	WESTHOUSES
23	HASLAND
24	STAVELEY
	Sheepbridge
25	SHEFFIELD
	Canklow
	Millhouses
26	NORMANTON
27	YORK
28	LEEDS
	Stourton
29	MANNINGHAM
	Keighley
	Ilkley
30	SKIPTON
	Hellifield
	Ingleton
32	LANCASTER
33	CARLISLE
34	PLAISTOW
35	TILBURY
36	UPMINSTER
37	SHOEBURYNESS

Letter designation for sub-sheds reappeared of course with the LMS reorganisation scheme of 1935. It became familiar through its adoption by BR and though given in Volume 1 is repeated below.

In a much earlier period an entirely different method of shed identification was employed and E. L. Ahrons refers to it in one of his series of articles after the First World War. The reference is part of a delightful story concerning sheds and their engines and there is every reason for repeating it here:

On one occasion in the early eighties a Midland locomotive disappeared for a time. It was one of the 800 class, No. 805, then stationed at Kentish Town and one fine morning it started

---

L.M.S. SHEDS IN 1947

1A	WILLESDEN	5C	Stafford	12C	Penrith	18A	TOTON	23A	BANK HALL	29A	PERTH
1B	Camden	5D	Stoke	12D	Workington	18B	Westhouses	23B	Aintree		Crieff
1C	Watford	5E	Alsager	12E	Moor Row	18C	Hasland	23C	Southport		Aberfeldy
		5F	Uttoxeter	12F	Beattock	18D	Staveley	23D	Wigan		Blair Atholl
2A	RUGBY				Lockerbie					29B	Aberdeen
	Market Harborough	6A	CHESTER	12G	Dumfries	19A	SHEFFIELD	24A	ACCRINGTON	29C	Dundee
	Seaton	6B	Mold Junction		Kirkcudbright	19B	Millhouses	24B	Rose Grove	29D	Forfar
2B	Bletchley	6C	Birkenhead	12H	Stranraer	19C	Canklow	24C	Lostock Hall		Arbroath
	Leighton Buzzard				Newton Stewart	19D	Heaton Mersey	24D	Lower Darwen		Brechin
	Newport Pagnell	7A	LLANDUDNO JUNCTION	13A	PLAISTOW	19E	Belle Vue	24E	Blackpool		
	Oxford	7B	Bangor	13B	Devons Road	19F	Trafford Park		Blackpool North	30A	CORKERHILL
	Aylesbury	7C	Holyhead	13C	Tilbury			24F	Fleetwood	30B	Hurlford
2C	Northampton	7D	Rhyl	13D	Shoeburyness	20A	LEEDS				Beith
2D	Nuneaton		Denbigh	13E	Upminster	20B	Stourton	25A	WAKEFIELD		Muirkirk
2E	Warwick					20C	Royston	25B	Huddersfield	30C	Ardrossan
2F	Coventry	8A	EDGE HILL	14A	CRICKLEWOOD	20D	Normanton	25C	Goole	30D	Ayr
		8B	Warrington	14B	Kentish Town	20E	Manningham	25D	Mirfield		
3A	BESCOT		Arpley	14C	St. Albans		Ilkley	25E	Sowerby Bridge	31A	ST. ROLLOX
3B	Bushbury	8C	Speke Junction			20F	Skipton	25F	Low Moor	31B	Stirling
3C	Walsall	8D	Widnes	15A	WELLINGBOROUGH		Keighley	25G	Farnley Junction		Killin
3D	Aston			15B	Kettering	20G	Hellifield			31C	Oban
3E	Monument Lane	9A	LONGSIGHT	15C	Leicester		Ingleton	26A	NEWTON HEATH		Ballachulish
	Tipton	9B	Stockport	15D	Bedford	20H	Lancaster	26B	Agecroft	31D	Grangemouth
		9C	Macclesfield					26C	Bolton	31E	Dawsholm
4A	SHREWSBURY	9D	Buxton	16A	NOTTINGHAM	21A	SALTLEY	26D	Bury		Dumbarton
	Craven Arms				Southwell	21B	Bournville	26E	Bacup		Yoker
	Ludlow	10A	SPRINGS BRANCH		Lincoln		Redditch	26F	Lees		
	Knighton	10B	Preston	16B	Peterborough	21C	Bromsgrove			32A	INVERNESS
	Builth Road	10C	Patricroft	16C	Kirkby-in-Ashfield	21D	Stratford-on-Avon	27A	POLMADIE		Dingwall
	Coalport	10D	Plodder Lane	16D	Mansfield			27B	Greenock Ladyburn		Kyle of Lochalsh
	Clee Hill	10E	Sutton Oak			22A	BRISTOL		Greenock Princes Pier		Helmsdale
4B	Swansea			17A	DERBY	22B	Gloucester	27C	Hamilton		Dornoch
	Llandovery	11A	CARNFORTH	17B	Burton		Dursley				Fort George
4C	Upper Bank	11B	Barrow		Overseal		Tewkesbury	28A	MOTHERWELL		Fortrose
	Gurnos		Coniston		Horninglow	22C	Bath	28B	Edinburgh		Tain
4D	Abergavenny	11D	Oxenholme	17C	Coalville		Radstock		Seafield *		Wick
4E	Tredegar	11E	Tebay	17D	Rowsley		Branksome	28C	Carstairs		Thurso
					Cromford	22D	Templecombe			32B	Aviemore
5A	CREWE NORTH	12A	CARLISLE KINGMOOR		Middleton Top	22E	Highbridge			32C	Forres
	Whitchurch	12B	Carlisle Upperby		Sheep Pasture		Wells				Keith
5B	Crewe South										

* Seafield had in fact been handed over to the LNER during the war but of course became part of the Scottish Region along with Edinburgh, etc., following Nationalisation.

The Midland was no different from other major companies in that engine yards with turntables, etc. were provided at important stations, yards and junctions. Barlow's great arch looms in the background of St. Pancras yard in pre-Grouping days. Perhaps the most interesting feature is the Great Eastern 2–4–0, the GER using St. Pancras as its 'West End Terminus' for many years prior to 1917. GE engines worked passenger trains to Lowestoft, Norwich and Yarmouth via Kentish Town and South Tottenham, the price being Midland access to the London Docks via Great Eastern metals.

Collection B. Hilton

out from St. Pancras with a 'special' for Northampton. On its arrival there, there was a sudden call for an engine to work a special goods train of boots or other 'perishables' — destination, Wigston. I am not sure as to the exact sequence of the subsequent movements of the engine, but they were somewhat after the following manner. The Northampton locomotive people had a good deal of frail human nature embodied in their make-up, and as 805 did not belong to them and they were hard up for engines, it was promptly requisitioned for the boots, with a fresh set of men. The London men returned home by train, taking their own head lamps which denoted the station of the engine, for in those days each Midland driver had his own set of lamps with his name and shed painted on them. There seems to have been an epidemic of special trains on that day, for no sooner had the engine turned up at Wigston than it was commandeered for a special goods to Birmingham. Eventually, it

wandered to Bristol, who sent it back to Gloucester, and the locomotive people at the latter shed, not knowing to which station it belonged, put it into a siding behind some coal wagons pending enquiries, and then proceeded to forget all about it.

A day or two later, Kentish Town found they were minus an important engine, and made enquiries from Northampton who promptly communicated with Wigston, &c., &c. The correspondence grew rapidly in volume on the snowball system, but there was a hitch somewhere, as somebody had omitted to record one of the chess-board moves made by the engine, so that at the return of stock at the end of the month the engine was reported as missing. A circular letter to all the locomotive depots on the line resulted in the eventual discovery of 805, grazing peacefully in the Gloucester siding, but it was some time before Kentish Town saw its long lost engine again.

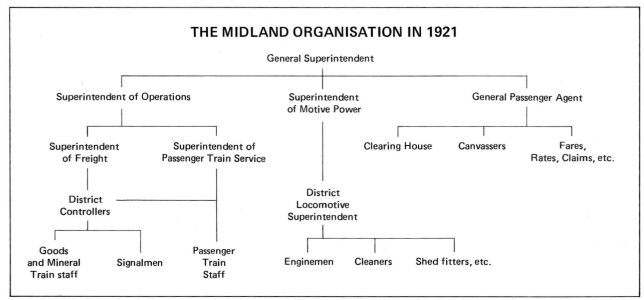

THE MIDLAND ORGANISATION IN 1921

CHAPTER ONE

The Midland Railway 'Engine Houses'

ARISING from the first great railway amalgamation, the Midland was created in 1844 from three lesser companies, the North Midland Railway, the Midland Counties Railway and the Birmingham and Derby Junction Railway. The original stock of less than a hundred locomotives rose to 499 by 1863 and by 1905 stood at 2,900. Staff in the Locomotive Department over the same period rose from 2,500 to 17,800. In a period of prodigious railway growth the Midland was especially successful, penetrating most areas of the country. The company had grown to such an extent that by 1904 (even before the acquisition of the London, Tilbury & Southend lines) a writer in the *Railway Magazine* noted:

"It is highly probable that those who 'christened' the Midland Railway, when, in 1844, it assumed its present name, would have selected a far more comprehensive title had they foreseen anything of the future greatness that awaited their undertaking. The modest designation of this most ubiquitous of all British railways is now as great a misnomer as is (at the opposite extreme) that of the Manchester and Milford Railway, for the Midland counties now represent but a small portion of the immense territory from which the Midland Railway draws its traffic.

Not content with its conquest of England, from the bleak hills of the north to sunny Bournemouth, and from the western port of Bristol to the Suffolk coast at Lowestoft, the mighty giant must needs invade the sister countries, and hence we have the unique spectacle of a single railway owning territory in all four divisions of the United Kingdom. In Scotland, it is true, its lines are only 'joint' and there its locomotives are never seen; while in Ireland its newly acquired territory is at present worked by rolling-stock which bears little resemblance to that on the parent system. In Wales, on the other hand, the Midland locomotives and coaches work not only the traffic on their own lines, but also exercise running powers over three of the other Welsh railways."

This 'most ubiquitous of modern railways' followed a steady, balanced course in everything it did and the development of the Locomotive Department and sheds reflected this. It declined to abandon the roundhouse concept, instead developing them further and resisting the temptation to build large new engines where traffic could be adapted to suit a smaller, already available type. By the Grouping it was the only major company, apart from the South Eastern and Chatham Railway, to rely entirely on four coupled locos for its express turns, odd in itself, but acquiring something of the perverse when the severe gradients abounding on the Midland system are taken into account. From the Lickey in the south to Ais Gill (Ais Ghyll for many years) major inclines were regular features. Even more surprisingly, the vast freight and mineral traffic, in terms of mileage the greatest single amount in the country, was handled by nothing larger than 0–6–0s, nearly 1,500 of them. The MR was able to operate its express services with less than sixty class '4' locomotives by strictly limiting the loads they were expected to handle and 'little and often' was a reasonable if over-simplified description of the operating practice. In the 1870s nearly all the shunting work was done by tender engines and there were only thirty-six non-passenger tanks on the line. Local passenger work was entrusted to a collection of older engines long past their prime, but by the close of Johnson's reign, a host of bustling 0–4–4Ts was available. There had certainly been a lack of engines for local work on the Midland which, according to E. L. Ahrons, 'was far behind the Great Western and London and North Western Railways in this respect. In 1875/76 Mr. Johnson set about remedying this deficiency.' In reality, passenger traffic was of relatively little importance, the wealth of the Midland resting firmly on coal. In 1912, for instance, when the much smaller London and Tilbury and Southend company was absorbed, total passenger receipts increased by over 50%!

Remarkable not only for their diminutive power and size, the MR's locos also displayed an extreme longevity, as Alan Rannie, MA, noted in 1946. Curved double frames and spring balance safety valves were common on many Midland engines at the Grouping and over twenty years later had still not completely disappeared. Ahrons, as early as 1919, was moved to comment on the extraordinary antiquity of some of the locos, even then: 'For long service some of the Midland goods engines can give points and a beating to any locomotives with which I am acquainted.' He went on to note that several goods locos had been at Peterborough shed for over fifty years and some double-framed goods engines at Nottingham were still at work, having been introduced in 1860/61.

The Midland therefore was a company possessing a high degree of stability and orderliness, operating at the heart of the British railway system. Its unchanging and

Nos. '2' and '3' sheds at Derby circa 1888, 'No. 2' on the left still at this time housing engines in steam.　　*Collection V. Forster*

Inside the original North Midland Railway 'round shed' designed by Francis Thompson in 1838. Actually polygonal in plan, with sixteen sides, it had a diameter of 130 feet and a conical roof over 48 feet high. By 1905 when this view was taken it had long been used for engine repair work.

National Railway Museum

Johnson 2—4—0 No. 131 and 0—6—0T No. 1720 outside the 'No. 3' shed at Derby. The early 'round sheds' had expanded to cover twenty-four roads, a total which formed the basis of all the subsequent roundhouse variations.

Collection J. B. Radford

unchanged ways led to a difficult period in LMS days but its sheds, particularly the well lit and spacious roundhouses, proved to be among the best run and maintained of all the varied LMS inheritance.

'ENGINE HOUSES' ROUND AND SQUARE

The 'Engine Houses' of the Midland and its immediate predecessors, in common with many other companies of this period, took the form of circular roundhouses. With the rapid growth in locomotive sizes this form of building was soon rejected by the majority of companies, but the Midland Railway persevered with the concept, abandoning its 'circular sheds' in favour of square buildings, again housing a turntable and radiating spurs. The first circular sheds of pre-Midland vintage had contained sixteen roads, but new ones were soon enlarged to cover twenty-four roads, a total retained for the subsequent square buildings. The square 'turntable unit' sheds came to be associated with the Midland to a degree only seen on two other railways, the Great Western and the North Eastern, and accommodation at any one depot could be doubled, trebled etc. by the simple addition of further sheds alongside, behind, in front, or wherever. The GWR and NER were rather more conservative in the arrangements they adopted, usually siting sheds in rows or compact squares but on the Midland almost any configuration was possible, according to site variations. Twenty-four road circular sheds had appeared

at most of the Midland's important locations by the late 1850s, including Leicester (adjacent to an earlier sixteen road building), Birmingham, Gloucester and Sheffield. Developments at Derby neatly illustrate the evolution of the Midland roundhouse. The town, now a city, was the hub of the system and the various 'generations' in roundhouse design were for many years all visible together, most of the circular sheds at other sites being swept away soon after their displacement by the new square buildings.

The first 'Round Engine Shed' at Derby was opened by the North Midland Railway in 1839 and was supplemented by a second, slightly larger building, of similar appearance, in 1847. Like many other buildings, the first roundhouse at Derby was designed by Francis Thompson and like all other 'circular' sheds was actually polygonal in plan. The roof beams were supported on cast iron columns, the high conical roof was slated and each of its sixteen roads was intended to stable two engines. Yet a third building was soon required and a further circular shed, to the same general design but enlarged to cover twenty-four roads, was erected in 1852. The whole series was eventually crowned by a large double square shed erected in the 1890s.

The decade of the 1860s was one of extraordinary expansion, even for a railway of the Midland's far-reaching ambition, climaxed by the completion of the London Extension and the opening of St. Pancras in October 1868. New sheds were required not only for London but at

Roundhouses were ever prone to inadvertent destruction! Techniques employed to minimise damage in later years made use of relatively thin brick screens supported by a pre-stressed concrete frame. Thus in LMS days if any engine repeated the exploits of Midland 0—6—0WT No. 1095A no damage of any structural import was sustained.

National Railway Museum

other major centres where traffic would inevitably increase. The best example of this was Burton, where a large new shed was erected less than two years after the opening of St. Pancras and the immediate upsurge in beer traffic to London. The anticipated stimulus to traffic from new routes was the major factor at this time in the opening of a number of new sheds, at Holbeck, Saltley, Nottingham, etc.

Beginning with the new London shed at Kentish Town, Matthew Kirtley, the Midland's Locomotive Carriage & Wagon Superintendent, instigated a new roundhouse design, of square outline and, once again, containing twenty-four roads. Originally conceived in 1864, when Holbeck was first planned, these early sheds were characterised by two different sets of gables, with a neat and aesthetically pleasing result. The roof pitches were arranged in series at 90° to each other, but this complex arrangement soon gave way to a more straightforward system. This later design made use of three great roof pitches arranged in parallel, resting on huge lattice girders, sup-

ported in turn on cast iron columns. They varied in detail, generally becoming more austere in appearance towards the end of the century and eventually outnumbering the slightly smaller and more elegant predecessors.

The Midland continued to build their square sheds to this basic plan for over thirty years and, although marginally larger, the final examples were more or less identical to their predecessors. They remained a feature of 'the steam railway' throughout LMS and BR days and one at least, Staveley, survived to see use as a diesel depot, the locos stabling around the turntable exactly after the manner of steam engines for decades previously.

Generally speaking, for the staff, roundhouses (at least the square variety) were distinctly preferable to the 'straight sheds' employed elsewhere. They were far less draughty to begin with (not the case of course in later years when a number of examples were left roofless and open to the elements) and they were by and large safer to work in. With increasing turntable sizes and larger locomotives, however, they became more and more cramped

Wellingborough (*Top*) and Burton were two sites where it was possible to see two generations of 'square shed' design alongside each other. In both cases the earlier buildings, dating from the 1860s, displayed the attractive transverse pitches with an abundance of decoration.

W. Potter and R. J. Essery

EARLY M.R. SQUARE ROUNDHOUSE (BELLE VUE)

SCALE — approx. 1 mm to 1 foot

(Some roof detail necessarily omitted)

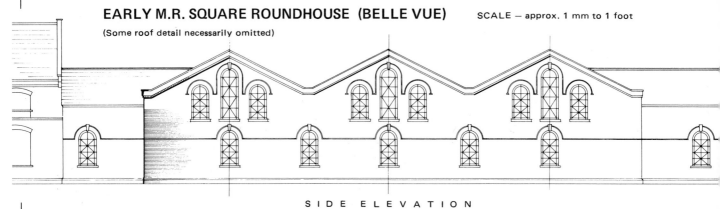

S I D E   E L E V A T I O N

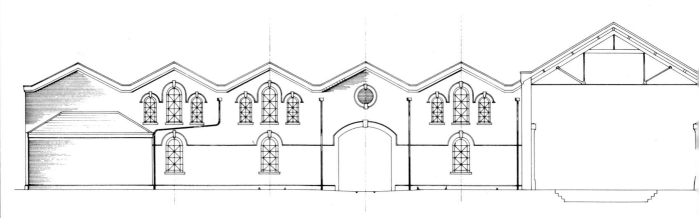

F R O N T   E L E V A T I O N   (S E C T I O N   T H R O U G H   F I T T I N G   S H O P)

M.R. FITTING SHOP (BELLE VUE)

SCALE — approx. 1 mm to 1 foot

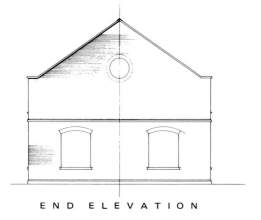

E N D   E L E V A T I O N

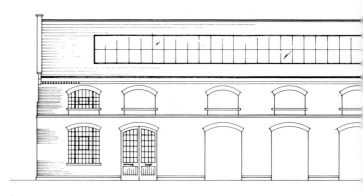

PLAN OF TYPICAL ROUNDHOUSE (SALTLEY)

Pits on all roads

Smoke ducts
on all roads

Drain

Column

SCALE — approx. ¾ mm to 1 foot

S I D E   E L E V A T I O N

STANDARD M.R. ROUNDHOUSE (DERBY)

END ELEVATION

CROSS SECTION

Turntable pit

SECTIONAL SIDE ELEVATION

SCALE – approx. 1 mm to 1 foot

The succeeding buildings carrying three high roof pitches did not acquire a markedly austere appearance until the 1890s and this view of Wigston, built in 1873, illustrates the point.

W. A. Camwell

The interior of Carnforth, opened the following year.

W. A. Camwell

Carnforth on 14th March 1937. No alterations have been carried out since the shed's construction in 1874 and all the standard features developed by the period can be observed. The 'coal sheds' were later abandoned and the roundhouses slightly enlarged and simplified but this distinctive Midland 'look' was maintained undiluted over a period of more than fifty years.

W. A. Camwell

Wigston and Carnforth were built to the same design but the precise position of ancillary buildings varied according to the particular site, evidenced by the relative position of the sandhouses at each shed.

W. A. Camwell

and awkward. There was considerable variation in the length of the pits and on only about four, for instance, was it possible to set a 'Jubilee' 4—6—0 for taking down the middle big end. Even with the final type of large LMS/BR roundhouse, as erected at Leicester and Upperby, care had to be taken when moving engines, especially when low in steam and, as a consequence, brake power. Any increase in turntable capacity meant a corresponding decrease in the length of the stabling roads and when through roads were provided, as at Durran Hill for the

GSWR 4—6—0s and at Toton for the 'Garratts', the stabling capacity was severely reduced. Turntable deficiencies incidentally caused a number of anomalies, notably at Kentish Town. This shed, although strictly a 'garage' under the later LMS scheme, continued to undertake its own mileage examinations, the 'concentration' depot at Cricklewood being unable to turn anything larger than a '5MT' 4—6—0. At Leicester, where the old circular sheds were retained until the last years of the Second World War, space (even though 42 ft. turntables were still in use) was

The Midland sheds were noticeably better maintained, even well into LMS days, than those of other pre-Grouping companies and flower beds in and around the yard were by no means uncommon! Wigston had an enthusiastic gardener who must have been particularly saddened by the shed's closure a few weeks after this photograph was taken.
W. A. Camwell

The 'new roundhouse' under construction at Leicester in the final years of the Second World War. Conditions at Leicester must have been truly appalling to prompt this level of investment in the war years. This design would have become the new LMS/BR standard had steam not been abandoned.

Authors' collection

The shed complete in May 1947.   *Authors' collection*

at such a premium that cast iron boxes were let into the walls at the end of each road, engines stabling with their buffers actually *in* the wall! Stabling an engine even without wartime blackout conditions was a hair-raising experience to say the least, and the imminent prospect of an engine emerging through the outside wall was one of the factors taken into consideration when, despite the prevailing economic stringencies, the decision was taken to rebuild the shed.

Some mishaps did inevitably occur, and by 1945 Kentish Town for one had received two extra openings in this way. The dividing wall between numbers '2' and '3' sheds had been partly demolished by a driver under the impression that he was on the through road and No. '3' shed had received an additional exit when another driver attempted to leave the shed whilst on tracks adjacent to the outgoing road. The problem even without the exigencies of war was simply one of staff losing their bearings whilst on the table, understandable enough at night, surrounded by noise and smoke and with poor or non-existent lighting. The LMS kept this kind of incident very

much in mind when designing the large new roundhouses which comprised a sturdy ferro-concrete framework, the bulk of the outside wall being a simple brick screen. This avoided serious structural damage on at least one known occasion about 1960, when a 'Duchess' slowly emerged, tender first, through the wall at Upperby.

Williams, in his famous 1876 work *'The Midland Railway'* has some interesting comments on the Running Department, at a time when the new roundhouses were being constructed. After a brief summary of work at the sheds, (the type of procedures etc. were the same on all railways and have been detailed in Volume One) ending (with typical contemporary imagery) with the 'red hot contents of the stomach' being dumped into the ashpits, he describes the facilities provided for the men. The Midland were comparatively enlightened in this respect and Williams describes 'two large messrooms, the smaller holding 100 men, the larger 400, spacious and well-lit. Also a fine 3-storey building erected for lodging with 22 bedrooms'. Accommodation 'holding' crews engaged on lodging turns were an early feature at many Midland

L.M.S. LEICESTER, NEW MOTIVE POWER DEPOT

The contractors had a special sortie flown for their customers, the LMSR, on completion of the main building and a number of these photographs were issued for publicity purposes. Traces of the engine stalls of the former 'No. 1' roundhouse are still visible in the lower right foreground, used for engine stabling right up until completion of the new building.

Collection V. Forster

L.M.S. RE-ROOFING DESIGN FOR EX-M.R. ROUNDHOUSES

to be demolished →

Existing wall of roundhouse →

SCALE – approx. 2 mm to 1 foot

S E C T I O N A L   S I D E   E L E V A T I O N   T H R O U G H   'A A'

A

A

S E C T I O N A L   E N D   E L E V A T I O N

Though the MR roundhouses survived well, the passage of time, fire, bombs and errant locos had taken their toll by 1945. Many were accordingly rebuilt in styles utilising concrete and steel in various combinations. Cricklewood is receiving the first of its new roofs in this photograph taken in early BR days.
British Railways

The new shed at Rowsley, resplendent amidst the Derbyshire hills on 24th November 1924. It was in purely Midland style and followed a lull in new building of some twenty years. Certain standards had been discarded since the days before the Great War and the shed was in worse condition by 1948 than many similar MR sheds built decades earlier. Secondhand rails serving as roof trusses were cited as one reason for the building's accelerated decline.

National Railway Museum

engine sheds and were comparatively comfortable and well-appointed.

The 'principal engine stations' with average number of engines in steam in 1876 were: 'Derby 94, Birmingham 72, Sheffield 47, Leeds 48, Toton 54, Nottingham 49, Leicester 52, Wellingborough 49, London 69'.

GOING STRAIGHT

The Midland Railway was a major builder of roundhouses but straight sheds were increasingly popular from the late 1870s. They had, of course, been occasionally employed by the constituent companies since the very earliest days, notably at Leeds (Hunslet Lane) and at Derby, but subsequently, the more important 'Engine Houses' took the roundhouse form, other designs tending to appear only

when the number of engines involved was very low. One or two roads were normally considered sufficient and successive generations of 'basic models' were developed. In the 1860s sheds with hipped slated roofs appeared, giving way to more ornate buildings, employing straightforward pitched roofs, in the late 1860s and early 1870s. St. Albans, Northampton and Overseal, among others, fell into this latter category and broadly similar buildings were erected at sites like Wirksworth and Rowsley.

The northlight pattern roof, beloved of the LNWR and L & YR, was a rarity on the Midland, but odd examples did appear, notably at Manningham, in 1887, and Bedford. The 1887 building was constructed in timber whilst that at Bedford, erected a year previously, was in brick.

The later, most familiar type of Midland straight shed can be considered to have made its debut in 1880, when

The standard straight sheds were built down to a minimum capacity of about two/four engines but never had less than two roads. The small example at Hitchin is still used today but had been closed for locomotive purposes for many years when this photograph was taken in July 1936.

W. A. Camwell

The Midland straight sheds approached the magnitude of the LNWR and L & YR 'steam sheds' at only one or two locations. The largest and best recorded, photographically, was Millhouses, shown here in the early years of this century.

Collection J. B. Radford

Kettering dated from a rather earlier period but the smoke flues in timber and the cast iron columns supporting the roof were features common to all the MR straight sheds.

R. J. Essery

a three road brick building opened at Pleck Junction, Walsall. The company described it as 'the new metal shed', its framework being of steel, but the general arrangement had been arrived at a few years previously with timber clad sheds at Skipton and Worcester. Brick was the preferred material, however, and with the exception of Stockingford in 1902, was adopted as the standard material.

The new design incorporated pitched slated roofs covering either two or three roads, with a variety of detail differences appearing over the years. These usually concerned the precise method of smoke ventilation, provision of windows, etc. The new sheds remained small and did not normally exceed four roads in width but accommodation varied. Keighley's four roads for instance were so short that they barely housed a single 0—6—0 apiece while Upper Bank, opened a year or so later and having only two roads, could stable twice the number of locomotives. The design was successively enlarged to accommodate six roads at Westhouses in 1890, and the maximum width was attained when the eight road shed at Millhouses opened in 1901.

The end of new construction by the Midland was now in sight and its last new shed, opened only two years later, was a three road affair at Kirkby-in-Ashfield. The last roundhouse, Toton 'No. 3', had been completed in 1901 and this period can, in a way, be regarded as the peak of the Midland's power and prosperity. Rowsley, a straight shed of standard design and construction, had been planned as early as 1900 but construction, delayed firstly by economic considerations and then by war, was not underway until 1922. It would have been the first Midland shed to be equipped with a mechanical coaling plant but in the event the depot was destined to open under LMS auspices.

The branch line engine sheds of the Midland, like those of any major company, least lend themselves to classification, with examples often inherited from absorbed companies. Two main themes appear on the Midland, however, one represented by the solid brick example at Leicester West Bridge, photographed in 1907 and the other a less substantial timber design, found at sites like Thornbury and Ingleton.

Courtesy Leicester Museum

MIDLAND RAILWAY STRAIGHT SHEDS

PLECK

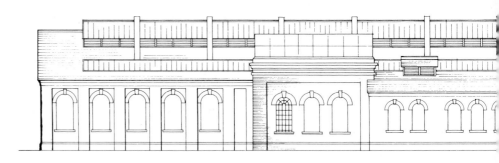

KIRKBY-IN-ASHFIELD

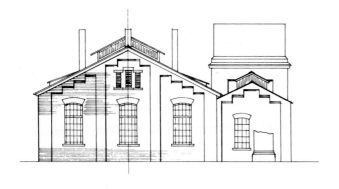

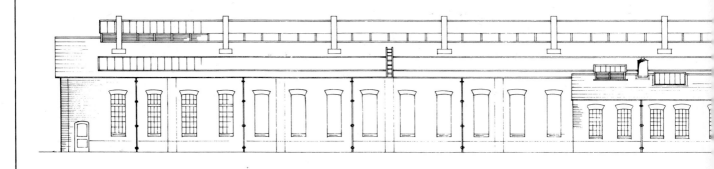

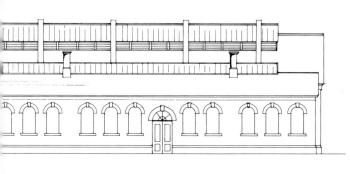

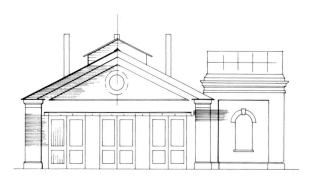

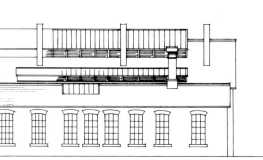

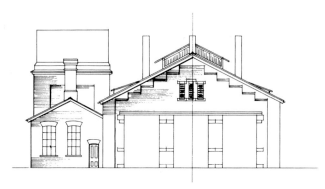

ROWSLEY

SCALE — approx. 1 mm to 1 foot

REPRESENTATIVE M.R. MINOR SHED (e.g. Bedford, St. Albans, Northampton, Overseal, etc. Details, of course, varied from site to

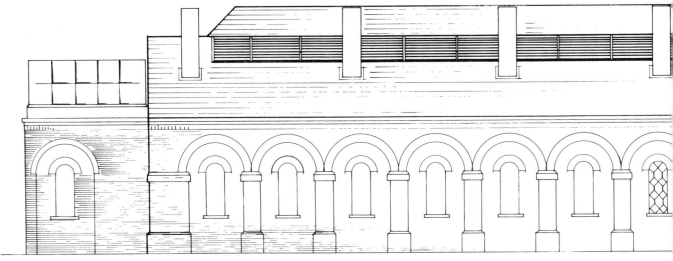

SIDE ELEVATION

WIRKSWORTH

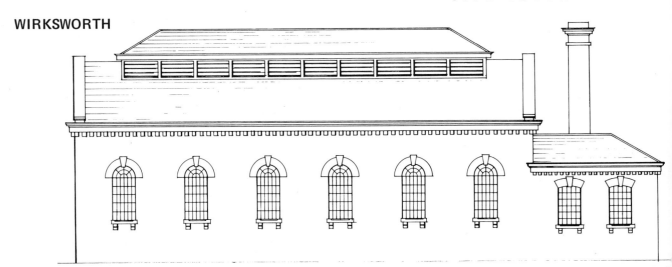

SIDE ELEVATION

SKIPTON
(STANDARD STRAIGHT SHED IN WOOD)

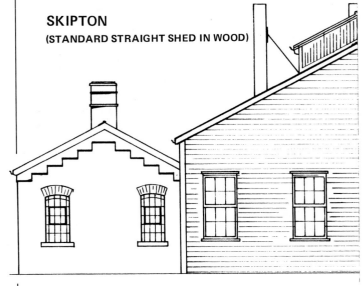

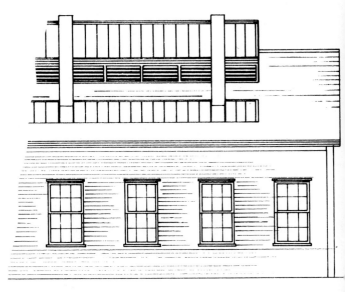

PART REAR ELEVATION

PART SIDE ELEVATION

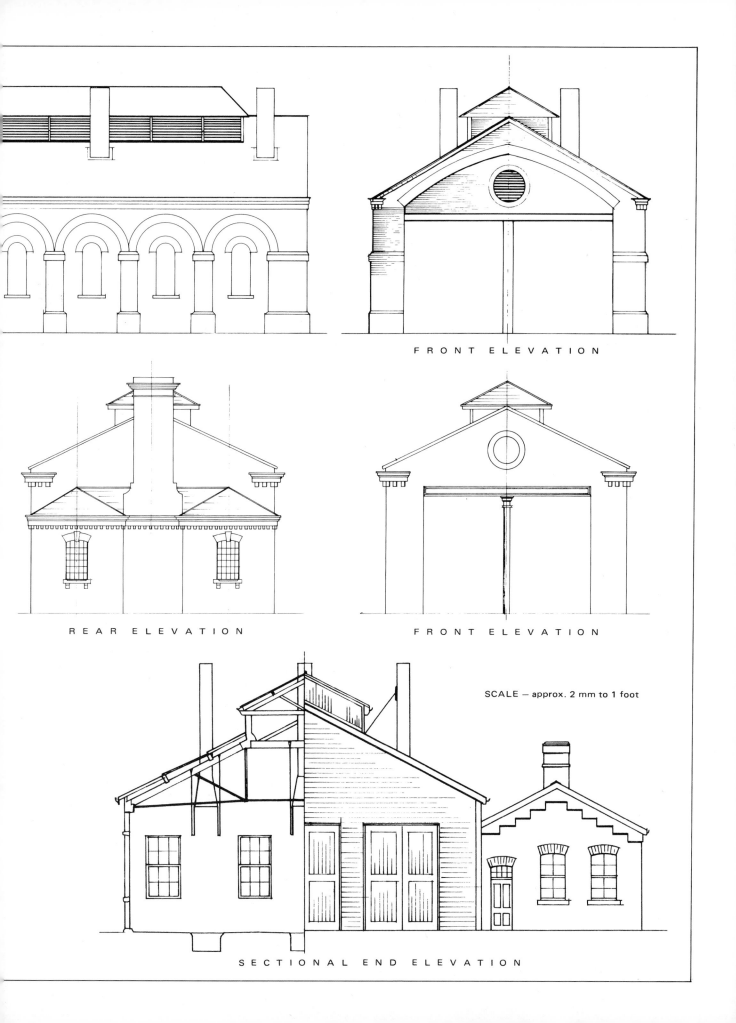

FRONT ELEVATION

REAR ELEVATION

FRONT ELEVATION

SCALE — approx. 2 mm to 1 foot

SECTIONAL END ELEVATION

The 'outstation shop' at Sheffield, Grimesthorpe. The restrictions imposed by this sort of arrangement, on engine size in particular, are immediately apparent. The kind of task being undertaken readily indicates the nature of the outstations, being extensions of Derby Works rather than running shed workshops. There is essentially little difference between this scene and, say, the old Derby 'No. 2' erecting shop.

National Railway Museum

CHAPTER TWO

'Outstation Shops'

THE Midland arranged its repair shops on a more elaborate basis than most other railways, beginning with small buildings attached or adjacent to early circular sheds like Gloucester and Saltley. Access was from small turntables, requiring the engine to be detached from its tender and hauled by capstan onto its stall in the workshop. With the general enlargement of the depots after 1868 the opportunity was taken to provide a strategically sited network of 'outstation shops' attached to the new square sheds. The new shops were under the supervision of the District Locomotive Superintendent but operated more or less independently of the running sheds, concentrating almost entirely on 'heavy' repairs. Sir Guy Granet carried out a comprehensive reorganisation of the MR in 1909, a major result being the separation of the running sheds from the shops. The latter remained under the CME but the District Locomotive Superintendents were now responsible to the Chief General Superintendent at Derby.

The 'outstation shops' in the heyday of the Midland were as follows:

Belle Vue	Leicester
Bristol	Nottingham
Carlisle (Durran Hill)	Peterborough
Cricklewood	Saltley
Gloucester	Sheffield
Kentish Town	Wellingborough
Leeds	

Seven of them, Belle Vue, Bristol, Carlisle, Kentish Town, Leeds, Saltley and Sheffield, remained in use through to LMS ownership, the remainder having closed or been turned over to 'light' repairs, operating simply as workshops for the adjacent running shed. Output from all the various LMS shops was reviewed on 8th June 1929, after which most of them suffered a sharp decline.

OUTPUT FROM LMS SHOPS

Shop	1927		1928		1929	
	'Heavy'	'Light'	'Heavy'	'Light'	'Heavy'	'Light'
CREWE	355	49	448	39	412	44
Bow	45	10	35	7	19	14
Carlisle Upperby	38	5	44	14	12	32
Rugby	40	7	46	23	14	42
DERBY	267	4	298	9	294	8
Belle Vue	9	1	7	7	1	37
Bristol	2	2	3	3	1	7
Carlisle Durran Hill	2	—	4	—	1	8
Kentish Town	14	5	18	13	11	47
Leeds	15	3	23	—	1	47
Saltley	16	1	6	39	2	55
Sheffield	4	2	7	1	3	24
HORWICH	221	31	220	104	192	84
Barrow	24	4	15	6	5	17
ST. ROLLOX	138	11	93	9	125	12
Kilmarnock	59	14	49	12	20	21
Inverness	16	10	10	12	10	15

After 1928 the surviving outstations progressively turned over to 'service' repairs only, and within four years all but two, Bristol and Leeds, had closed completely, with most of the others converted for road lorry maintenance. The two survivors were closed in their turn in early BR days.

The three largest surviving shops on the Midland Division of the LMS operated with the following staff complements on 19th April 1930:

	Kentish Town	Leeds	Saltley
Boilersmiths	6	3	4
Boilersmiths Mates	—	1	—
Carpenters and Joiners	2	1	2
Coppersmiths	2	1	1
Fitters	28	20	18
Tender Fitters	2	2	2
Fitters Mates	1	1	—
Holders Up	4	3	5
Labourers	16	10	10
Machinists	2	2	1
Millwrights	2	—	—
Painters	5	3	5
Smiths	2	2	2
Smiths Strikers	3	4	1
Tinsmiths	2	1	1
Tubers	7	4	5
Turners	5	3	5
Turners (Wheel)	2	2	1
Others (except juniors)	6	7	5
Apprentices	11	7	10

Following the review of 1929, on 23rd July there had, in fact, been a proposal to reopen some of the shops, at Gloucester and Nottingham, and estimates were given for re-equipping them. A fascinating 'might have been', the abortive proposals are listed below and if nothing else, serve to compare costs with those of today.

	£
GLOUCESTER	
1 New Overhead Travelling crane	1750
Fixing and wiring	500
1 Wheel lathe	1500
1 Shaping Machine	250
1 Planing Machine	350
1 Drilling Machine	200
	4550
Alterations to old crane ex-Derby 8 Shop	200
Wiring and putting up	300
	5050

NOTTINGHAM

1 New Overhead Travelling Crane	1750
Fixing and wiring (current on site)	300
1 Wheel lathe	1500
1 Planing Machine	350
1 Drilling Machine	200
	4100
Alterations to old crane ex-Derby 8 Shop	200
Wiring and putting up	500
	4800
Total for 2 Shops	£9850

Nottingham already has 20″ Stroke Shaping Machine

Gloucester and **Nottingham** each have axlebox boring lathe

Increased mileage resulting from the introduction of 'service' repairs, with a reduction in total locomotive stock and improved output from the main works, meant that neither shop reopened. The main problem with the MR shops was really that they had been outgrown by modern locomotives, and were deficient in both head room and crane power. Access was from small turntables, 18 ft to 25 ft in diameter, or a traverser and only the smallest locomotives could be accommodated.

All companies had been required by law since 1911 (when the Board of Trade Railway Accounts & Returns Act had been passed) to submit annually details of their classified locomotive repairs. They fell into two categories, 'heavy' or 'light', according to the actual work undertaken and on the Midland (and later the LMS) were as follows:

Heavy Repairs

Any *one* of:

1. Reboilering
2. Boiler taken off frames
3. New tyres to four or more wheels

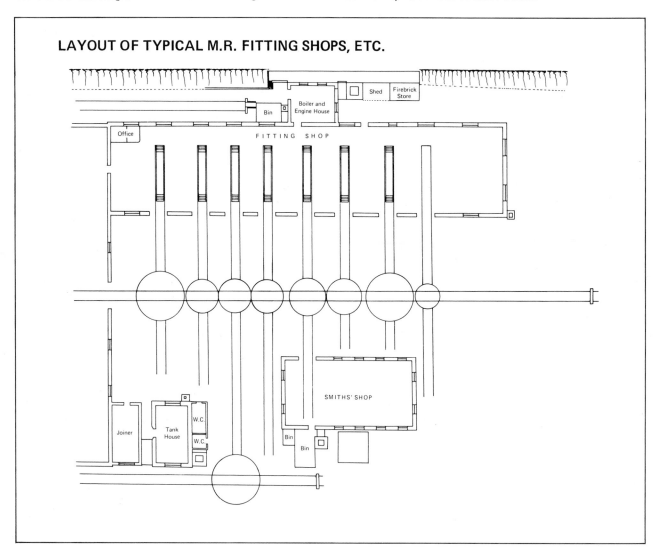

LAYOUT OF TYPICAL M.R. FITTING SHOPS, ETC.

Shear-legs, either hand, electrically or hydraulically powered, normally stood inside when provided at roundhouses but were invariably placed outside at straight sheds. This somewhat spartan arrangement was in force at Buxton MR shed, a depot far better equipped than its much larger ex-LNW neighbour.

A. G. Ellis

Any *two* of:

1. New cylinders
2. New axle(s)
3. Retubing
4. Turning wheels, refitting axleboxes, overhaul of motion or brake work
5. Boiler repair whilst in frames involving the renewal of not less than 15% of stays

Light Repairs

1. New cylinders
2. New axle(s)
3. Replacing more than 50% of boiler tubes
4. Turning four or more wheels and refitting axleboxes
5. Overhauling motion
6. Fitting patch to boiler
7. Re-lagging boiler
8. Fitting four or more new axleboxes
9. Welding, patching or straightening frames
10. Reboring cylinders and refacing ports
11. Removal and repair of tanks

The terms 'General', 'Service', 'Intermediate' or 'Casual' were strictly for internal use and had no meaning as far as the Board of Trade was concerned, the official 'annual return' being described only as 'heavy' or 'light'.

A 'general' repair, involving as it invariably did the removal of the boiler, automatically qualified as a 'heavy' repair, but 'service', 'intermediate and 'casual' work could fall into either of the two main categories. 'General' and 'Service' repair work was scheduled, i.e. carried out to a pre-arranged programme, based on time in traffic and mileage (although boiler condition was the controlling factor) whilst 'casual' repairs were performed on an *ad hoc* basis. They were normally required in the event of minor collision or other damage.

The MR running sheds themselves were equipped with a variety of facilities, notably shear-legs, used for hot box repairs as well as bogie and driving axle examinations on a periodical basis. All machine work and whitemetalling would be carried out in the shop. As at 21st June 1923, full facilities (i.e. shear-legs, tyre turning and axlebox boring equipment) were available at Belle Vue, Bristol, Carlisle, Kentish Town, Leeds, Leicester, Nottingham, Peterborough, Saltley, Sheffield and Wellingborough. No other sheds were equipped to perform tyre turning but shear-legs and axlebox boring machinery was supplied at Burton, Buxton, Gloucester, Hellifield, Toton and Upper Bank. Shear-legs, necessary for any running repairs involving lifting or wheel removal, were in addition provided at the following locations in June 1923, a number of them 'sub-sheds': Bedford, Bournville, Brecon, Carnforth, Coalville, Cricklewood, Derby, Hasland, Heaton

In roundhouses the shear-legs were necessarily placed on one of the longer roads, usually number 16 in the furthest corner from the entrance. This scene in 1920 is typical of most of the Midland roundhouses.

Collection R. J. Essery

Despite Aspinall's criticism, the Midland did possess at least one wheel drop, installed at Grimesthorpe and recorded by the official photographer on 14th July 1920.

Collection J. B. Radford

Mersey, Kettering, Kirkby, Lancaster, Liverpool, Manningham, Mansfield, Millhouses, Normanton, Skipton, Staveley, Stourton, Trafford Park, Walsall, Walton, Westhouses, Wigston, Worcester and York.

The Midland, like the GWR, was a great proponent of shear-legs, and wheel drops were rare at their sheds until after the Grouping. Aspinall of the Lancashire and Yorkshire Railway many years before had pointed out the eccentricity of this policy, declaring *"I cannot understand why two of our largest railways consider it better engineering practice to lift sixty tons of engine rather than lower two tons of wheels!"* On the Midland shear-legs came in three main types, hydraulic, electric and hand operated. The major depots were usually equipped with one of the first two types but when neither source of power was available the staff had to make do with the hand operated units. They were, however, (an example of the Midland's inexhaustible benevolence) allowed an extra fifteen minutes per lift.

On the Midland and its contemporaries, every task had an exact, laid-down time for its execution, a practice continued well into the LMS period. 'Basis' times were pro-

vided for all the various operations and in order to gain bonus payment the man concerned had to *improve* on the figure. The minimum the fitter was supposed to achieve was a saving of one third but generally he would be expected to complete the job in half the 'basis' time. For this he would be paid at time and a half and in the former case time and one third. If no saving was obtained the man concerned was paid at 'day rate'. The system could only be applied to operations having a known work content and was restricted to 'stopped' engine work and mileage examinations only, fitters engaged on 'running' repairs being unable to earn the bonus payments. This caused so much ill-feeling that the whole scheme was eventually withdrawn in the 1920s.

It was possible to complete the tasks within the times expected by the management, but the work was arduous and the disappearance of the system was probably applauded by the majority of men.

The staff complements necessary at each individual shed was also carefully calculated and investigations by the LMS established, for instance, that 330 man hours were necessary per year to adequately maintain the stan-

0—6—0 No. 3176 under the shear-legs at Derby in the early years of the LMS. This set was later removed, leaving Derby a surprisingly ill-equipped depot.

W. Potter

dard '4F' 0—6—0, i.e. about one hour per day. Accordingly, on the basis of an eight hour working day one fitter could be expected to look after eight '4F's per day. Different classes of course varied as to the time allowed and 'concentration' depots normally had several additional staff. A similar formula existed for boilersmiths, varying according to the quality of water available in the district. Despite the multitude of changes and procedures imposed by the LMS, old traditions refused to die and a wealth of regional and local practices continued to flourish, even until the demise of steam and the advent of the diesels.

With LMS ownership, following closure of the out-station shops, no 'heavy' repairs and very few 'light' repairs were undertaken at running sheds, with even the latter normally confined to 'TRD' work ('Tube removal for dirt'). The other big companies, the SR, LNER and GWR, continued to undertake much more extensive repair work at their depots and for this reason they were generally better equipped. No effort was thus spared on the LMS to get an engine 'into the works', Crewe, Derby, etc. This it was virtually impossible to do unless the engine had received severe accident damage or required major boiler repairs and/or all its tyres turned or renewed. The LMS system worked reasonably well but it was often a struggle

at the sheds to keep run-down engines at work in the final months before 'shopping'. Some classes, notably the '5MT' 4—6—0 (with whitemetalled axleboxes) and the '4F' 0—6—0, became particularly rough riders in these periods and it then became a constant battle between fitting and footplate staff, the latter sometimes refusing to take engines into traffic. Prayers for a failure requiring works attention were not unheard of! The very robustness and simplicity of the steam locomotive made the problem worse, the most run-down engine usually being capable of 'just one bit more'. Incredible feats were far from rare, a Derby '3F' 0—6—0 at one time working a freight quite comfortably on only one cylinder, the other having broken up completely! Later engines were also capable of withstanding almost any mistreatment, a mechanical stoker-fitted '9F' 2—10—0, for instance, working a 55 wagon train from Birmingham to Carlisle without *any* piston rings! The fitter at Saltley had forgotten to fit them during a valve and piston examination but, although the engine consumed some ten tons of coal, it still managed to work the train. It would not have been possible without a mechanical stoker but the incident illustrates the ability of the steam locomotive to keep going despite the most adverse conditions.

CHAPTER THREE

'Coal and Water'

AS with its predilection for roundhouses, the Midland's practice with regard to the coaling of its locos somewhat paralleled North Eastern Railway practice. The company eschewed the squat 'coal holes' favoured by the old enemy, the London and North Western and, at least following Johnson's appointment, went in for high, spacious coal stages. They were the final development and were not displaced until the LMS innovations of the 1930s.

Simple 'coal sheds', rectangular or tapering in plan, were provided until the 1870s, Holbeck, Wellingborough and Kentish Town being among the principal sites to receive them. They were superseded by the high level coal stages, those at the busiest depots having two roads. Engines could take coal from either side of these large 'double' stages, while the smaller 'single' versions were 'blank' on one side.

The obsolete and inconvenient 'coal sheds' largely disappeared, although they did linger on at a few locations, the unfortunate staff at Manningham being compelled to make do with theirs, for no obvious reason, until the 1960s. The shed at Wellingborough had escaped the destruction usual on the installation of the new high level stage and served as a shelter for the giant 2—6—0/0—6—2 'Garratts' sent to the shed in the early 1930s, housing the

Compound 4—4—0 No. 1028 alongside the coal stage at Derby in 1926. The immaculate loco featured in a series of publicity photographs on that day, taking No. 1028 through the servicing sequence.

National Railway Museum

The 'coal shed' with its crane pedestal in use at Carnforth, September 1934.   *W. Potter*

Coal was processed in what amounted to an appallingly inefficient manner and only cheap labour delayed the advent of mechanisation for so long. The coal here had already been won from the ground by hand, transported and stacked, again by hand, and is now being lifted in similar manner, for locomotive use. The unfortunate ladies owe their presence on this laborious task to the Great War and the ceaseless demand for men.

Collection J. B. Radford

Variations on the 'coal shed' theme (this one is St. Albans, 1937) were tried in the years before the general introduction of high level stages, with a separate roof section affording shelter to the coal crane. A greatly enlarged version of this building served the 'No. 3' roundhouse at Derby. *A. G. Ellis*

wheel drop provided by the LMS. Other sites to retain such structures included Wigston and Carnforth (until closure) and Leicester (until rebuilding in the 1940s).

A number of MR types were converted to oil burning in 1926 in an attempt to combat the effects of the coal strike, and engines were refuelled from tank wagons stabled on the coal ramps. The practice was abandoned as coal supplies became more readily available. The railways went to some lengths to secure adequate supplies of coal at economic prices, the whole question being examined in

great detail by the Coal Supplies Office of the LMS. Extra coal stacking sites were brought into use, the purpose being to buy in summer when supplies were cheap, lifting for use in winter when prices were high. This worked well until the Second World War and the following years of austerity when lack of coal and the men to stack it made the system difficult to operate. Not all depots had the space available and supplies were generally concentrated at one or two sheds in a district. At Highbridge in the period 1949-1950, for instance, the stack amounted to

Coal stages, like sheds, were occasionally built in wood, witnessed by this somewhat ramshackle example nearing the end of its career at Hellifield in 1961.

British Railways

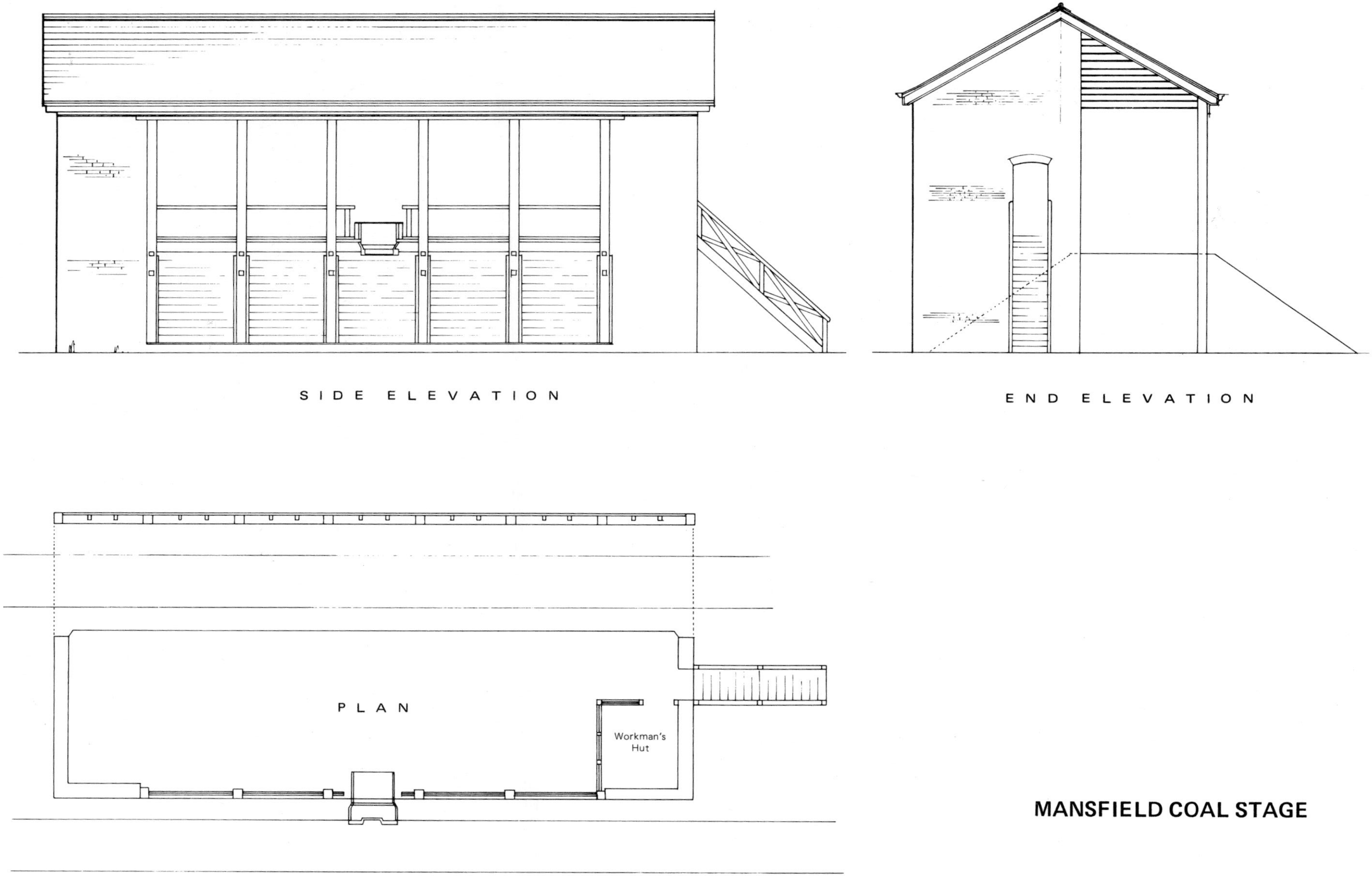

END ELEVATION

SIDE ELEVATION

PLAN

Workman's Hut

MANSFIELD COAL STAGE

SCALE — approx. 2 mm to 1 foot

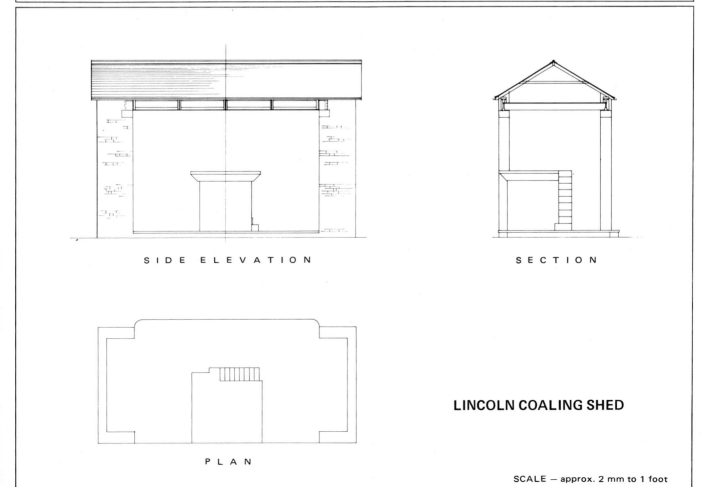

KIRKBY-IN-ASHFIELD COAL STAGE

E N D   E L E V A T I O N

S I D E   E L E V A T I O N

Water Crane retaining wall

P L A N

SCALE — approx. 1 mm to 1 foot

S I D E   E L E V A T I O N

S E C T I O N

LINCOLN COALING SHED

P L A N

SCALE — approx. 2 mm to 1 foot

Coaling up at the new Derby stage in 1909.   *National Railway Museum*

The LMS in its early years had a brief flirtation with oil firing, engines being fuelled at Derby from tank wagons parked at the end of the coaling ramp. The year is thought to be 1926, the coal strike prompting the experiment. It was abandoned as coal supplies were gradually resumed.

Collection R. S. Carpenter

The Midland that never was. Rowsley would have been the first MR shed equipped with mechanical apparatus, originally designed with an overhead bucket-carrying system to enable coaling to take place on several roads. In the event the LMS was responsible for the equipment, providing this more or less conventional concrete bunker.

Collection J. B. Radford

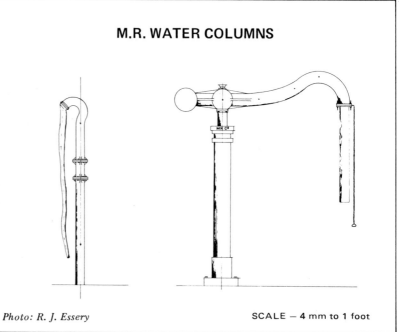

M.R. WATER COLUMNS

Photo: R. J. Essery   SCALE — 4 mm to 1 foot

The unmistakable Midland water tank, in this case the imposing structure at Nottingham. Built in all sizes, the base normally served as a store of some kind and would be constructed of virtually any material, but most commonly brick.

R. J. Essery

The various tanks required for the Midland's water softening plant at Derby Works were also in conventional company style.

National Railway Museum

about 4,000 tons, a total which fell off when the Southern Region took control. The softer Welsh coal preferred by the SR authorities did not take kindly to such handling and stacking on this scale gradually declined.

WATER SUPPLY

Some of the most conspicuous features of the Midland were its standard water tanks. Unmistakeable products of a highly standardised railway, the boxlike plate iron design, supported by a solid brick or stone base, was employed at innumerable locations. Sheds, yards, water troughs, etc. would have one of suitable size supplied either by a company pump from an adjacent well or from the local corporation. The feed would thence be by gravity to water columns, standpipes, etc. The diagram produced overleaf shows a fairly typical arrangement at an average shed. The actual location is Bournville, a standard roundhouse, but the principle was of course identical where straight sheds were concerned. Water softeners do not appear to have seen much use on the Midland, at least as far as locomotive running was concerned, but certainly such equipment was not unknown. The complex example illustrated here supplied Derby Works for various industrial processes and a second unit followed for use at the shed in LMS days. A list of softeners installed by the LMS was provided in Volume One.

Perhaps the most familiar MR water column style.

R. J. Essery

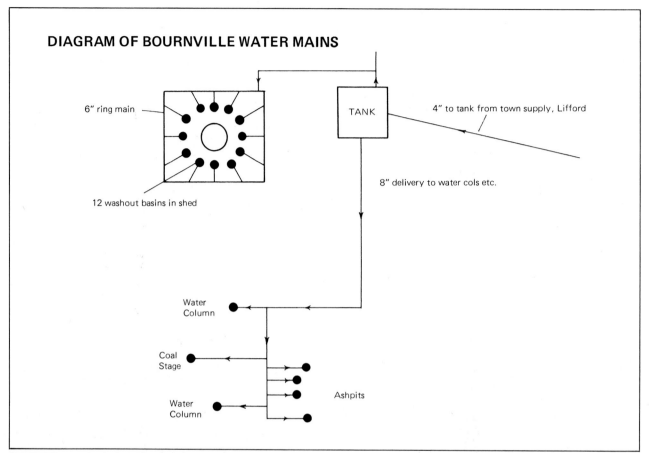

DIAGRAM OF BOURNVILLE WATER MAINS

6" ring main

12 washout basins in shed

TANK

4" to tank from town supply, Lifford

8" delivery to water cols etc.

Water Column

Coal Stage

Water Column

Ashpits

The small shed at Wirksworth was provided with a standard tank supported on a wooden base (*left*) whilst the store beneath the tank at Burton was in brick.

R. J. Essery

Compound 4—4—0 No. 1028 on another stage in its servicing sequence for the photographer in 1926. The turntable is the 60 ft unit installed outside 'No. 4' shed, the only feature to emerge of the erstwhile second double roundhouse.

Collection J. B. Radford

TURNTABLES

The early circular roundhouses were too small to cope successfully with even a 42 ft turntable and this size was standard by the 1860s. They were provided outside on occasions, to supplement the original 39 ft turntables and were installed as a matter of course when the new square sheds were introduced in 1868. By 1876 it was necessary to increase the diameter to 46 ft. (A 'new improved' 46 ft turntable for Skipton supplied by Cowans Sheldon was ordered in December 1876 and two others, at Nottingham and Saltley, were ordered in the same year) but within a few years 50 ft turntables were necessary. These units, like most of the company's turntables, were supplied by either Eastwood Swingler Ltd. or Cowans Sheldon of Carlisle. In later years Derby Works joined the fray, tendering for the new 60 ft turntable required at Normanton and ordered by the station Joint Committee in 1909. The competition was as follows:

	Cost	Delivery Date
Cowans Sheldon & Co.	£720	14-16 weeks
Eastwood Swingler & Co.	£760	3-4 months
A. Handyside & Co.	£707/10s/0	16-20 weeks
Patent Shaft & Axletree Co.	£840	4½-5 months
Ransomes & Rapier Ltd.	£700	12-14 weeks
MR Loco Works	£658	19 weeks

MR tender accepted.

50 ft turntables had been supplied to most sheds by the late 1890s and several of 55 ft were supplied between 1899 and 1902. 60ft tables had first appeared in 1900 at the new Saltley 'No. 3' shed, and these remained the largest in use on the system. The following details (kindly provided by J. B. Radford Esq.) were issued by headquarters in 1911:

ENGINE TURNTABLES

Engines which can turn	Stations
60 feet Table	Avonmouth, Derby, Carlisle, Chinley, Cheadle Heath, Gowhole, Kirkby, Leicester, Millhouses, Morecambe, Normanton Junc., Nottingham, Sheffield (pass'r) & Grimesthorpe, Stockingford, Saltley, St. Pancras.
55 feet Table All engines	Belle Vue, Canklow, Chesterfield, (54 ft), Kentish Town (3), Leeds, Mansfield, Peterborough, Wellingborough, Toton.

A photograph taken inside Derby 'No. 4' shed, 27th August 1936, on the commissioning of the new 60 ft turntable from Ransomes & Rapier Ltd.

Collection J. B. Radford

Turntables could certainly cause problems and those of the Midland were no exception. This particular incident took place at Leeds station and illustrates the wonders a breakdown gang could perform with simple jacks.

National Railway Museum

50 feet Table

All engines *except*
1000 to 1004
700 to 779
685 to 694

with bogie tenders

Aireside (Leeds), Appleby, Bedford, Blackwell, Bournville, Bradford, Bristol, Burton, Cheltenham, Colne, Cricklewood (2), Derby (3), Gloucester (2), Hawes Junc., Hellifield, Hereford, Hope, Ilkley, Keighley, Kettering, Lancaster, Lincoln, Marple, Normanton Junc., Nottingham, Olney, Ripley, Stourton, Walsall, Westhouses, Wolverhampton.

46 feet Table

All engines *except*
1000 to 1044
990 to 999
700 to 779
685 to 694
523 to 562
483 to 522*

* when rebuilt with
G7 boilers

Bath, Belle Vue, Birmingham (Lawley St.), Bromsgrove, Broome Junction, Carlisle, Leeds, Nottingham, Rugby, Saltley, Sharpness, Sheffield, Skipton, St. Pancras, Trent.

45 feet Table

All engines *except*
1000 to 1044
990 to 999
700 to 779
670 to 694
328 to 377
378 to 402*
403 to 472
473 to 482*
483 to 562

* when rebuilt with
G7 boilers

Carlisle (G & SW Rly), Malvern, Marple.

42 feet Table

All engines *except*
1000 to 1044
990 to 999
700 to 779
600 to 694
300 to 562
2200 to 2229*
2230 to 2239*

* Americans

Ashby, Brent, Bristol (2), Burton (2), Carnforth, Chaddesdon, Clifton Down, Coalville, Coalville Junc., Derby, Eckington, Hasland, Hitchin, Hucknall, Leeds, Leicester (2), Luton, Manningham, Nailsworth, Newark, Normanton, Northampton, Nottingham, Nuneaton, Overseal, Rowsley, Saltley, Shackerstone, Stamford, Staveley, Stonehouse, St. Pancras, St. Albans, Sutton Bridge, Swansea, Teversall, Thornbury, Toton (2), Wellingborough, Wigston, Wirksworth, Worcester.

The familiar outside turntable at Derby gave way to a vacuum operated 70 ft example during the depot's modernisation and Stanier 4–6–0 No. 5044 is making use of it here on 27th August 1936.

Collection R. J. Essery

40 feet Table   Buxton, Derby (2), Evesham, Tamworth.
(will turn)

No. 1 Class pass'r   All No. 1 class and 2 class Goods except
     1 to 191   Nos. 3333, 3387, 3326*
217 to 221
& all tank engines

* These engines were in fact '3 F's and the official reasoning here is
   not quite clear. There are also several omissions, for instance
   2—4—0s Nos. 192-216 and 222-281.

This list must have been more advisory in nature than
instructional, for the largest Midland engines, including
the Lickey banker could be accommodated on a 50 ft
turntable, though larger diameters made the task less
exacting. A Stanier class '5' could make do with a 55 ft
table easily enough and while 'Claughtons' and 'Jubilees'
could also be dealt with, the care and time required
meant it was not feasible on a day to day basis. 60 ft
turntables were really the necessary minimum and the
Midland's introduction of these as early as 1900 indicated
a high degree of awareness of running shed daily life (the
existence of these larger units also placed less constraint
on Derby if ever a 4—6—0 passenger type came under dis-
cussion). It seems in fact to be beyond argument that the
Midland was considerably more 'houseproud' than most
other companies when it came to engine sheds. Turntable
pits, for instance, until about 1920 at least, were boarded
over and railed off. The decking was kept scrubbed and
clean and any member of staff foolish or misguided enough
to take a short cut *across* them instead of taking the long
way round would inevitably incur the wrath of authority!

The Midland turntable that will ever have a place in railway literature. The moorland wind at Garsdale was capable, once engines were on
the table, of rotating them more or less indefinitely and the sleeper pallisade was erected to combat this embarrasing phenomenon.
L & GRP

CHAPTER FOUR

The Sheds

Building 'on the LNWR system' was certainly cheaper, but did have its drawbacks! Bedford, largely roofless on 19th March 1949.

H. C. Casserley

BEDFORD

The shed at Bedford was a two road brick affair with a pitched slated roof and its opening was arranged to coincide with the St. Pancras Extension. The new shed began operating in 1868, a coal crane and shear-legs later being provided. The turntable ('the foundations had been agreed and approved with Mr. Cox at £160' on the 1st of September 1868) was at first of 42 ft diameter but was later enlarged to 46 ft. On 19th November 1885 the Locomotive Committee considered two proposals for a new shed, to hold sixteen engines, one at £10,260 'on the LNWR system' and one costing £11,550 'on the Midland system'. On 1st January 1886 Johnson submitted a plan for a four road shed 'built in the same way as the LNWR Co's sheds', estimated cost £9,010. This was revised in April to £6,160, Johnson agreeing to make use of the existing turntable, coal stage etc. H. Hicks' tender of £4,221.14s.7d. was accepted shortly afterwards and the shed was in use before the end of the year. This and the timber structure at Manningham were the only two on which the MR chose sheds akin to Webb's northlight pattern designs and they were not repeated. It seems that

herein lies one of the reasons why the LNWR 'steam sheds' fell into such a parlous state, their very economy contributing to their more rapid deterioration.

The new Bedford avoiding line would have cut the new shed off from its facilities and in June 1893 it was accordingly agreed that a new turntable, coaling stage etc. should be provided, at an estimated cost of £5,850. Tenders were received in November and the new facilities opened early in 1894, the new station avoiding line in turn being brought into use some months later, on 7th October. There had incidentally been an earlier, markedly different proposal for an engine shed at Bedford. This was for a roundhouse and arose on 18th November 1873, the old shed housing only four locos out of an allocation of sixteen. It was to have stood in the fork of the London and Hitchin lines south of the station but in the event was not proceeded with. The small shed at Hitchin, the former southern limit of the Midland's London route, remained as a sub-shed for many years.

Bedford's principal workings were the St. Pancras passenger turns and goods work on the main line and to Northampton, handled over the years by 2—4—0s, 4—4—0s and 0—6—0s. Local passenger duties like the Hitchin branch trains were dealt with by several 0—4—4Ts. Some

The rebuilt shed, in solid modern style, on 24th April 1960.

W. Potter

Ex-MR '3F' 0−6−0 No. 43449 rests inside the shed on 14th April 1962, after working the Hitchin branch goods. This was one of the last duties worked by these engines and they were replaced by 2−6−4Ts in March of the following year.

S. Summerson

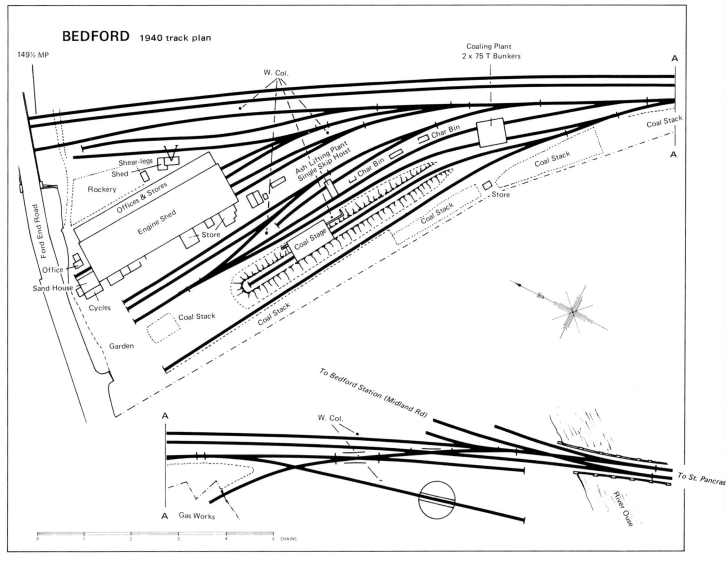

BEDFORD 1940 track plan

149½ MP

W. Col.

Coaling Plant
2 x 75 T Bunkers

A

A

Coal Stack

Shear-legs

Shed

Rockery

Offices & Stores

Engine Shed

Store

Office

Sand House

Cycles

Coal Stack

Garden

Ford End Road

Ash Lifting Plant
Single Skip Hoist

Char Bin

Char Bin

Coal Stack

Store

Coal Stack

Coal Stage

Coal Stack

Coal Stack

To Bedford Station (Midland Rd)

A

W. Col.

A   Gas Works

To St. Pancras

River Ouse

0   1   2   3   4   5   CHAINS

of the '800' class 2—4—0s, Nos. 820-829, were transferred to Bedford in 1880 and seven of this class were still there as late as 1914. Four 2—4—0s remained as late as 1933 and the last, No. 20216 was not transferred away until 1941. Various 4—4—0s followed the 2—4—0s, usually after spending a number of years at more important sheds and 0—6—0s, latterly '3F's, were a feature of the shed (No. 43428 by 1961 had been at Bedford for over thirty years) until displaced by 2—6—4Ts in March 1963. Their final duties were the Hitchin goods, their axle loading being the heaviest permitted on the branch.

In the 1930s Bedford was noted for its MR '700' class '3P' 4—4—0s, used mainly on the St. Pancras services. The shed was responsible for the longest turn then worked by these engines, which brought one daily to Nottingham via Leicester, returning to St. Pancras around 5.25 p.m. via Melton Mowbray, preceding the up 'Thames—Forth Express' to Kettering and following therefrom. The 4—4—0 concluded its diagram with a passenger train St. Pancras—Bedford. From late 1938 this turn was taken over by the new 'articulated diesel multiple unit train' numbered 80000-80002, which was based at Bedford. By 1953, the Johnson 0—4—4Ts had disappeared, (the last, No. 58091, was transferred away in September) replaced by Ivatt 2—6—2Ts Nos. 41269-72 and No. 41329 and a BR version

of the same design, No. 84005. Larger BR tanks Nos. 80044, 80045, 80046, 80060 and 80061 had also appeared, in theory able to work the St. Pancras passenger turns and local goods alike, and displacing both 4—4—0s and 0—6—0s. However, their limited water capacity made them unsuitable and BR 4—6—0s Nos. 75040-75044 were drafted in as replacements in January 1955.

The LMS had provided coal and ash plants by 1938 and a new 60 ft vacuum operated turntable had appeared in 1935, but the dilapidated roof was not replaced until BR days, in 1951/2. By 1962 only one steam passenger turn remained, the 8.21 a.m. to Kettering and, although a solitary class '5' No. 45238 was still active, the number of stored locos at the shed was beginning to increase. The official changeover to diesel power came in August 1963 and from January 1964 the official allocation comprised shunters Nos. D4135 and D4136 and type '2s' Nos. D5279-83. The last steam engine to use the shed in fact was preserved Highland Railway 4—6—0 No. 103 during the filming of *Those Magnificent Men In Their Flying Machines* in May 1964.

Midland shed No. 14, Bedford had become 15D under Wellingborough in 1935, was recoded 14E in April 1958 and took the code 14C from September 1963. It is still standing today, empty and without tracks.

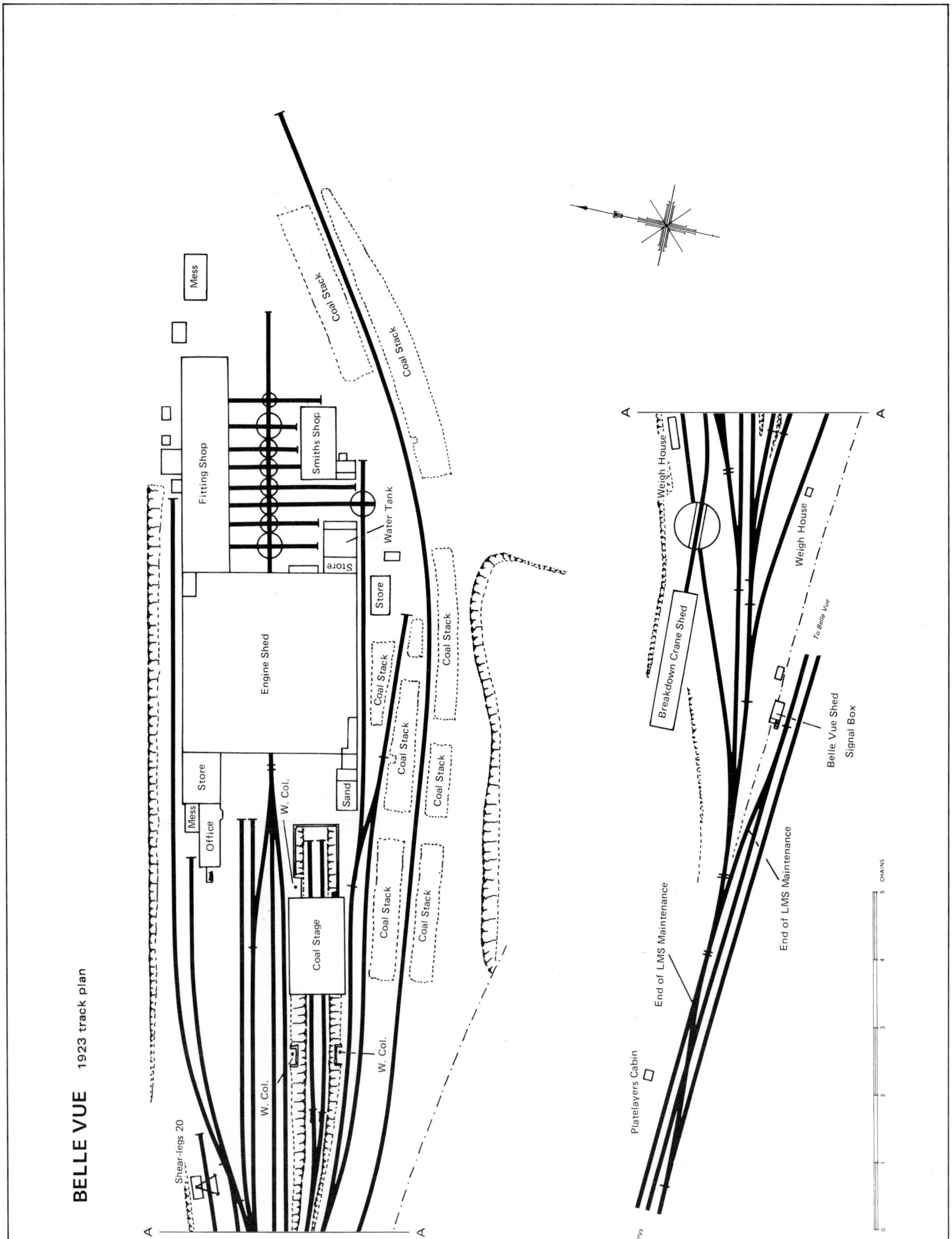

BELLE VUE 1923 track plan

Mess

Coal Stack

Coal Stack

Fitting Shop

Smiths Shop

Water Tank

Store

Engine Shed

Store

Coal Stack

Store

Coal Stack

Mess

Office

W. Col.

Coal Stack

Coal Stack

Sand

Coal Stack

Coal Stack

Coal Stage

W. Col.

Coal Stack

W. Col.

Coal Stack

Shear-legs 20

A

A

Weigh House

Breakdown Crane Shed

Weigh House

To Belle Vue

Belle Vue Shed
Signal Box

End of LMS Maintenance

End of LMS Maintenance

Platelayers Cabin

To Ashburys

A

A

0   1   2   3   4   5 CHAINS

The shed and yard in April 1936, viewed from the heights of Gorton (ex-GCR shed) coaling plant.   *W. Potter*

BELLE VUE

Known simply as 'Manchester' in Midland days, the shed here opened in 1870. The plans for a new 'square shed' with a 42 ft turntable had been drawn up in March of the previous year and the cost of the new depot was estimated at £19,000. A coaling shed was also provided as well as the usual four road fitting shop at the rear. The new depot increased steadily in importance and an additional turntable 46 ft in diameter was installed in the yard after only seven years. A breakdown crane shed and a second set of shear-legs were provided on spurs off the new turntable and a large new 'double' coal stage was erected in 1882. Increasing repair work made further expansion necessary and around 1892 the shops were more than doubled in size, giving Belle Vue an abundance of facilities for this type of work. It is slightly surprising in view of all this that the shed remained a single roundhouse, despite the lavish coaling arrangements and workshop accommodation. It had, in fact, been intended at some time to erect a second roundhouse but the idea never came to fruition. The shed was equipped with a new 55 ft inside turntable at a cost of £1,586 in 1899 and in 1908, £65 was expended on a footpath 'from Belle Vue shed to Ambrose Street, to enable enginemen to get to and from shed without walking on the Great Central Railway'.

Belle Vue was shed No. 21 and over half of the hundred or so locos officially allocated were outstationed at two major sub-sheds, 21a Trafford Park and 21b Heaton Mersey. Further locos were serviced by arrangement with other companies at Newton Heath L & Y, Northwich CLC, and Lower Darwen L & Y. Ahrons has a few words to say about 'Manchester' following the introduction of new Sharp Stewart 4—4—0s in 1893, ostensibly for the new Sheffield-Liverpool/Manchester services:

> 2213-2217 were at Manchester but the authorities there thought them too good for the short runs to Sheffield and put them on the London Expresses to Leicester. Instead of the new engines, two of the old 4—4—0s, Nos. 1342 (7 ft) (later No. 324) and 1666 (6′ 9″) (No. 357 after 1907) were almost invariably used between Manchester and Sheffield.

The generation of express locomotives prior to this had been 2—4—0s of course and before their transfer to Bristol in 1880 Nos. 1282-1301 (157-176) had mainly been at Belle Vue. Used mostly on the London expresses, they were 'very celebrated engines and justly had an excellent reputation amongst the men'. Freight duties were handled by 0—6—0s but 'Crab' 2—6—0s had appeared by 1929. Most of Belle Vue's passenger turns had been handed over to Trafford Park on its opening in 1895 and 0—6—0s formed the basic allocation for many years. By 1950 seven class '5's were available, together with eight '8F's.

Under proposals first put forward in 1946, the high pitched roof was replaced in the usual concrete style, giving the shed a squat appearance, and the turntable diameter was increased to 57 ft. No mechanical aids were provided in the yard and the shops by 1939 had been converted to road lorry maintenance. The shed received the code 19E in 1935 and, although theoretically part of the Midland Division, certain administrative responsibilities passed to the District Locomotive Superintendent at Longsight. This was also the case with Heaton Mersey and Trafford Park. All three sheds were formally absorbed in the Western Division of the London Midland Region in November

A view snatched from a train at speed in early LMS days. The high level of running repairs at Belle Vue required a second set of shear-legs, erected on a stub siding off the outside turntable.

W. H. Whitworth

1948. A separate district for the ex-Midland and Cheshire lines sheds in the Manchester area was created by BR in February 1950 with Trafford Park as the main shed and Belle Vue as a 'garage', 13B. The whole lot was dismembered on 22nd May 1950 after the briefest existence and Belle Vue found itself this time as 26G under Newton Heath ex-L & YR shed. A further recoding, to 26F, followed in October 1955, but by then the shed only had some six months of active existence remaining. Its allocation shortly before the final recoding totalled only 32 engines, most of them 0—6—0s or 'WD' 2—8—0s, which had replaced the '8F's. There were five Stanier two cylinder 4—6—0s, the remaining stock being two ex-L & Y saddle tanks and a couple of old MR '1F' tanks, Nos. 41702 and 41814. Belle Vue was the first of the Manchester sheds to be dispensed with and finally closed its doors on 16th April 1956. The shell of the building survived until at least the mid-1970s.

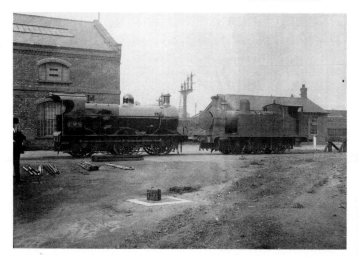

Engines awaiting repair at the rear of Belle Vue shed around 1925; a '3F' 0—6—0 and an ex-L & YR 0—6—0T, No. 1356.

Collection R. Carpenter

The Belle Vue breakdown crane.
Real Photographs

Inside Bournville, 31st August 1919, with a collection of 2—4—0s and 0—6—0s. From left to right: Nos. 18, 3536, 129, 2625 and 19.

W. L. Good

BOURNVILLE

Bournville was a standard roundhouse, opened compara- tively late, in 1895. It was one of the last to be built and stood alongside the 'Birmingham West Suburban Line', opposite the junction of the Lifford Canal branch. Coded 3a, it was provided with a 50 ft turntable, a 'single' coal stage and housed some twenty-five locos outstationed from Saltley. Accommodation was more than adequate and the expected rise in traffic, for which the shed was to be responsible, never fully materialised. There were a number of factories and works in the immediate area and the shed was close to the junction of the Camp Hill line with the Birmingham-Gloucester main line, the Worcester-

Birmingham canal passing nearby. The complement stood at only fifteen engines in 1929: four 2—4—0s, a pair of 4—4—0s, half a dozen 0—6—0s, three of the Deeley 0—6—4 tanks and a pair of Johnson '1F' tanks. It had increased to twenty-nine by 1945, notably with the introduction of several 2—6—4Ts on the suburban services. The 0—6—4Ts had been engaged on local passenger work as well as some quite important turns, like the Birmingham-Leicester expresses, as late as 1924 but following various mishaps in the 1930s they were downgraded and subsequently withdrawn, several remaining stored by the side of the shed.

The shed was passed by in the LMS modernisation programme although a mobile canteen, 'presented by the men of the Argentine Railways' was provided inside the

2—4—0 survivor at Bournville, No. 20002, on 2nd March 1935.

H. C. Casserley

Bournville in September 1936. The shed was far from being a 'strategic' depot and for much of its existence could almost be described as a 'retirement home' for elderly engines.

W. Potter

A Midland type which long found refuge at Bournville. Outside framed 0—6—0 No. 2603 by the coal stage in March 1935.

H. C. Casserley

The presence of various stored locos over the years contributed to the shed's peaceful atmosphere. The two long sidings at the western side of the roundhouse held an interesting succession of engines and on 17th March 1935 contained a number of ex-LNWR 4—6—0 goods engines, Nos. 8723, 8786, 8820, 8832, 8841, 8842 and 8869.

W. A. Camwell

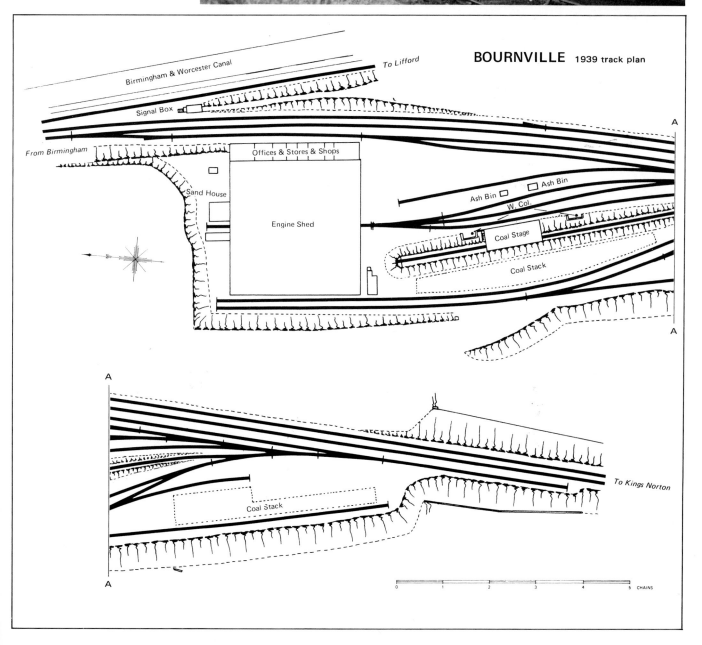

BOURNVILLE 1939 track plan

Birmingham & Worcester Canal

To Lifford

Signal Box

From Birmingham

Sand House

Offices & Stores & Shops

Engine Shed

Ash Bin   Ash Bin

W. Col.

Coal Stage

Coal Stack

A

A

A

A

Coal Stack

To Kings Norton

0   1   2   3   4   5 CHAINS

'Ancient and Modern' inside Bournville. Kirtley double-framed 0—6—0 No. 22630 accompanies new 2—6—4T No. 2556 in August 1936.
W. Potter

A view in August 1947. Engines comprise 2—6—2T No. 178, 4—4—0s Nos. 1064, 439 and 1039, and 0—6—0s Nos. 22863 and 3583.
J. V. Skirrow

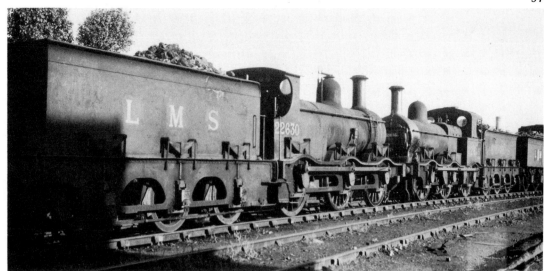

The ancient double-framed 0–6–0s of Midland vintage lingered at Bournville even into BR days and prompted numerous enthusiasts' visits. No. 22630, with Johnson boiler, is paired here on 29th June 1947 with Belpaire-boilered compatriot No. 22846. The latter was the last of its type to remain at the shed.

N. S. Eagles

shed itself. The turntable diameter was increased from 50 to 57 ft around 1948. The shed went out of action in 1956 when an engine fell into the pit damaging the table which was sent to Swindon for repair, the locos being forced to use Saltley and Bromsgrove for boiler inspection and wash-outs.

Closure was planned as early as 1959 but in the event was deferred until January 1960. Coded 21B since 1935, Bournville finally closed on 14th February 1960, with 'Black Five' No. 44843, the last loco 'off shed'. Left in store were 4–4–0s Nos. 40439, 40443, 40511, and 40568 and 0–6–0s Nos. 43490, 43675, 43693, 43858, 44084, 44227, 44406, and 44515. They were removed shortly afterwards (40439, 40443 and 40511 were in fact

sent to Toton, finishing their days on freights in January 1961) and the whole site cleared. The depot had been very much a backwater in latter years, particularly after the abandonment of the Birmingham suburban service round the Camp Hill line, but was notable for a number of Kirtley double-framed 0–6–0s, mainly used on the Halesowen branch. Of these engines, three had acquired Johnson boilers, Nos. 22630, 22818 and 22834 and three had Belpaire boilers, these being Nos. 22846, 22853 and 22863. The last to remain at the shed was No. 22846, withdrawn in 1949. The Kirtley 'horseshoe' tender from No. 22834 is now preserved with 2–4–0 No. 158A in the National Collection. The site at Bournville is now occupied by modern industrial development.

The depot from a passing train on 1st June 1957. It was never considered necessary to install mechanical aids at the under-used depot.

N. E. Preedy

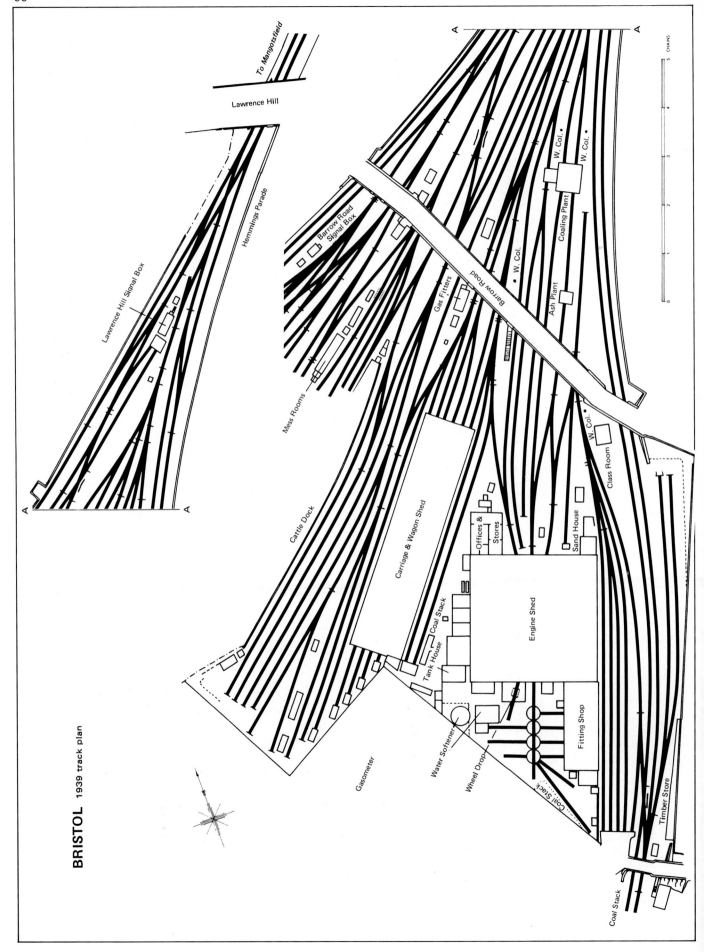

BRISTOL 1939 track plan

To Mangotsfield

Lawrence Hill

Hemmings Parade

Lawrence Hill Signal Box

Barrow Road Signal Box

Mess Rooms

Gas Fitters

Barrow Road

Cattle Dock

W. Col.

W. Col.

Coaling Plant

Ash Plant

W. Col.

Carriage & Wagon Shed

Coal Stack

Tank House

Offices & Stores

Sand House

Engine Shed

Class Room

W. Col.

Gasometer

Water Softener

Wheel Drop

Fitting Shop

Coal Stack

Timber Store

Coal Stack

CHAINS
0 1 2 3 4 5

The yard at Bristol was neatly bisected by the stone bridge carrying Barrow Road. A flight of steps leading down from this public road formed the shed entrance and the viewpoint of this 1936 photograph.

L & GRP

BRISTOL

The Midland leased the Bristol and Gloucester Railway in 1846 and inherited a small shed put up by that company. It was fairly well equipped for this early period, for by 1849 it was resolved 'to construct a new engine pit under the shear-legs at Bristol'. The coke stage was enlarged in 1859 and in 1866 following 'additions to the skylights' a contract was awarded for the thorough cleaning of the shed and the repair of all the doors and windows.

Estimates were ordered to be prepared for a new building on 17th October 1871 and this was quickly accomplished, the figure of £20,000 being arrived at by 31st of the same month. The shed, a standard roundhouse with 42 ft turntable, was ready in 1873 and a four road fitting shop at the rear opened the following year. The shed's principal duties were expresses on the Birmingham line, but freight was also very important. Ten of the famous '800' class 2—4—0s built by Neilson in 1870, Nos. 820-829, (53-62 in 1907) went to Bristol and worked exclusively on the Birmingham trains. They were replaced in 1880 by the '1282' series of 2—4—0s which again did not work north of Birmingham. After 1888, however, the shed did acquire a longer working, the 'Scotch Express' to Derby using 6′ 6″ 2—4—0s Nos. 1295 and 1296. Some of the 7′ 9″ '115' class singles succeeded the 2—4—0s following their construction in 1892. Goods traffic had remained in the hands of relatively elderly double-framed engines and Bristol had to wait until 1892 before any of the new

0—4—4T No. 1267 in May 1935. On the far side of Barrow Road bridge is the original Midland coal stage, demolished on modernisation by the LMS.

H. C. Casserley

'1357' (3020-3129 series in 1907) 'express goods' 0—6—0s, first introduced in 1878, were made available. In 1875-76 new 0—4—4Ts Nos. 1274-1281 (1248-1255 in 1907) had arrived and these engines remained on the local services to Bath and Clifton Downs until the mid-1880s.

The '4P' compound 4—4—0s (in the late 'twenties and early 'thirties these comprised Nos. 1023-1031, noted for their outward cleanliness and obviously fine mechanical condition) were the largest engines on the Birmingham expresses until 'Black Fives' and 'Jubilees' arrived in the

'Barrow Road' shed, as it became known in BR days, in 1963.

T. W. Nicholls

late 1930s. The compounds were able to work west of Derby when the viaduct near Wichnor was strengthened in 1924 and replaced '700' class 4—4—0s on the West of England line. Three 2—4—0s remained at the shed as late as 1933, No. 92 (No. 20092 from 1934) one of the last Kirtley single-framed 2—4—0s; No. 155, built by Johnson in 1876, and later 6′ 6″ engine No. 157. Both the Johnson engines survived to be renumbered in the 20,000 series, No. 20155 transferring to the service department as 'Engineer South Wales' at Abergavenny ex-LNWR shed.

'Jubilees' and 'Black 5's came in the late 1930s and the number of 'Jubilee' 4—6—0s had increased to twelve following Nationalisation. However, some of the two-cylinder 4—6—0s were transferred away, freight remaining in the hands of MR and LMS 0—6—0s throughout the 1950s. At least one ex-LYR 'pug' was also at Bristol for many years. No. 11212 had gone there in the 'thirties and was still there twenty years later as No. 51212, accompanied in 1954 by No. 51202. The latter engine had replaced Sentinel No. 7190 originally built for the Somer-

The dirt and grime of the twilight of steam.

R. J. Essery

The gas holders at the rear of the shed were another 'landmark' at Bristol and overshadowed the shed itself.　　　*R. J. Essery*

The four tracks on the east side of the shed were also overlooked by a public road and were invariably full of locomotives in steam, although stored engines were depressingly in evidence in latter years. It was much photographed and this view, taken in the 'sixties, is fairly typical, with ex-Great Western types intermingled with BR and ex-LMS engines.

Photographer unknown

The Bristol coaling plant, installed around 1938/9. It was of the 'No. 2' type, having a pair of 75 ton bunkers. Dozens of these structures were provided by the LMS, in bewildering variety, and drawings etc. were provided in Volume One of this series.

T. W. Nicholls

For many years an outside turntable was located in the area shown on the right of this picture. *T. W. Nicholls*

set and Dorset Railway and indeed the engines off the latter system were often to be found at Bristol (as well as Gloucester) for repair work not possible at Bath.

Bristol was Midland shed number 8 with sub-sheds at Bath and Thornbury (closed in 1944) and on the reorganisation of 1935 it became a 'concentration' depot, 22A, of a district which included Gloucester and the former S & D sheds. A new 60 ft turntable was supplied in 1927 at a cost of £3,212 and new coal and ash plants with an improved yard layout were completed in 1938-39. It was transferred to the Western Region as 82E from February 1958 and ex-GWR engines were increasingly in evidence, especially following the closure to steam of Bath Road shed in September 1960. The MR depot was by now more generally known as 'Barrow Road' to distinguish it from the two ex-Great Western sheds in the city and the announcement came in 1960 that it would become 'the residual steam depot for Bristol'. St. Philip's Marsh shed duly closed in 1964 and there was a further influx of pannier tanks, 'prairies' and so on. The shed survived to become virtually the last point on the Western Region able to service steam locomotives and finally closed on 14th October 1965. It remained disused for a time but has now been completely demolished.

The ash handling plant at Bristol, of ferro-concrete construction, was the sturdiest of a number of designs employed by the LMS and again described more fully in Volume One. *R. J. Essery*

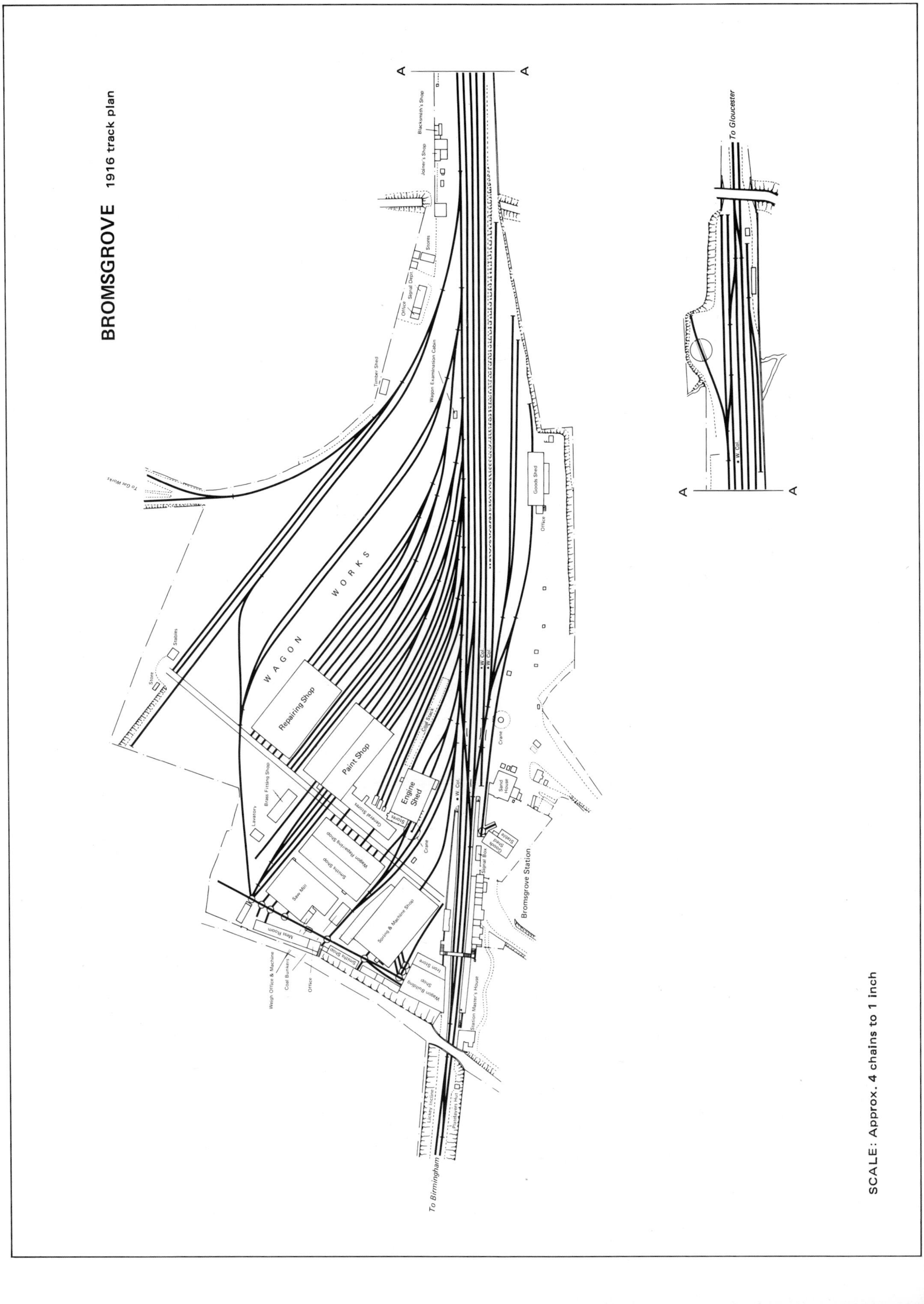

BROMSGROVE 1916 track plan

To Gloucester

A A

A A

• W. Col

Blacksmith's Shop

Joiner's Shop

Stores

Office Signal Shed

Turntable Shed

Wagon Examination Cabin

To Gas Works

W A G O N

W O R K S

Stables

Store

Repairing Shop

Paint Shop

Goods Shed

Office

Coal Stack

Crane

• W. Col
• W. Col

Engine Shed

Brass Fitting Shop

Lavatory

Smiths Shop

Wagon Assembling Shop

• W. Col

Sand House

Smiths Shop

Saw Mill

Smithy & Machine Shop

Spring Box

WORKS
SIGNAL BOX

Signal Box

Crane

Iron Store

Mess Room

Wagon Weigh Office & Machine

Coal Bunkers

Office

Smiths Shop

Wagon Building Shop

Bromsgrove Station

Station Master's House

Lickey Incline

Goods Hall

To Birmingham

SCALE: Approx. 4 chains to 1 inch

Bromsgrove shed in May 1949. The building had a somewhat rambling and crowded aspect, the whole displaying great individuality.

H. C. Casserley

BROMSGROVE

Banking engines were required from the outset when the Lickey Incline, over two miles at 1 in 37½, opened in 1840. A shed was built by the Birmingham and Gloucester Railway alongside their works and, although altered and extended over the years, remained in use until the end of steam. The depot existed primarily to house and service the Lickey banking engines and the history of the shed is bound up with the successive generations of these locos.

The first bankers were four or five USA-built Norris engines which were supplemented in 1845 by a large 0–6–0ST *Great Britain*, specially designed by J. E. McConnell and constructed in Bromsgrove shops.

Four new well tanks for banking duties on the Lickey Incline were built between 1860 and 1863 and these were

succeeded by standard Johnson '1F' 0–6–0Ts. In June 1892 Nos. 210, 211, 212, 215 and 216 (1720-1724 after 1907) were at the shed. Bromsgrove's three roads were numbered upwards from north to south and until 1892 a turntable was supplied on No. 3 road. In that year it was transferred to a site about 640 yards south of the shed. This was equipped with a coal stage and rest room for crews and became known as 'Bromsgrove South', those banking engines 'on duty' stabling there between trips up the incline and back again. The turntable and coal stage had indeed figured prominently in a variety of alterations carried out in the period 1855-57. Messrs. J. Cowley had been the proud recipients of a tender amounting to £19.1s.5d. for unspecified 'alterations to the turntable' and Messrs. Hiltons' tender of £94.0s.0d. had also been accepted for 'alterations to the coke stage' and the erection

MR 0–6–0 No. 2905 outside the shed in 1921.

Collection R. Carpenter

The shed was repaired and thoroughly 'tidied up' by BR but nevertheless retained much of its charm. Part of the wagon works can be seen in the background, 11th August 1956.

T. J. Edgington

of a cokesman's cabin. At the same time it was 'ordered: that the ash pit at the entrance to the station be removed'. The 42 ft turntable formerly at Hendon was ordered to be enlarged in January 1892 to 46 ft for use at Bromsgrove.

The depot was coded 4a, a sub-shed of Worcester, but carried out all its own washouts and minor repairs. A large reservoir cut into the red sandstone south of the Alvechurch Road bridge supplied the works and station but the shed tank was fed from an adjacent borehole, with a delivery hose inside the shed itself. Worcester, the parent shed, had closed in December 1932 and facilities at Bromsgrove were improved. Two years later Bromsgrove became 21C, a 'garage' of Saltley, retaining this code until transfer to the Western Region as 85F in February 1958.

The shed's most famous engine, the 0–10–0 'Big Bertha' (its Derby nickname), arrived shortly after construction in 1919 and spent its entire working life there. MR No. 2290 'Bertha' was renumbered 22290 in 1947 and 58100 in 1948 and standard '3F' tanks replaced the old Johnson engines assisting her. By 1906 '1F's Nos. 1932-1938 had become the regular bankers and Nos. 1934-1938 remained at Bromsgrove until September

One of the ex-GW tanks drafted in by the WR as replacements for the LMS tanks is just visible inside the shed on 5th July 1959.
W. T. Stubbs

1941, when they were replaced by similar LMS built '3F' tanks. In 1954 these were Nos. 47276, 47301, 47303, 47305, 47308, 47425, 47502 and 47565. MR '3F' No. 47234 had remained as a shunting engine until 1951 before being transferred away. Potential replacements for 58100 which had been tried over the years included ex-LNW 0–8–4T No. 7953, in 1929/1930, and ex-LMS Garratt No. 4998 was also tried on the incline in 1934, but was soon found unsuitable. LNER Garratt No. 69999 had two spells on the incline, the first having been from March 1949 to November 1950, returning as an oil burner during the summer of 1955 before withdrawal in December.

Sadly, 'Big Bertha' (she was also known as 'Big Emma') was withdrawn the following year, '9F' 2–10–0 No. 92079 afterwards becoming the main Lickey banker. Pannier tanks replaced the '3F's, No. 92223 succeeded 92079 on takeover by the WR in 1958 and the shed was recoded 85D in January 1961. Bromsgrove's bankers became redundant with dieselisation on the Bristol-Birmingham main line and the shed closed on 27th September 1964. It was still standing intact in about 1975.

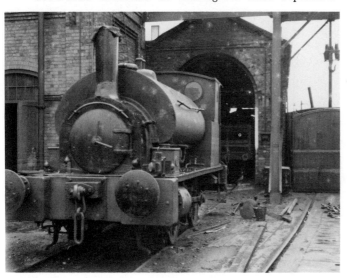

Ex-Caledonian 0–4–0ST No. 56020 stabled at the rear of Bromsgrove in 1955. It was originally sent there to serve the oil burning ex-LNER Garratt on its second sojourn on the incline, as a pump and heater for the big engine's oil supply. *Pendon Museum*

Burton sheds and yard in 1946.   L & GRP

BURTON

In 1900 Messrs. Bass & Co. despatched 113,825 wagons of beer, the great majority running over Midland metals. There were no less than thirteen other breweries in Burton at this time and the value of the town to the Midland Railway can be readily appreciated. A coke stage and pit had been provided at the station in 1849 and an engine shed was in use from June 1859, under foreman Thomas Ryder. It was rather small and in 1861 the Way and Works Committee ordered 'that some land near the Engine Shed at Burton about 13 feet in width be purchased from the Marquis of Anglesey'. Some two years later in October 1863 further instructions were issued, 'that the shear-legs at Burton be lengthened, and the sand furnace be rebuilt and a roof erected between the Shed and Tank House'. The turntable was enlarged the following year, but the ever increasing needs of the country's beer drinkers meant that additional accommodation was already overdue. The Midland's share of the traffic rocketed with the extension to London and in February 1868 it was decided to purchase more land from the Marquis, eight acres in all, at £500 per acre. An estimate was obtained for a single roundhouse on the site in March 1869 and a standard building with coal stage, etc. opened in 1870.

Most of the shed's duties were freight of course with a high proportion of shunting turns. Among various tanks a succession of elderly tender locos were consigned to Burton at the end of their working lives to shunt the brewery sidings and yards. Much of the work was, however, carried out by the breweries' own locomotives or Burton's allocation would have been far higher. (As well as innumerable horses, Bass, for instance, owned over a dozen engines and Allsopp's half that number).

Over one hundred locos were at Burton shed in its heyday in the 1930s, a handful of them Johnson '2P' 4—4—0s and '1P' 0—4—4Ts for the various local passenger turns. Until the 'twenties the 4—4—0 duties had been

handled by '156' class rebuilt 2—4—0s, a number of them based at Burton for many years. MR short wheelbase tanks, including Johnson 0—4—0STs Nos 1510 and 1506 and later Deeley side tank versions, examples of which were still at work in the 'sixties, (41516 was the last to remain) were always a feature at Burton. Indeed small tanks had been part of the Burton scene for many years, a fact noted by Ahrons in 1919. 'Some of the oldest Midland shunting engines are kept there to attend to the beer. Officially these old engines are recorded as dating back to 1847/8, but this is a clerical anachronism for in actual truth there is nothing older than 1857/8 in them and only five of them remain at work.' He was in fact referring to five surviving Kirtley well tanks, three of the small variety, Nos. 1601, 1602 and 1603 which began life as 2—2—2 passenger engines in 1848/55, undergoing conversion to 0—6—0WTs in 1872 and two large well tanks, Nos. 1600 and 1604. The rest of the allocation consisted almost entirely of 0—6—0s of all types with ex-LNW locos formerly housed at Horninglow very much in evidence. There were twenty-two rebuilt '2P' and '3P' 4—4—0s for local passenger work to Derby, Coalville, Leicester etc, with a few 0—4—4Ts. 'Crab' 2—6—0s supplemented the '4F's in the 1930s on the celebrated London beer trains. No. 16020, a Caledonian Railway 'pug', was also allocated to Burton during and after World War Two.

The second roundhouse, 'No. 2' shed, with a 50 ft Cowans Sheldon turntable was added on spare ground between the original shed and the main line in 1892. This was the only significant development at Burton until dieselisation by BR, the depot remaining something of a backwater. Both turntables were enlarged by the LMS, the original 42 ft example in 'No. 1' giving way to a 57 ft table and the 50 ft unit in 'No. 2' being increased to 55 ft. The shed was Midland Railway No. 2 and took over responsibility for Horninglow ex-LNWR shortly after Grouping, while the North Staffordshire Railway shed was closed and demolished. The 1935 reorganisation saw the

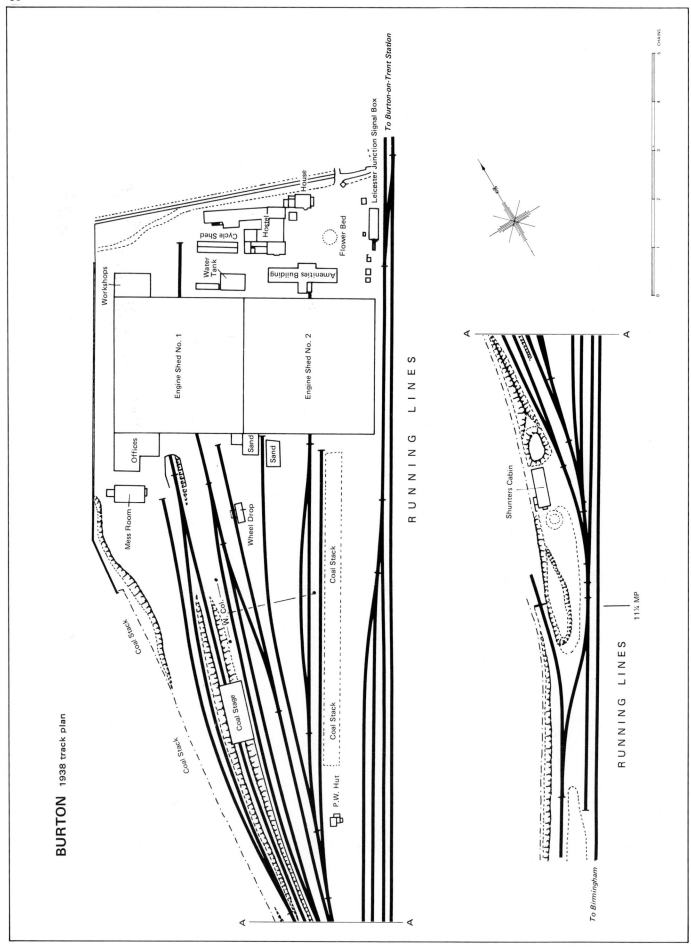

BURTON 1938 track plan

Workshops

Cycle Shed

Hostel

House

Water Tank

Amenities Building

Flower Bed

Leicester Junction Signal Box

To Burton-on-Trent Station

Engine Shed No. 1

Engine Shed No. 2

Offices

Mess Room

Sand

Sand

Wheel Drop

Coal Stack

Coal Stack

Coal Stack

Coal Stack

Coal Stage

W. Col.

P.W. Hut

A

A

RUNNING LINES

Shunters Cabin

A

A

11¼ MP

To Birmingham

RUNNING LINES

5 CHAINS

0 1 2 3 4 5

A similar view, from a passing train, on 28th April 1957.

W. Potter

Elderly ex-MR 0–6–0 No. 58130 at Burton in May 1953.

H. C. Casserley

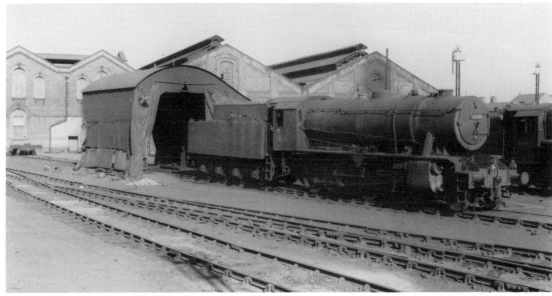

'WD' 2–8–0 No. 90602 on the wheeldrop road in later BR days. These covered wheeldrops were installed at many depots by the LMS, replacements for the old MR shear-legs.

R. J. Essery

The stark exterior of Burton's 'single' coal stage. The building remained in use until the end of steam but, like many of these structures, required extensive repairs over the years, with large portions rebricked. Unusually for a unit of this size, timber was employed for the 'blank' side. The stages at Kettering and Mansfield embodied this feature but were on a much smaller scale.

R. J. Essery

shed coded 17B under Derby, eventually becoming part of the Toton district as 16F in September 1963. A wheel drop had been installed by the LMS and latterly Burton was the only depot in the district with such facilities, the shear-legs at Derby itself having disappeared by at least 1944 (the steam breakdown crane subsequently being pressed into service!). Burton was consequently kept busy on hot axle box repairs, etc, with engines larger than a '4MT' 2—6—4T having to be sent from Derby. Burton also had a properly equipped machine shop, including wheel lathe, in contrast to Derby, ostensibly the 'concentration' depot.

In the mid-1950s there were 96 locos at Burton, over half of them still 0—6—0s. '8F' 2—8—0s had begun to arrive and three BR standard locos, 2—6—2Ts Nos. 84006, 84007 and 84008, had been sent new to the shed for local work like the Tutbury autotrain. With the onset of dieselisation and with an increasing proportion of the beer traffic moving by road, the number of engines declined steadily. Something of an anomaly resulting from this was a fleet of some twenty 'Jubilee' 4—6—0s sent to Burton in the early 1960s to end their working lives. Grandiose proposals for a large diesel depot on the site of the two roundhouses were eventually abandoned in view of the drastic decline in BR's share of the town's goods traffic but a small servicing shed was eventually opened on the old coal stacking ground. The sheds were abandoned and sold off to a private firm, in whose hands they remain.

Stanier locos, including some of the 'Jubilees', Burton's 'swan-song', predominate in this view taken on 9th August 1964. *W. Potter*

Canklow, 3rd July 1966, retaining to the end its Midland features. The shed by this time was only available for servicing visiting steam locos.

W. Potter

CANKLOW

The Midland empire expanded to the extent that in some cities one engine shed was insufficient for the traffic and the number of engines involved. This was particularly so in the Sheffield area where eventually three large depots were necessary. Grimesthorpe in the industrial heart of the city was first, followed by Millhouses and Canklow at the turn of the century. The purchase of land for the new engine shed at Canklow, costing £6,025, was approved on 1st July 1898 and as there was no suitable site available a considerable amount of earthworks were involved, C. Barker & Sons winning the contract, of over £6,900, for preparation of the site at 'Masborough'. Messrs. E. Brown & Sons' tender of £15,032.12s.5d. was accepted

on 15th December 1898 and the shed, referred to in the early years as 'Canklow Junction, Masborough' opened in 1900 on the west side of the MR's North Midland line opposite Canklow Wood. Equipped with a 55 ft turntable and a 'single' coal stage, adequate for this size of depot, it operated, at first, some forty locos. They were officially outstationed from Grimesthorpe, the parent shed, Canklow's code being 25b. 'Coal and iron' was the main product of the district and the shed's allocation, consisting entirely of 0—6—0s and a few shunting tanks, reflected this.

There was a previous shed, or rather depot, in the district in North Midland Railway days but its exact location has not been established. Later, in 1854, tenders were let for the construction 'of an engine shed and tank

Canklow a month later, on 1st August 1966. The various tanks were all stored, following their withdrawal from the Staveley Works duties.

Ken Fairey

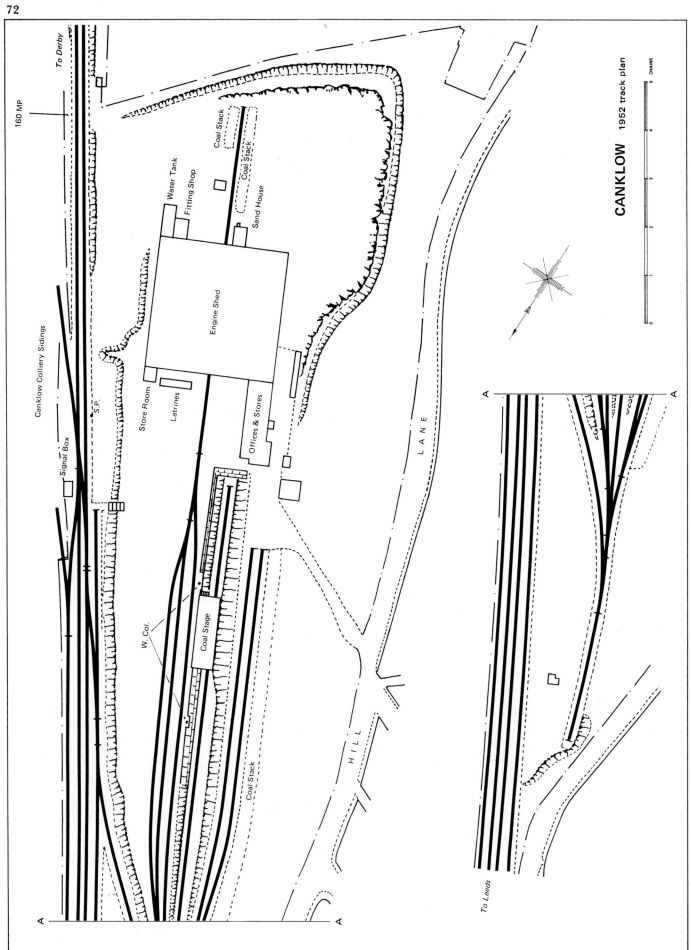

To Derby

160 MP

Canklow Colliery Sidings

Signal Box

S.P.

Water Tank

Fitting Shop

Coal Stack

Coal Stack

Sand House

Engine Shed

Store Room

Latrines

Offices & Stores

W. Col.

Coal Stage

Coal Stack

HILL

LANE

To Leeds

A — A

CANKLOW   1952 track plan

0   1   2   3   4   5   CHAINS

A reminder of the shed's earlier days, when MR 0−6−0s were responsible for the great bulk of the goods traffic. Nos. 58170 and 43225 keep company with a modern successor, 2−8−0 No. 48209.

L. Hanson

house at Masborough' and in 1881 gas and water were laid to the 'new engine shed', the allocation a year previously being a single 0−6−0, No. 268. Certainly a turntable and assorted buildings were in use for locomotive servicing by 1889, sited in the fork of lines south of Rotherham station.

Canklow's subsequent history can be described briefly as few developments of any note occurred over the sixty or so years of its existence. The shed retained its MR pitched roof and the coal stage, yard layout and even the type and numbers of locomotives allocated changed only gradually.

0−6−0s and 0−6−0Ts formed the bulk of its allocation and half a dozen 'G3' 0−8−0s had found their way there by 1930. No. 9631 was present as late as 1946. The shed became 19C in 1935 by which time '4F's represented an increasing proportion of the 0−6−0 stock. '8F' 2−8−0s arrived during the war when the complement rose to

nearly seventy locomotives. Unusually, in the 1940s, several '3P' 4−4−0s were also at Canklow, for freight duties, the last survivor of this class, No. 40726, being withdrawn from the shed in 1952. Canklow was also notable in retaining about eight old '2F' 0−6−0s until the mid-1950s and by that time there were fifteen of the Stanier 2−8−0s, Garratts were frequent visitors, and '43000' moguls had arrived. '9F's appeared at the end of the decade. The shed was transferred to the Eastern Region as 41D in February 1958 and by February 1965 was one of the last two ER steam sheds, with thirty-seven locos. Millhouses had closed in January 1962, its engines and duties transferring to Canklow which in turn closed on 11th October 1965. Its allocation had been transferred away the previous May but the facilities remained available for the dwindling number of visiting steam locomotives until about September 1966. Although in poor condition the building was still standing in October 1980.

Freight and shunting engines at Canklow on 9th September 1951, including '1F' No. 41805 and Garratt No. 47969.

W. Potter

Coalville in 1907.   *Courtesy Leicester Museum*

COALVILLE

There was a small one road shed here from the earliest years, with offices and stores on the north side and a turntable at the rear. This 'table was enlarged following orders in 1857 'that the Engine Turntable at Coalville be lengthened'. Some of the rebuilt '50' class 2—4—0s were stationed in the area in the 1880s employed on locals to Leicester and freight, mainly coal, also tended to be relatively local in nature. According to Ahrons, 'around 1890 2—2—2 No. 35 was quartered at Coalville and worked local trains to Leicester. The road, however, between

Leicester and Coalville is a very heavy one and quite unsuitable for small single engines so that I do not understand what induced the Locomotive Running Department to station this engine in this District'. In any event, the number of engines required was steadily increasing and a new shed, a three road brick built affair, with standard small coal stage, 50 ft turntable, shear-legs, etc. opened in that year, plans and estimates having been prepared as early as 1st February 1889. These totalled £5,750, excluding land, and the building was intended to house nine locomotives. Edward Woods' tender of £3,536.12s.9d. for the shed itself was accepted on 19th September 1889 and the necessary land was purchased in November. The depot was finally completed in the following year but the water supply was found to be inadequate, a new well becoming necessary in 1893, at a cost of over £800. A sub-shed of Leicester and coded 10b, it eventually housed around thirty locomotives, a handful of 2—4—0s and 0—6—0Ts and the rest a collection of Kirtley and Johnson 0—6—0s.

Elevated to 'garage' status under Derby as 17C in 1935, various small improvements followed. The ash pit was renewed in 1939 and extended in 1944 and the deep well from which the shed drew its water received a new pump. Softening apparatus for the supply was also provided. New 'G3' 0—8—0s, Nos. 9631-9634, had arrived in 1931 and '8F' 2—8—0s appeared at the shed during the Second World War, the latter only to be transferred away when traffic subsequently declined. Of twenty-one locos allocated in January 1954, all but one, a '3F' tank No. 47449, were ex-MR or LMS 0—6—0s. Most notable were three

The original single road shed.   *Courtesy Leicester Museum*

The yard in BR days. The pit on the right indicates the site of the original shed.   *R. J. Essery*

Left: The coal stage, battered but unbowed, soldiered on until the end of steam power at Coalville. *Right:* The rear of the coal stage and the archaic contents of its gloomy interior. All the photographs on this page were taken in 1964.

R. J. Essery

The coal stage approach.   *R. J. Essery*

Midland '2F's, Nos. 58163, 58247 and 58264, (the latter two retaining Johnson cabs) necessary for the Leicester West Bridge workings over the former Leicester and Swannington Railway with its restricted clearances. Three of the '2F's were retained at Coalville, the last of their class, until displaced by a BR Mogul No. 78013 with slightly modified cab, in December 1963. The loco was taken through Glenfield Tunnel before modification to check the clearances between the eaves of the cab roof and the tunnel wall, in places found to be only half an inch! Had the engine failed the staff would have been trapped on the footplate! The last '2F' to remain in service, No. 58182, was put to work in Coalville goods yard, 'spare' until a second modified 2—6—0 became available.

The shed had been recoded 15D under Wellingborough in April 1958 and on 11th May the following year it received its first diesel 0—6—0 shunter No. D2508. In September 1963 it was again recoded, 15E, but closed only two years later in October 1965, its last allocation consisting mainly of '8F' 2—8—0s. The rails were removed and the building, though still intact in August 1967, has now been demolished.

One of the specially retained '2F' 0—6—0s, No. 58143, on the Coalville turntable on 3rd May 1962. The crew have gone to lunch after a trip from Leicester.

R. C. Riley

More detail at Coalville in February 1964, showing the tank and the site of the original shed. *R. J. Essery*

The water softener introduced by the LMS. (Drawings of this type of unit were provided in Volume 1 together with their general distribution over the LMS system). The steam locomotive was a profligate machine and produced a range of often unpleasant waste products. Ash, clinker, smoke, etc. were familiar enough but even processes designed to increase efficiency contributed to the range of unsavoury by-products. The sludge precipitated by the softening process had to be removed in tanks (usually old tenders sufficed) for disposal, and one or two, stained and begrimed, were usually stabled near to the plant. Chemicals necessary to initiate the process came in large drums and again numbers of these, both full and empty, could usually be found scattered around the immediate vicinity.

R. J. Essery

Ashford-built 2–8–0 No. 48619 glides past the coal stage on 3rd May 1962.

R. C. Riley

Top left: Coalville after closure, 29th July 1967. *Left:* The offices occupied the north side, together with the inevitable cycle shed. *Above:* Offices etc., and general dump, February 1964.

D. Banks & R. J. Essery

The rear of the shed in February 1964. The sand house on the right, along with the shed itself, was reclad in corrugated sheeting.

R. J. Essery

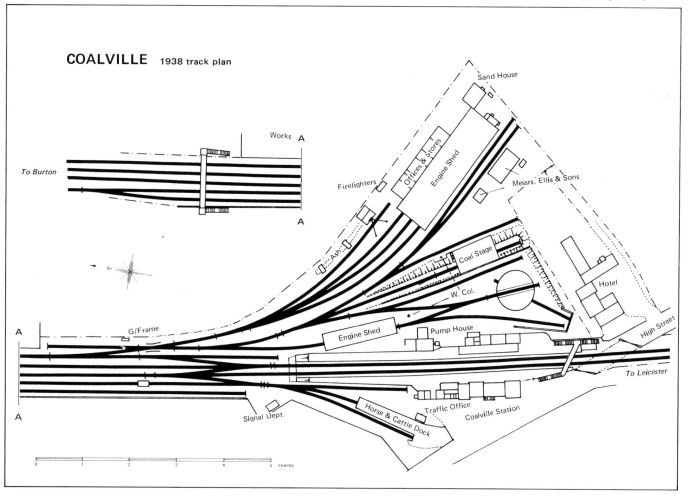

COALVILLE 1938 track plan

To Burton

Works A

A

Firelighters

Offices & Stores

Engine Shed

Sand House

Messrs. Ellis & Sons

Ash

Coal Stage

W. Col.

Hotel

A

G/Frame

Engine Shed

Pump House

High Street

To Leicester

A

Signal Dept.

Horse & Cattle Dock

Traffic Office

Coalville Station

0 1 2 3 4 5 CHAINS

Looking south over the Cricklewood complex in BR days, the two rebuilt roundhouses just right of centre. The major road parallel and to the west of the main line is the Edgware Road, meeting the North Circular Road at 'Staples Corner' in the centre foreground. The east-west engine loop describes a great tear drop, diving under the North Circular bridge and connecting the 'up' and 'down' sides.

Aerofilms

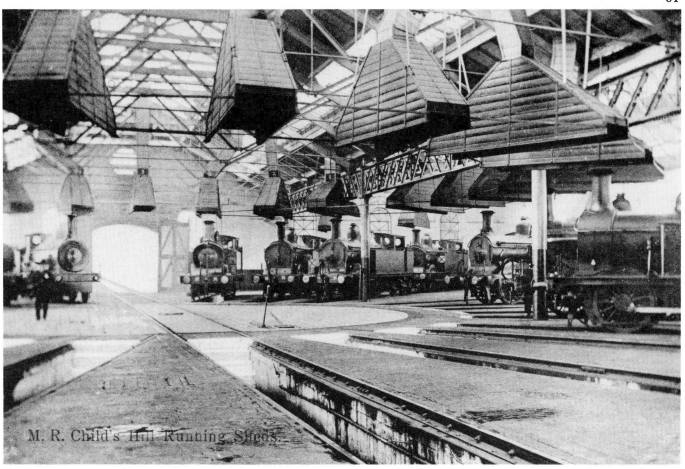

Inside 'Childs Hill Running Sheds' in the early years of this century.

Collection O. Carter

CRICKLEWOOD

Traffic, notably coal, increased greatly following the opening of the London Extension and the main sorting sidings were laid out in open country beyond the margins of the capital at Brent. A small shed, 'Hendon', was opened in 1870 to house 4 locos; it had a turntable costing £588.5s.7d. and a coaling crane at £67 was also provided. This shed, although it remained extant over 80 years later, was inadequate for the burgeoning freight traffic and was in use for little more than ten years, a new standard round-house opening in 1882. Known until around 1900 as 'Childs Hill' it had been built for £14,967 by G. Lilley & Sons. The vast Brent sidings continued to grow apace and in 1893 a second roundhouse was added. The new 'No. 2' shed contained a 50 ft turntable supplied by Messrs. Eastwood Limited and, a measure of Cricklewood's increasing importance, a fitting shop for 6 locos was built alongside. The coal stage was doubled in size to serve the enlarged shed which eventually acquired an allocation of around 70 locomotives. The majority of these were 0—6—0s and 0—6—0Ts but Cricklewood did have a limited number of passenger turns, using Johnson 0—4—4Ts and latterly 2—6—2Ts. In later years, the shed also became responsible for a number of Tilbury boat trains, 'Crab' 2—6—0s being favourites on these turns. Over 300 trains a day were marshalled at Brent and there were 8 pilot duties alone, for many years in the charge of Johnson 0—6—0Ts. The endless procession of coal empties to Wellingborough

and beyond were worked by successive generations of MR 0—6—0s, supplemented by LMS '4F' versions from 1924. From the late 'twenties of course 0—8—0s and Garratts took over an increasing proportion of the coal traffic.

The 0—6—0s remained the principal freight type, in terms of numbers at least, until after the Second World War, '8F' 2—8—0s not arriving until about 1948. They had of course been familiar as visitors for a number of years. Nine were stationed at Cricklewood by 1954, aided by 'Crab' and '4MT' 2—6—0s. BR '9F' 2—10—0s later appeared and a considerable number of these powerful locos were eventually provided, finally ousting the assorted 0—6—0s, Garratts, etc. from main line work. During the same period most of the pilot turns were given over to diesel shunters. Garratts from Toton and Wellingborough were frequent visitors until the 1950s but unlike at their home sheds, no special accommodation was built for them at Cricklewood. The giant locos normally stood on the 'Brent Ash Pits' within the 'Brent Empty Wagon Sidings' on the opposite side of the Acton Wells junction line from the shed. Locomotives simply requiring turning and fire cleaning were dealt with here, obviating the need to enter the shed yard and for many years a turntable was provided. Garratts were turned on the Brent East to West engine loop which passed under the viaduct to the north of the complex right alongside the North Circular Road. Engines appeared on this loop with a suddenness that could be startling for pedestrians and motorists alike. The steeply graded line down to the loop was a grassy and relatively secluded area with something of the atmosphere of a

Early years and a surprisingly rural setting at Cricklewood.

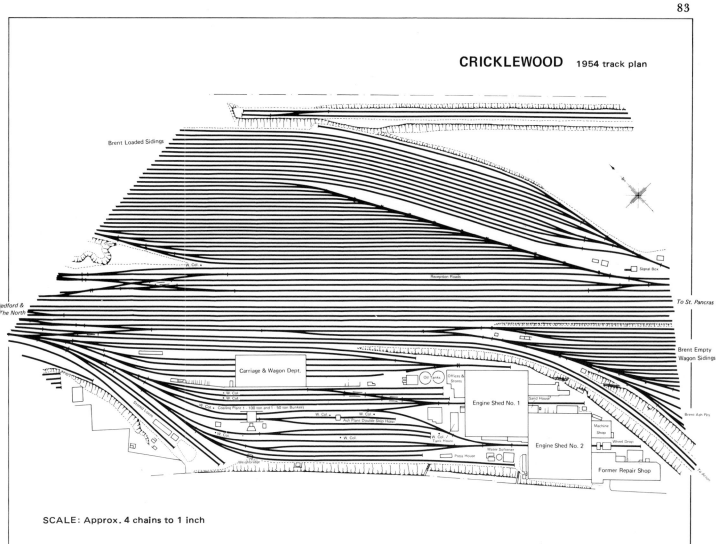

CRICKLEWOOD 1954 track plan

Brent Loaded Sidings

W. Col.

Reception Roads

Signal Box

Bedford & The North

To St. Pancras

Brent Empty Wagon Sidings

Carriage & Wagon Dept.

Oil Tanks

Offices & Stores

Engine Shed No. 1

Sand House

Brent Ash Pits

Stored Locos

W. Col.
W. Col.

Coaling Plant 1 - 100 ton and 1 - 50 ton Bunkers

Ash Plant Double Skip Hoist

W. Col.

W. Col.

W. Col.

Machine Shop

W. Col.

W. Col. /
Tank House

Engine Shed No. 2

Wheel Drop

W. Col.

Press House

Water Softener

Former Repair Shop

To Acton

Weighbridge

SCALE: Approx. 4 chains to 1 inch

Cricklewood yard with Garratt No. 4995 temporarily stored.

N. S. Eagles

84

Cricklewood's coaler differed in appearance from the majority erected by the LMS. It was in fact a precursor of the main construction programme initiated in 1933 and was in use when the LMS had these publicity photographs taken in August 1932. Rotating bunkers like the one carried by this member of the class were intended to ease the fireman's task on the mighty Garratts. They required great care on the part of the shed staff, however, and could easily be 'over-rotated' and become jammed. The complete emptying of the bunker was afterwards the *easier* part of the restoration! Like most subsequent coaling plants, two bunkers, enabling different quantities of coal to be delivered, were provided but, unlike later practice, in this case they were of different capacities: 100 tons and 50 tons.

BBC Hulton Picture Library

Left: The coaler in 1957. *Centre & right:* Two further views taken to illustrate the principles of the new 'one-man coaling plant'. Plants such as this worked splendidly until the inevitable wagon plank became stuck fast and halted operations. Terrible trials might then have to be endured by the luckless shed staff! Other problems came about when wagons were wrongly marshalled and it was not unknown for wagonloads of firebars, old rail chairs or firebox bricks to be dumped unsuspectingly into the bunker. This sort of disaster was eclipsed on one infamous occasion at Cricklewood when a load of detonators found their way into the plant. The authorities spent a fraught few hours tracking down locomotives which had inadvertently been transformed into potential bombs!

W. Potter and BBC Hulton Picture Library

country branch, a lunch spot favoured by some staff in the summer months! One interesting aspect of Cricklewood's activities was the handling of Midland Division locos passing to and from Bow Works, 'running in' from the depot for a week or so on local trips before returning to their home sheds.

The repair shop had been closed and let to a private concern in the 1920s and the turntable in 'No. 1' shed was enlarged to 55 ft in 1933. New coaling and ash handling apparatus was provided by the LMS but badly needed roof renewals ('No. 2' was actually roofless by 1948) fell to BR. Both sheds were rebuilt in early BR days employing the usual concrete style, the first to be dealt with being 'No. 2', 'No. 1' following a few years later.

Cricklewood was shed No. 15 in MR days and became 14A, the Midland Division's London 'concentration' depot, in 1935. Despite this the administrative head-

quarters remained at Kentish Town which, unlike Cricklewood, could accommodate the larger express passenger 4–6–0s. Passenger services into St. Pancras were finally dieselised in 1963, Kentish Town then ceasing to be used for stabling purposes. Some of its locos went to Cricklewood but the main shed's own days were numbered. A large new diesel maintenance depot had opened on the opposite side of the main line, by the former carriage shed and on 9th September 1963 as 'Cricklewood East' it took over the 14A code, the steam shed becoming 14B 'Cricklewood West'. A dwindling number of '8F's, '9F's and 'Black Fives' on freights continued to use the shed throughout 1964 but steam was finally banished on 14th December. Diesels, mainly Derby Sulzer type '2's, used the shed, officially a 'stabling point' for a while but it was eventually demolished and the site cleared, the privately owned former repair shop the only portion of the shed to survive.

Diesels continued to use the old shed for quite a lengthy period but the general air of abandonment and dereliction was beginning to take a hold when this photograph was taken in July 1967.

W. T. Stubbs

The interior of Derby 'No. 4' in pre-Grouping days.

The scene from the engineer's offices in the late 1880s.

Collection J. B. Radford

DERBY

For a long time Derby was the Midland's most important depot with an allocation of very nearly a hundred locomotives as early as 1876. Despite this, the engines at Derby were possibly the worst housed on the system and new 'square shed' accommodation was not provided until comparatively late, in 1890. To trace the various developments at Derby it is necessary to look at the pre-Midland era when three companies, forerunners of the Midland itself, were operating from the town. The Birmingham and Derby Junction Railway and the Midland Counties Railway opened in 1839 and the North Midland Railway the following year. All three had engine sheds with that of the North Midland providing most interest. It formed the basis of subsequent designs and its layout, enlarged from sixteen to twenty-four roads, was duplicated at a number of locations. Of the other two companies, the Birmingham and Derby Junction erected a three road straight shed in brick and the Midland Counties a broadly similar building. Expansion of the locomotive workshops eventually put paid to the two latter sheds (although the MCR building found subsequent new use) but increased accommodation was required even before amalgamation of the three companies in 1844. A second polygonal roundhouse was thus opened in February 1847, housing sixteen engines. A larger roundhouse, with twenty-four roads and generally similar in appearance, opened in 1852, built by George Thompson at a cost of £6,500, to the designs of John H. Saunders, the MR Architect. Termed 'No. 1', 'No. 2' and

'No. 3' sheds, the stabling room they provided was found to be increasingly inadequate. 'No. 1' was soon given over to repair work and by 1888 'No. 2' was required for 'spare engine' storage.

New buildings were urgently required (shed room as at February 1888 was: ' '2' shed — 16, '3' shed — 24, with 99 engines regularly in steam, plus ex-Works engines') and on 2nd November that year Messrs. Walkerdine were successful with a tender of £15,003. 4s. 9d. for a wholly new depot. The proposals had originally envisaged four new square sheds, arranged in two offset pairs, but Messrs Walkerdine's tender covered only the first of these, 'No. 4' shed. The new depot, a twin roundhouse with no dividing wall, came into use in 1890, but the second pair never appeared, part of the site eventually being occupied by a new 60 ft turntable, supplied by Eastwood Swingler in 1900 at a cost of £1,065. This was the only portion to appear of the abortive 'No. 5' shed, and a second proposal, in June 1902, for a new engine shed was also subsequently abandoned. It was to be a single standard roundhouse (with room for a second alongside) for freight locos, and the drawings prepared envisaged a site at the Spondon end of the Chaddesden Sidings. It was not to be, however, and a turntable and coal stage remained the only facilities available for visiting freight locos.

Fittingly coded shed number 1, Derby was the premier depot throughout most of the Midland era. It was important for both freight and passenger traffic and all of the standard MR types were in use over the years. 2—2—2s Nos. 1-10 were the main express engines in the 1860s whilst Nos. 35-39 of the last batch of this type, turned

Kirtley 0—6—0s Nos. 2537 and 2749 at Derby in 1931.

L. B. Lapper

out by the nearby works in the 1860s, were employed on Nottingham and Lincoln workings. '50' class 2—4—0s followed, succeeded eventually, of course, by the various larger 4—4—0 engines. There were over 120 engines at Derby in the 1890s, including three of the little Kirtley singles, nineteen 2—4—0s and eight 4—4—0s. The freight stud consisted of no less than seventy-seven Kirtley double-framed 0—6—0s. Great changes had occurred by 1914, particularly on the passenger locomotive side, with nearly twenty class '2' 4—4—0s, nine Johnson singles and the last thirty class '3' Belpaire 4—4—0s, Nos. 750-779 allocated to the shed. Among the goods engines were the only two '4F's built by that date, Nos. 3835 and 3836. The small three road ex-North Staffordshire Railway shed on the opposite side of the main line closed within a few months of Grouping and its duties were absorbed by the far larger MR shed.

Derby had no repair shop, a feature rendered unnecessary by the close proximity of the works but 'running in'

turns for newly overhauled engines were naturally a prominent feature of the shed's duties. Having the works so close by was not such a great advantage, from the point of view of the depot engineering staff, as might have been expected. Because the shed had very little in the way of repair facilities, even relatively minor items like hot big ends (which would normally take about three to four hours to remedy at a well equipped depot) on some occasions might well take up to a week. There were several reasons for this — differences in priorities, etc. — but principally, while the shed ran engines on a seven day basis, the works were on a six, later five and a half day week. The problems connected with lack of equipment would not have been so noticeable in early days when the CME controlled both the works and the running sheds, but after Sir Guy Granet's reorganisation of the MR in 1909, transferring the sheds to the General Superintendent's Department (one of the reasons, incidentally, for Deeley's resignation) the time necessary for repairs at

Immaculate '2P' 4—4—0 No. 700 outside the shed.

A. G. Ellis

Locomotives arranged around the 70 ft outside turntable at Derby, 24th September 1961.   *R. C. Riley*

The shed from the coaler, 11th August 1966. Steam had only a few months remaining at Derby and as part of the alterations for diesel working the turntable was removed.

Ken Fairey

Nos. 22979 and 4197 at Derby on 13th March 1938.

Collection R. S. Carpenter

Derby became a problem. Even as late as 1956 Derby 'No. 4' had only one machine, a hand operated grindstone reminiscent of a village smithy! There was a compressed air supply, but it was an entirely unofficial 'home-made' arrangement, of which the works knew nothing! Engine lifting required the use of the breakdown crane and this and other activities could be carried out much more expeditiously at Burton, with its wheeldrop and machine shop.

Coded 17A under the 1935 rearrangements, Derby still had over a hundred locos in the mid 'thirties, a total which increased to nearly 140 engines in the 1950s. They were serviced with the aid of a coaling plant erected by Henry Lees & Co. and two steel framed ash plants, by Babcock and Wilcox Ltd., which had appeared by 1937. Among various standard LMS locomotives in use were 'Crab' 2—6—0s Nos. 13098 and 13099 (red livery) arriving new in 1929 and joined by sister engines Nos. 13145-13148

The coal stage constructed prior to the opening of 'No. 4' shed, in 1931. The Derby building appears to have been the largest example of this particular type and survived well into LMS days.

Gordon Coltas

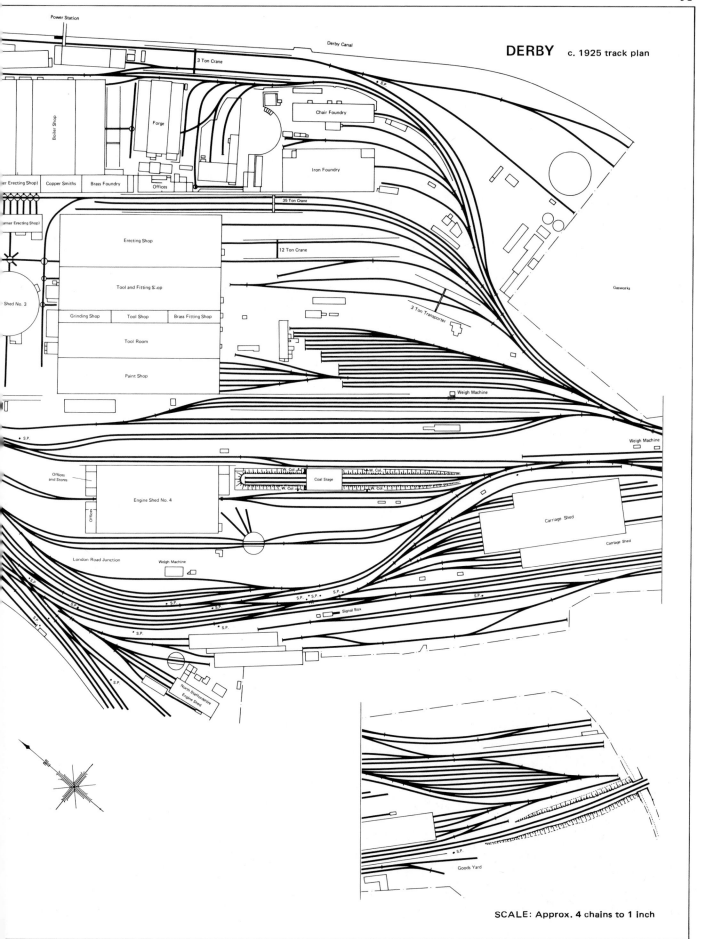

DERBY c. 1925 track plan

Power Station

Derby Canal

3 Ton Crane

S.P.

Boiler Shop

Forge

Chair Foundry

Iron Foundry

er Erecting Shop)

Copper Smiths

Brass Foundry

Offices

35 Ton Crane

Gasworks

omer Erecting Shop)

Erecting Shop

12 Ton Crane

Tool and Fitting Shop

3 Ton Transporter

Shed No. 3

Grinding Shop

Tool Shop

Brass Fitting Shop

Tool Room

Paint Shop

Weigh Machine

Weigh Machine

S.P.

Offices
and Stores

Engine Shed No. 4

Offices

W. Col.

Coal Stage

W. Col.

W. Col.

W. Col.

Carriage Shed

Carriage Shed

London Road Junction

Weigh Machine

S.P.

S.P.

S.P.

S.P.

S.P.

S.P.

Signal Box

S.P.

S.P.

S.P.

North Staffordshire
Engine Shed

S.P.

S.P.

Goods Yard

SCALE: Approx. 4 chains to 1 inch

The shed from the main footbridge in April 1954. The offices alongside the northern wall survived the demolition of the roundhouses and were still in use well into the 'seventies.

Photomatic

in 1930. Stanier 4—6—0s subsequently appeared and there was a large influx of both two-cylinder and three-cylinder varieties. Ivatt Moguls, class '4' and '2' and BR standard '5MT' 4—6—0s joined the Stanier types after 1948.

At the centre of the old Midland system and with duties to most of its extremities, Derby nevertheless fell into a steep decline following dieselisation and closures in the early 'sixties. It was recoded 16C in September 1963, with nominal responsibility for the C & HPR sheds at Cromford and Sheep Pasture, under the new Toton District, and the number of locos in use fell steadily. The 'Jubilees' and 'Black Fives' on the St. Pancras expresses gave way to BR/Sulzer 'Peaks' entirely in 1962 and full closure to steam came in March 1967. A few locos, notably saddle tanks off the High Peak, remained 'dead' for a while and odd steam visitors continued to arrive, particularly Eastern Region 'B1' 4—6—0s, but a new diesel depot, 'Etches Park', had by now taken over all servicing work. The buildings were demolished in 1969 leaving only the offices at the north end.

A smoky September afternoon at Derby in 1950.

B. Hilton

The original locomotive belonging to the contractor for the Dursley branch would have fitted snugly into the little building. The arched entrance was subsequently replaced by a concrete lintel, the doors being dispensed with in the process.

B. Mathews

DURSLEY

The line from Coaley Junction to Dursley, along the valley of the River Cam, opened to goods traffic in August 1856 under the auspices of the Dursley and Midland Junction Railway. It was worked at first by the Midland and following a brief period of independent operation was completely absorbed, on 1st January 1861. The small brick built shed, located some distance from the station, was of particular interest in that its construction had been for other purposes and had preceded that of the branch itself. It was

purchased in 1856 at a cost of £270 and at first (presumably) housed the contractors' engine.

The branch was originally worked by a small 0—4—0 saddle tank which was taken over by the Midland and numbered 156. No. 202, a slightly larger well tank locomotive (a Kirtley rebuild of a Fairbairn well tank absorbed from the Little North Western Railway) took over and by 1880 Kirtley 2—4—0 No. 57A was recorded working the branch on many occasions.

The branch locos making use of the shed from the 1880s onwards were the ubiquitous Johnson '1F'

The cramped terminus.

Lens of Sutton

'Dursley Engine Shed Siding' on 12th September 1936. 'Listers Works' dominated the shed and indeed the very town itself.

W. A. Camwell

0–6–0Ts, which were not finally displaced until 1956. Ex-Severn & Wye tanks, Nos. 1606 and 1608, based at Gloucester may also have made use of the shed in the period before 1921. In 1884 the water supply was assured with the payment of £50 to a Colonel Graham, 'for a perpetual supply of water to the Dursley Locomotive Tank'. Following the Grouping, Johnson 0–4–4Ts took over but within five years the '1F's had regained their dominance. Nos. 1691, 1720, 1727, 1742 and 1748 supplied by Gloucester were regular performers over the years, No. 41748 being the last to go, in 1957. In 1956 following transfer to the Western Region, the light axle-load '16XX' pannier tanks increasingly took over.

Passenger services were withdrawn in 1962, the last 'Dursley Donkey' running on 10th September and the shed itself was closed on the same day. BR '2MT' Moguls worked the goods service in the last years and would have made use of the water tank. Along with most of the other buildings on the branch, the shed has now been demolished.

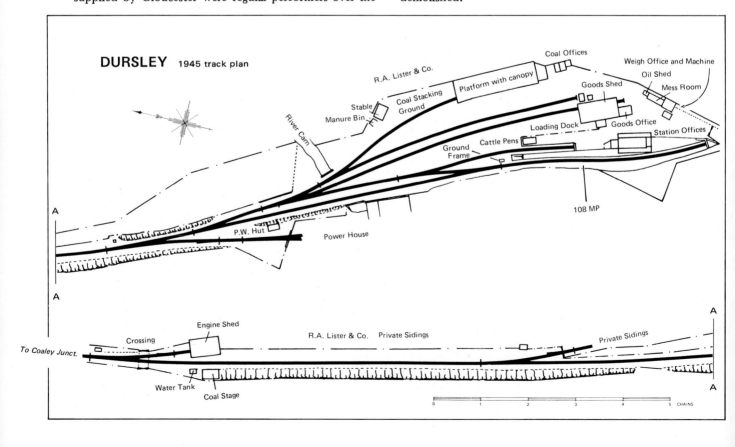

A busy yard at Gloucester, on 26th March 1948. The old 'outstation repair shop' in the background had been out of use for some years by this time, and a standard LMS wheeldrop was available for the necessary repair work.

W. Potter

GLOUCESTER

The Birmingham and Gloucester Railway opened in November 1840 from Gloucester to Cheltenham and throughout to Birmingham a month later. Amalgamation with the Bristol and Gloucester Railway came in 1845 and the following year an agreement was made for the Midland to lease both railways, the whole route eventually becoming a 'second main line' of the MR. The station at Gloucester was originally a terminus and was provided from the first with a 'small engine shed' ordered to be repaired in 1849. In the same year the company began searching for a suitable site for a larger shed and on 5th June plans were inspected. The proposed site proved too expensive but it was eventually resolved 'that a circular engine shed be built on the company's own ground between the present transfer shed and the passenger shed'. A tender of £4,085 for this building plus £965 for a smithy and stores was accepted a few months later and in 1850, the following year, the engineer was happy to report that the new engine shed 'would be ready for use on the 8th day of July'.

The inside turntable was enlarged in 1869 and by 1883 a further 50 ft turntable had been provided in the yard. The site ocupied by the shed was then required for station alterations (the replacement of the old Midland terminus by a through station) and in 1892 a new square building was proposed on land at Barnwood, between Horton Road and Cheltenham North Junction. This opened, complete with shear-legs and a 50 ft turntable from Cowans Sheldon, in 1895. A four road fitting shop was subsequently added. On the opening of the new shed the company decided on additional facilities near to the new

Spare ground at Gloucester was for many years put to good use and potatoes at least were seldom in short supply. The year is 1932.

L & GRP

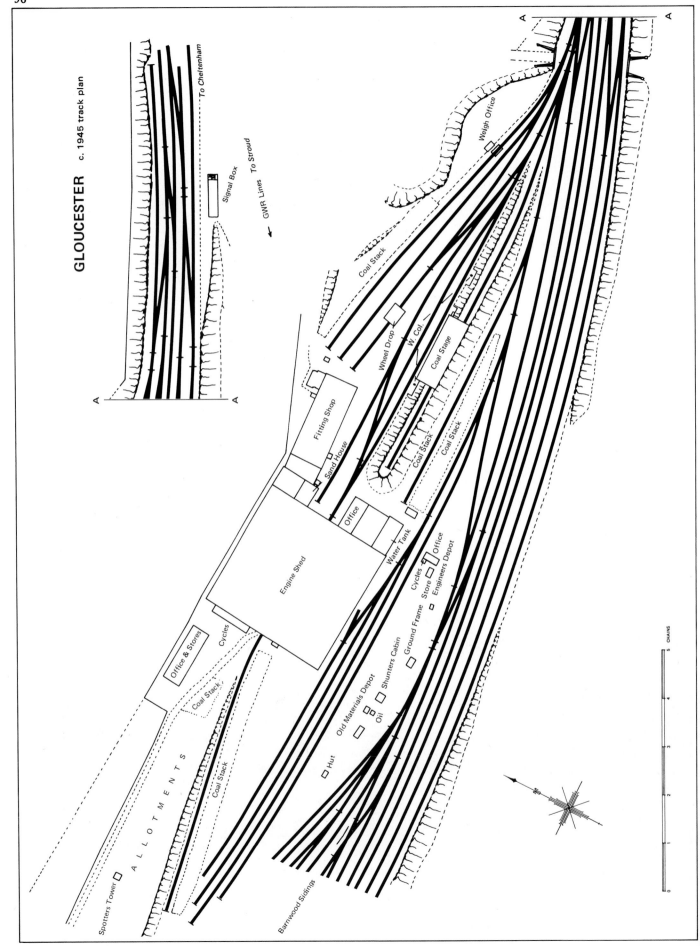

GLOUCESTER   c. 1945 track plan

To Cheltenham

To Stroud

GWR Lines

Signal Box

Weigh Office

Coal Stack

Wheel Drop

W. Col.

Coal Stage

Coal Stack

Coal Stack

Fitting Shop

Sand House

Office

Water Tank

Cycles

Store

Office

Engineers Depot

Ground Frame

Shunters Cabin

Oil

Old Materials Depot

Hut

Engine Shed

Office & Stores

Cycles

Coal Stack

Coal Stack

ALLOTMENTS

Spotters Tower

Barnwood Sidings

0   1   2   3   4   5   CHAINS

Engines on the wheeldrop road at Gloucester in June 1959. The LMS '4F's were 'poorly shod' with inadequate axleboxes and rapidly ran 'rough'.

Photomatic

Two of Gloucester's dock shunters on 19th June 1960.

P. J. Kelley

The shed in September 1964 after closure.

Collection S. Summerson

station: 'New engine turntable, water crane, ash pit and sidings to be installed in lieu of those which were removed along with the old engine shed in consequence of passenger station alterations. Cost £1,301.'

Gloucester was less important than Bristol and Saltley, at the two extremities as it were, of the Midland's 'West of England' route. Its duties tended to be of a secondary nature, goods and passengers southwards to Bristol and Bath and northwards to Evesham, Worcester and Birmingham. The passenger engines thus tended to be somewhat elderly and were often 'secondhand', displaced from more important duties elsewhere. The '170' class 2—4—0s for instance originally worked Derby-Manchester expresses but after 1880 Nos. 180 to 188 were stationed at Gloucester, and were still there in the 1890s, assisted by No. 231 of the '230' class 2—4—0s, converted from 2—4—0Ts in 1870. A dozen or so miscellaneous saddletanks, the entire stock of the Swansea Vale Railway, were promptly sent to Gloucester for dock work when the Midland absorbed that local company in 1874. Most of them were withdrawn in the 'nineties. Two or three 0—4—0Ts were always maintained at Gloucester for working the High Orchard branch to the docks; Nos. 1428A and 1429A in 1892, Nos. 1505, 1519 and 1522 in 1914, and latterly No. 41537, withdrawn from Gloucester shed in September 1963. When the Severn & Wye Railway was jointly taken over by the MR and GWR in 1894 six tanks were absorbed by the Midland and of these Nos. 1606 and 1608 were at Gloucester for many years, until withdrawal in 1924.

The allocation rose to something over sixty engines, mainly tanks, '2P' 4—4—0s and '2F' and '3F' 0—6—0s, Nos. 1000 and 1001, the first two Compounds, arriving from Holbeck in the 1930s. The depot was responsible for sub-sheds at Stroud, Nailsworth, Evesham, Dursley and Tewkesbury, the latter two only surviving into BR ownership. After the closure of Worcester by the LMS in 1932, Gloucester took over the locos and workings, apart from one duty which required a Gloucester '2P' 4—4—0 to be stabled at Worcester GWR shed. The depot was Midland number 7 and from 1935, 22B in the Bristol area. Ex-L & YR 0—6—0s arrived in the 1930s in the shape of Nos. 12131, 12140 and 12141, the first 'foreigners' to work on the West of England line and 'pug' 0—4—0STs followed for the dock workings. The number of engines at Gloucester subsequently declined and the only new LMS arrivals were Midland-derived '3F' tanks and '4F' 0—6—0s. The L & Y 0—6—0s were also later transferred away.

Known, particularly in later years, as Barnwood, the shed received very little in the way of modern equipment, although a new 55 ft turntable was installed in 1935. The shed's prospects took a turn for the worse on its transfer, as 85E, to the Western Region in February and pannier tanks and other types began making use of the wheel drop. The shed was recoded 85C in January 1961, but closed on 4th May 1964, its locos and men transferring to the nearby ex-GWR Horton Road shed. It was subsequently demolished.

'Midland Style' epitomised. The neat standard straight shed at Gurnos on 19th April 1953.   *B. K. B. Green*

GURNOS

A small wooden shed was opened in 1865 at Gurnos Junction, some twelve miles out on the line from Swansea. By November 1895 the coal stage required rebuilding and on 15th July 1897 the shed itself, in dilapidated condition, was recommended to be rebuilt. The General Purposes Committee agreed to this and a small two road shed opened in 1900. Local contractor David Rees had his tender of £2,670.14s.8d. accepted in October 1898 but for some reason this was shortly afterwards cancelled. He appears not to have lost out, however, for his second tender was accepted on 27th June the following year, this time for £2,730.7s.3d., the Midland paying a small penalty for their faint-heartedness!

The new shed serviced engines working local passenger and goods traffic up the Afon Twrch valley to the MR station at Brynamman East, to Colbren Junction and along the valley of the River Tawe to Swansea. Gurnos, or 'Ystalyfera' was near Ynisgeinon Junction, the centre of this little system and several 0—6—0Ts were oustationed from the parent shed, Upper Bank (MR No. 6), for many years. Upper Bank, about a mile north of St. Thomas' station, the Midland's Swansea terminus, had around 30 engines, most of them Johnson '1F' 0—6—0Ts, with up to ten of them working from Gurnos. Some of the first MR '3F' tanks (forerunners of the LMS standard 0—6—0T) were also based in the district and were of course used at Gurnos. It was coded A33 (Western 'A' Division) by

1926 and became W33 in the Western Division under Swansea LNW in 1930, 'coal tanks' and 5′ 0″ 0—6—2Ts subsequently putting in sporadic appearances. Under the 1935 scheme Upper Bank became 4C with Gurnos once more a sub-shed and in the ensuing years standard '3F' tanks gradually replaced some of the old MR engines. By 1948 only four or five locos were normally based at Gurnos, including auto-fitted '3F' tanks (Nos. 7477-7481) mainly employed on two-coach push/pull units provided for the Brynamman-Swansea service. On Nationalisation, both sheds were transferred, along with other former LMS lines in South Wales, to the Western Region, again as sub-sheds of Swansea Paxton Street (ex-LNW), now 87K. Pannier tanks were increasingly in evidence and by 1956 '67XX' 0—6—0PTs had largely replaced the LMS engines.

Both sheds became the responsibility of 87D Swansea East Dock on the closure of Paxton Street in September 1959, when the regular allocation at Gurnos totalled five engines, two panniers and three standard LMS tanks. Three of the locos worked in and around Gurnos but two carried out 'long distance' work. One of these was the early morning pick-up to Swansea Harbour sidings and return and the other a pick-up goods to Pantyffynon. '67XX' panniers were normally employed on both these duties as well as shunting at Gurnos Junction. Shunting at Ynisygeinon Junction sidings was still the preserve of '3F' tanks. Gurnos eventually closed on 2nd April 1962 and the last few locos, all pannier tanks, were transferred to Upper Bank.

0–6–0Ts at Gurnos in June 1950.

Photographer unknown

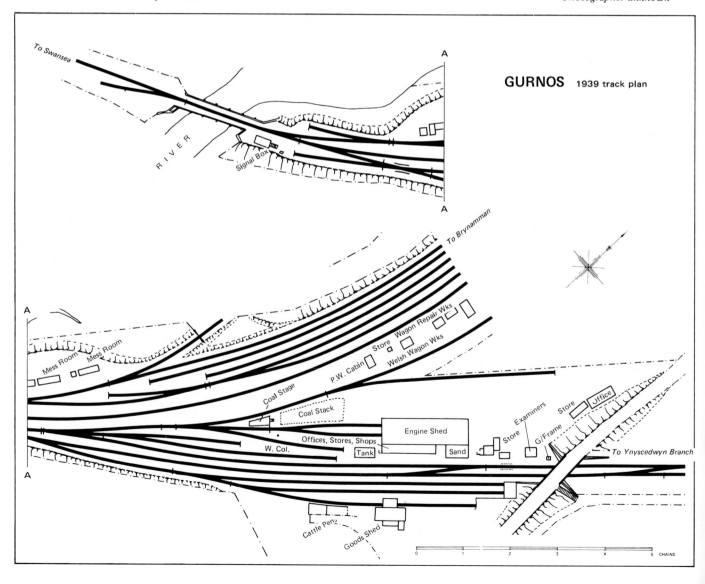

Hasland in 1930.   *G. Coltas*

HASLAND

Hasland was the Midland's Chesterfield depot, a standard roundhouse whose early history is complicated by the company's intermittent use of the alternative name 'Clay Cross'. The earliest mention in the minute books is on 15th October 1861 when it was ordered 'That plans and estimates for an Engine House and Turntable to be built at Chesterfield to accommodate the Passenger Traffic upon the opening of the Erewash Valley extension Branch be prepared.' An 'additional line' was laid to the turntable 'at Clay Cross' in early 1865 and on 18th April 1871 a 'steam shed for two locos at Chesterfield' was ordered to be built. A tender of £3,860 for the shed was referred to the Finance and General Purposes Committee on 2nd January 1872 but some three years earlier, on 2nd March 1868, plans and estimates had also been received for a shed housing six locos at 'Clay Cross' and costing this time only £3,100. By 1874 the proposal at 'Clay Cross' had

The shed in early BR days. Hasland's advancing dereliction is evident when compared with the photograph above.   *Photomatic*

As an interim measure, repeated at a number of other sheds, the central roof pitch was removed, leaving some covered accommodation at least. Elsewhere these half measures were usually succeeded (eventually!) by an entirely new roof; at Hasland subsidence rendered this pointless and, but for parts of the surrounding walls, the shed was dismantled. Conditions were still not too bad when this photograph was taken on 3rd September 1955; the shear-legs just visible on the right were another subsidence casualty.

H. C. Casserley

altered to a roundhouse design, the turntable costing £893. 18s. 1d. The name 'Hasland' now comes into more common usage and the roundhouse here together with a row of cottages for the men and their families eventually opened in 1875. Plans of the shed were still occasionally labelled 'Clay Cross' even in LMS days. Somehow in all this the company, between 1862 and 1869, had in fact contrived to erect a small shed, at 'Clay Cross' itself. Two locos were allocated to the tiny brick built shed, which remained in use, despite giving the appearance of imminent collapse, even into BR days, engines employed presumably on local works shunting.

The depot was Midland shed No. 23, the 1935 changes leaving it 18C in the Toton district. It remained isolated

and little known in its bleak setting and, although a coaling plant was installed in 1935, the next significant event was the removal of the roof in 1959, BR not bothering to provide a replacement. The building had suffered seriously as a result of subsidence from the extensive local coal mining operations and the removal of the roof became necessary for safety reasons. No replacement was provided, the walls not being considered safe enough to stand one! Latterly all that remained was a pair of walls, the remainder having been pulled down or collapsed under its own weight!

Some seventy or so locos were allocated in the 1920s; six 4—4—0s, with a similar number of 0—4—4Ts for passenger work and several 2—4—0s surviving until the 'thirties for minor and standby turns, works pilots, etc. The great bulk of the locomotive stud, however, consisted of 0—6—0s, most of them engaged on mineral trains with '1F' tanks on local iron works shunts. 0—4—0 tanks were also used on this work, Nos. 1518 and 1532 being resident for many years. Standard '3F' tanks began to replace the old Johnson locos in the early 1930s, the new engines represented at first by Nos. 7111, 7112, 16509 and 16712. Some of Toton's Garratts (a total eventually of sixteen), by now well past their prime, were concentrated at Hasland in the 1950s for the iron ore traffic between Wellingborough and York, working on occasions right through to Middlesborough, but all had been withdrawn by 1958. The last one to remain was No. 47994, the sad giant forced to stable in the shed yard. No special accommodation was provided for these engines at Hasland, even though as early as 1945 a batch of ten had been allocated. Two, Nos. 4984 and 4997, had appeared as early as 1933.

A closure rumour of 1959 to the effect that both Hasland and Barrow Hill would shortly close, with their locos concentrated at Staveley ex-Great Central shed, proved unfounded, but the inevitable came in 1964. Re-coded 16H only a year previously, the shed closed on 7th September and the crumbling remains were demolished. The site is now a corporation refuse tip.

The yard at least enjoyed some modern facilities, a lightweight 'Stranraer' type of coaler being provided to forestall the imminent collapse of the coal stage shelter. The Garratts had disappeared by the time this photograph was taken on 13th April 1958, 2—10—0s and '8F's working most of the remaining freight traffic.

W. Potter

'Before The Fall'. Hasland in earlier days, with curious additions. These new smoke vents, provided along with replacement roof cladding, were necessarily removed when subsidence began to take a hold.

Collection B. Mathews

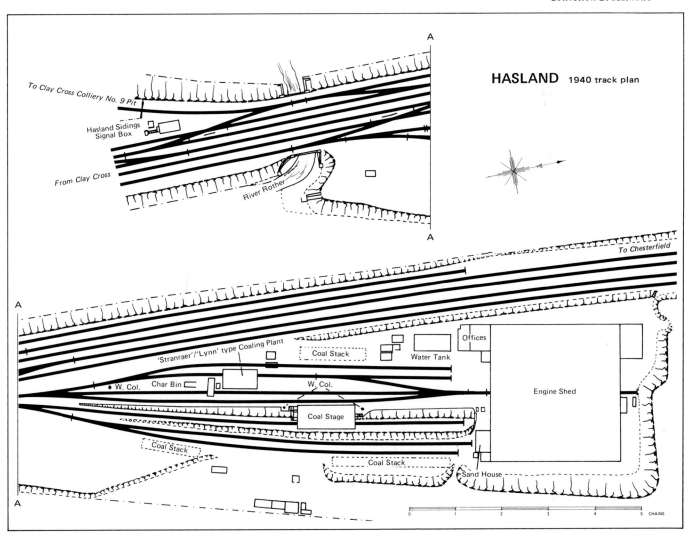

HASLAND 1940 track plan

To Clay Cross Colliery No. 9 Pit

Hasland Sidings Signal Box

From Clay Cross

River Rother

To Chesterfield

'Stranraer'/'Lynn' type Coaling Plant

Coal Stack

Offices

Water Tank

W. Col.

Char Bin

W. Col.

Engine Shed

Coal Stage

Coal Stack

Coal Stack

Sand House

0 1 2 3 4 5 CHAINS

Heaton Mersey with original roof, in May 1933. The Midland's share originally comprised the offices and four roads on the right.

W. Potter

HEATON MERSEY

Heaton Mersey shed, Stockport, opened in January 1889. It was similar to, and in a way the forerunner of, the much larger joint shed at Trafford Park, opened a few years later. It was a straight shed with eight roads, the Midland occupying the four nearest the river (in latter years at least) and although the coal stage and 50 ft turntable were shared, the rest of the facilities, offices, sandhouse, etc., were duplicated, as at Trafford Park. The Midland stabled rather more locomotives at Heaton Mersey than at the larger Trafford Park depot, at least after 1900 and the allocation included a much higher proportion of freight engines.

About three years after opening the Midland's complement consisted of a pair of 4—4—0s, three 0—4—4Ts and fourteen Johnson 0—6—0s. By 1902 five new 0—6—0Ts Nos. 1952-1956 in 1907) were at the shed for the Manchester South District passenger trains, succeeded after 1907 by new Deeley 0—6—4Ts Nos. 2005-2011. These latter engines were not displaced in their turn until 1935, when new Stanier 2—6—2Ts arrived for these duties. Several three-cylinder 2—6—4Ts also worked from Heaton Mersey for a brief period when first built, prior to their acceptance for work on the LTSR lines to Tilbury and Southend.

A tired looking ex-MR 0—6—0 outside the decaying shed on 12th March 1948.

H. C. Casserley

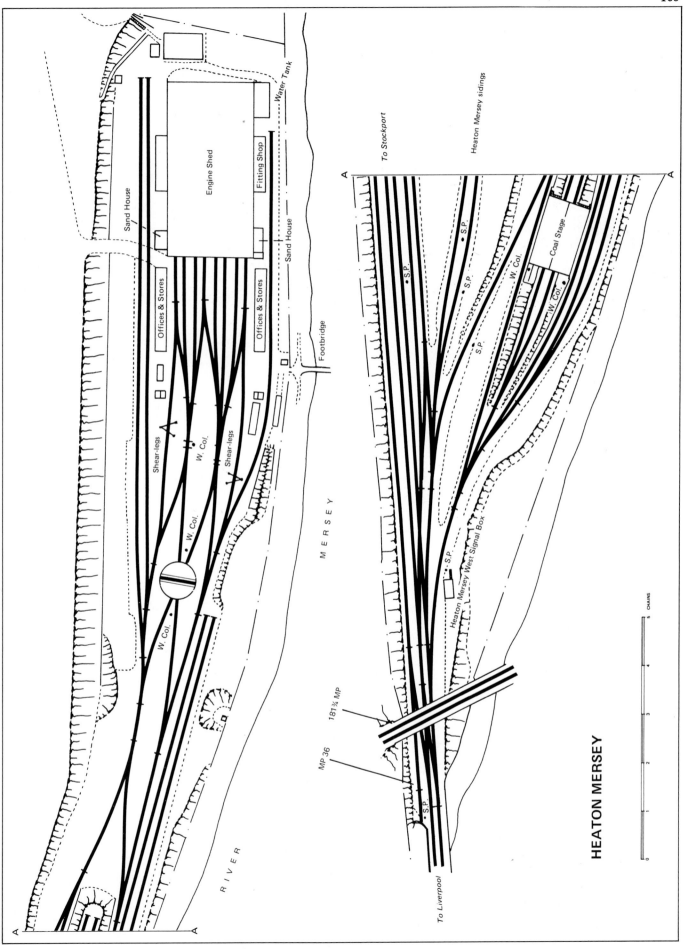

Sand House

Engine Shed

Fitting Shop

Water Tank

Offices & Stores

Offices & Stores

Sand House

Footbridge

Shear-legs

W. Col.

Shear-legs

W. Col.

W. Col.

W. Col.

M E R S E Y

R I V E R

To Stockport

Heaton Mersey sidings

A

A

S.P.

S.P.

S.P.

S.P.

W. Col.

W. Col.

Coal Stage

S.P.

Heaton Mersey West Signal Box

S.P.

18 1¾ MP

MP 36

S.P.

To Liverpool

A

A

0   1   2   3   4   5. CHAINS

HEATON MERSEY

Above: The great 'double' coal stage, by the banks of the Mersey in June 1935. *Below:* The stage in its last years. This method of coaling, with iron tubs, remained in use at Heaton Mersey until the end.

W. Potter and R. J. Essery

The joint involvement at these CLC sheds with the Great Central provided extra interest but also a number of problems, only really resolved by the demise of steam. Artisan staff on the GC section of the LNER did not enjoy the same conditions as their fellows on the LMS, rates of pay and conditions of service being rather inferior. The ex-GC men were governed by conditions extant in Gorton Works whilst LMS men were paid under 'Award No. 728', resulting in strict lines of demarcation at sheds like Heaton Mersey and Trafford Park. Ex-GC men would only work on LNER engines and, even when the older regional types had been replaced by standard locomotives, would only attend to those working 'GC' diagrams!

Heaton Mersey was Midland shed number 21B, under Belle Vue, and was one of four former sub-sheds given plates in early LMS days. It was recoded 19D under Sheffield in 1935 but, as at Trafford Park and Belle Vue, supervision came from the District Locomotive Superintendent at Longsight ex-LNWR depot. The shed was part of the short-lived '13' district, which combined the former MR and CLC depots in Lancashire, and was coded 13C for a short period to May 1950, when it was recoded 9F. In January 1957 it became 17E, part of another unworkable organisation, the expanded Derby District, but like Trafford Park, it reverted to its former '9' code, in April 1958. Mercifully this was the last recoding and the shed's plates stayed in place until closure ten years later.

The old northlight pattern roof was in dire condition by 1948 and in 1952/3 BR erected a new steel-framed example similar to the new designs appearing around that time on the Southern Region. The turntable was also increased in size, to 70 ft, and resited a short distance to the west. By the time of the BR rebuilding there were less than ten 0—6—0s remaining at Heaton Mersey, while the '8F' total stood at nearly twenty-five. Remaining

engines were a pair of Horwich Moguls, Nos. 42775 and 42788 and four Stanier 2—6—2Ts, Nos. 40089, 40094, 40113, and 40124. Only fourteen ex-LNER locos remained, all Great Central types, with half a dozen each of the 'J10' 0—6—0s and 'N5' 0—6—2Ts and a pair of 'Large Directors', Nos. 62663 *Prince Albert* and 62665 *Mons*.

It appears that supervision at Heaton Mersey was mainly in the hands of LNER staff until Nationalisation, but certainly during the war, LMS outside foremen were charged with the care of both companies' engines. The LMS maintained a full clerical section dealing with all local matters, mileage, overtime, etc. whilst the LNER were content with only a single clerk, most of the work being the responsibility of Gorton.

'9F' 2—10—0s and 'WD' and '8F' 2—8—0s came to predominate at Heaton Mersey in the final years and, although it was intended to erect a diesel depot alongside the steam shed, the continuing decline of traffic rendered this unnecessary and it closed completely on 6th May 1968. The buildings were reduced to rubble shortly afterwards.

Heaton Mersey on 10th September 1966. BR provided a new roof in corrugated sheeting in the early 1950s. *W. Potter*

Heaton Mersey West signal box, which controlled entry to and from the shed.
R. J. Essery

The turntable. Spreading out beyond are the extensive Heaton Mersey sidings.

R. J. Essery

Hellifield in October 1937. Engines, left to right, are 0—6—0 No. 3330, 4—4—0s Nos. 740 (at rear) and 747, 0—6—0 No. 3586, 4—4—0 No. 470 and, on the shear-legs road, 0—6—0 No. 3999.

G. S. Lloyd

HELLIFIELD

The plans for a new engine shed at Hellifield were drawn up in 1879 and construction was more or less complete in 1880. It was a standard straight shed design with twin roof pitches and four roads. The shed stood just to the north of the station and was supplied with a standard 'single' coal stage.

Hellifield was a major junction and the shed's activities were fully described in the *Railway Magazine* of 1903:

During the summer season the loco depot at Hellifield (MR) can claim its fair share of work. Out of a staff of 80 men there are 22 sets of drivers/firemen while there are 19 classes of locos

at their disposal. During normal times trains are worked by them between Carlisle, Manchester, Leeds, Bradford and Morecambe, and until recently, Nottingham and Lincoln. In the summer work increases to include heavier special passenger traffic totalling up to, at times, 5,000 miles per week with an extra 1,200 miles of banking or pilot work.

In addition, there was considerable freight traffic, minerals originating locally as well as wagons sorted and marshalled in the two nearby yards. A large carriage shed stood near to the engine shed. Hellifield at its peak in 1910 had 28 engines allocated, including 'two locos specially fitted for snow plough work'. Winter was a force to be reckoned with over the Settle and Carlisle and in 1909 two large independent snowploughs were built on

LMS '2P' 4—4—0 No. 40685 accompanies partially dismantled Fowler 0—4—0 diesel No. ED1 at Hellifield on 8th July 1961.

F. Dean

Locomotives by the coal stage in October 1937. Amongst the familiar 0—6—0s and 4—4—0s (Nos. 3893, 472 and 738) is ex-LNW 0—8—0 No. 9319.

G. S. Lloyd

Hellifield coal stage, executed unusually in wood.

British Railways

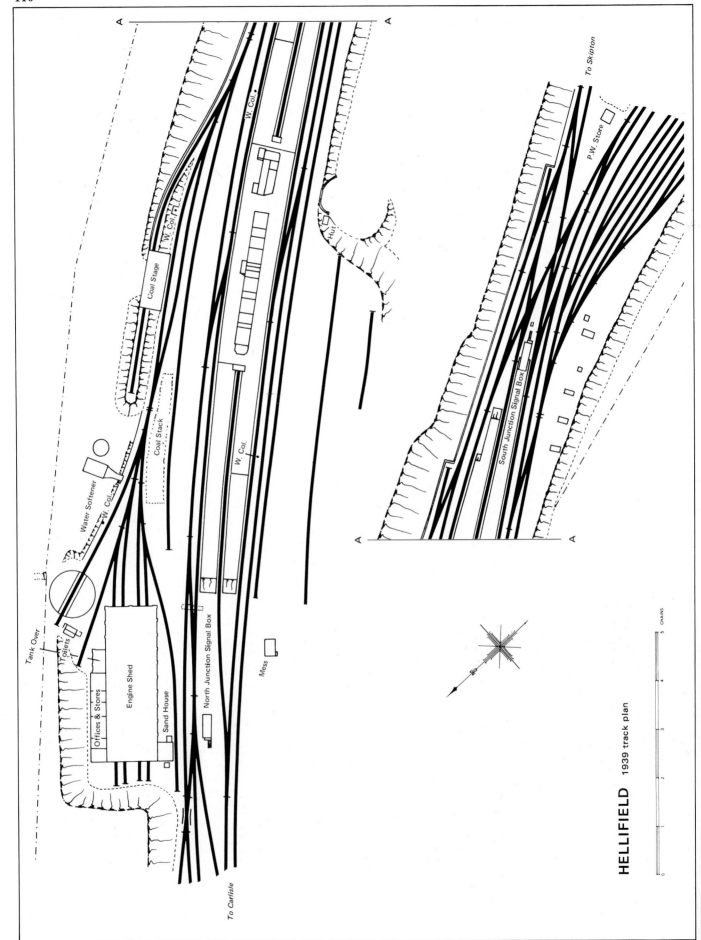

To Skipton

P.W. Store

South Junction Signal Box

Hut

W. Col.

W. Col.

Coal Stage

Coal Stack

W. Col.

Water Softener

W. Col.

Tank Over

Toilets

Offices & Stores

Engine Shed

Sand House

North Junction Signal Box

Mess

To Carlisle

0   1   2   3   4   5   CHAINS

HELLIFIELD 1939 track plan

The familiar Hellifield snowploughs.
National Railway Museum

the frames of redundant double bogie tenders and these 'Hellifield Ploughs' were an important feature of work at the shed.

Hellifield ex-L & Y shed closed in 1927 with its remaining duties and men transferring to the ex-Midland shed, bringing L & Y 0—6—0s and 2—4—2Ts into the 'MR' fold. 4—4—0s Nos. 236-239 went new to Hellifield in 1895 and were chiefly employed on 'Scotch express' workings to Nottingham, introduced shortly afterwards. 2—4—0s were of course the main passenger type up to the 1900s, the most notable being Nos. 1306-1311 arriving at Hellifield in 1885, subsequently performing as Ais Gill pilots for many years. The shed was coded 30a, a sub-shed of Skipton, becoming 20G in 1935 and by the end of the Second World War housed some thirty locomotives, '4F' 0—6—0s, '2P' and '4P' 4—4—0s, a 'Crab', No. 2893, and several '8F' 2—8—0s. The remaining engines were of Midland origin apart from several remaining ex-L & YR 'Radial' 2—4—2Ts. A 60 ft turntable replaced the old unit and repairs were carried out to the roof in 1940. Within

ten years the allocation had dropped by nearly half following a traffic decline exacerbated by a policy of concentrating traffic on alternative routes and modern '3MT' and '2MT' 2—6—2Ts had replaced many of the ex-MR engines on local work. A new repair shed with wheel drop, etc. had been erected at the rear of the shed in 1948 and district repairs kept Hellifield busier than could otherwise have been expected. This was especially so after 1960 when the official 'concentration' shed, Accrington, went over to diesel operation and the shop at Fleetwood was converted for railcar repairs.

Hellifield became 23B under Skipton in the BR scheme of 1950, but reverted to its former code in September 1951. It was then coded 24H in the Accrington district, in March 1957, and finally closed on 17th June 1963. It was renovated a year or so later and housed a number of preserved engines for some years, including the Gresley 2—6—2 *Green Arrow*, but following their departure it was abandoned to the combined mercies of the local climate and vandals. It has now been demolished.

Hellifield shed on 11th July 1954.

W. A. Camwell

Two of Ilkley's 0—4—4Ts, Nos. 6403 and 1413 outside the shed on 14th August 1939.   *R. J. Buckley*

ILKLEY

The Otley and Ilkley Joint Railway, under the auspices of the Midland and the North Eastern Railways, opened throughout to a terminus at Ilkley in 1865 and a small shed for the use of both companies was reported open from 1st July the following year. For such a small shed, Ilkley is exceedingly well documented, detailed accounts of its history appearing in at least two splendid books, *The Railways of Wharfedale* by P. E. Baughan and *North Eastern Engine Sheds* by K. Hoole. The old shed was close to the station and complaints, mainly channelled through the 'Ilkley Local Board' had been increasingly vociferous regarding the generation of 'black smoke', the bane of engine shed foremen. The MR's new line through to Skipton opened fully in 1888 and the opportunity was taken to transfer the building to a site ('on the opposite or north side of the line') where it would give less offence, the dignitaries of the Local Board evidently agreeing to bear part of the costs. A site for eight engines was eventually decided on to the east of the station and by July 1892 the new shed was nearing completion, C. Murgatroyd's tender of £3,795.15s.8d. having been accepted on 6th November the previous year. (The canny officials had in the meantime borne their ratepayers' interest firmly in mind by adamantly refusing to contribute their agreed share of the costs!) Orders were given on 30th December 1892 for the old building to be removed and a carriage shed erected in its place.

Small passenger tanks were the usual engines in immediate pre-Grouping days, comprising three or four Johnson 0—4—4Ts from Manningham for the Midland services and a similar number of 'BTP' 0—4—4Ts for the NER. In 1880 the MR complement had consisted of four 2—4—0s, three old Kirtley engines and a new Johnson example. By 1892,

shortly before the new shed was opened, the total had been reduced to three, all Kirtley engines dating from 1866. P. E. Baughan relates that new 2—6—4T No. 2303 went to Ilkley in 1928 'for the fast business trains to Bradford' and in the same year four ex-L & YR 'Radial' 2—4—2Ts replaced the old Johnson engines. Stanier 0—4—4Ts, beginning with Nos. 6402, 6403 and 6404 in 1932, followed by 6400 in 1936 and 6401 in 1939 were allocated to Manningham and all were to be found working from Ilkley on occasions. They had disappeared by 1947,

2—6—2Ts eventually replaced the elderly 0—4—4Ts; some of them are stabled here on 17th November 1957.

B. Hilton

Ilkley shed and its pleasantly rural backdrop on 21st June 1947.

H. C. Casserley

replaced by an interesting pair of locos, ex-Caledonian 0—4—4Ts Nos. 15130 and 15192, and LNER 'G5' 0—4—4Ts had long since supplanted the old 'BTP' engines. By 1951 when LMR crews manned all the engines (including 'G5's from Neville Hill, ex-LNER) the following were outstationed from Manningham: '2MT' 2—6—2T No. 41265, and 2—4—2T Nos. 50621, 50622, 50633, 50634 and 50795. The CR tanks had enjoyed only a brief sojourn

and the 'G5' at this time was No. 67290, supplied by Neville Hill.

From 3rd April 1954 all work was handled by LMR engines. The shed closed with dieselisation on 5th January 1959 and was afterwards demolished. As a sub-shed of Manningham it had officially been part of the North Eastern Region since January 1957, but this had made no effect on the locomotive types allocated.

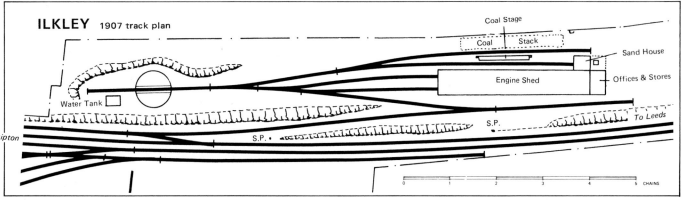

ILKLEY 1907 track plan

Coal Stage

Coal   Stack

Sand House

Engine Shed

Offices & Stores

Water Tank

S.P.

S.P.

To Leeds

Skipton

0 1 2 3 4 5 CHAINS

The building was extraordinarily long relative to its width and was obviously designed to suit a restricted site. Two reversals were necessary before engines could gain entrance to the shed, seen here on the same cold November day in 1957 as the view opposite. By this time the roof had been modified, involving the removal of the original central raised vent and the smoke 'pots'.

B. Hilton

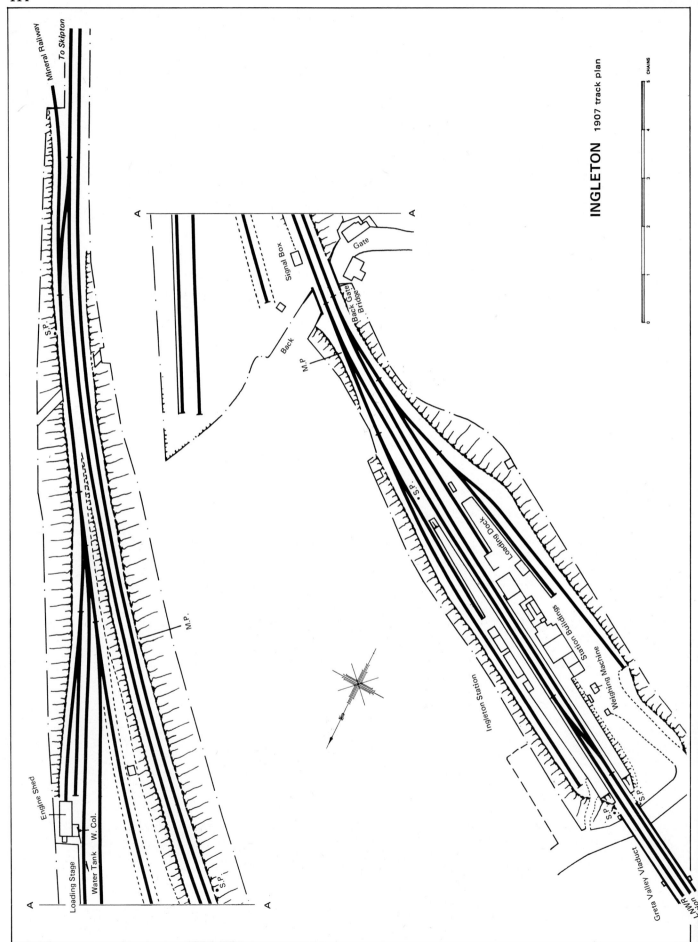

INGLETON 1907 track plan

The tiny Ingleton shed, of obviously Midland parentage. This was probably the general arrangement based on the shed at Hemel Hempstead and deemed in 1877 'as being suitable for similar locations'.

W. H. Whitworth

INGLETON

A turntable was 'ordered to be put down at Ingleton Station' on 17th December 1861 and a new water tank was requested seven years later. This was refused (a presage of troubles to come) but a small water tank along with sand furnace was provided when the engine shed eventually opened in 1878. Estimates had been received the previous year, and plans submitted for 'a wooden Engine Shed' with siding, to cost about £820. Messrs. Barrats were the successful contractors, offering to build the shed for £446.17s.6d.

Officially a sub-shed of Skipton, it was of standard Midland design, in timber with a pitched slated roof, and engines were coaled from open wagons placed in a short adjacent siding. There was an end-on junction with the LNWR at Ingleton and the stations of the two rivals were separated by a spectacular viaduct crossing the Greta River. The water supply was never adequate on the Midland side of the valley and in hot summers the company's branch engine, for many years 0—6—0T No. 1692, was forced to trundle across and make use of the *Premier Line's* supply. The 0—6—0T went to Lancaster Green Ayre for boiler washouts and repairs, an 0—6—0 usually being provided in its place. The Midland gained the final ascendancy, however, after the Grouping when the LNW 'Thornton' station and engine shed were closed and passenger traffic concentrated at the ex-MR station.

Fowler '3MT' 2—6—2Ts came to be the usual branch engines in later years with No. 40021 on the duty in July 1951. The locos were provided by 11D, Tebay and the shed's last function in early 1954 was to stable the engine off the 8.38 p.m. Low Gill train. The services were staffed by local men using Tebay engines, but the shed was finally closed on 30th January 1954. The line closed the following day and the shed has now been demolished.

The shed on 11th October 1936.

W. A. Camwell

Various ex-MR engines at Keighley shed in 1935.   *W. A. Camwell*

KEIGHLEY

There was a small one road shed at Keighley for many years, completed in 1869 when gas fittings were supplied at a cost of £58.9s.11d. The original company was the Keighley and Worth Valley Railway and their line had opened to passengers some time before, on 15th April 1867. The MR was in charge of operations from the first and took over the line completely in 1881. Described as an 'extension of the Engine Shed' a brand new four road structure on the same site replaced the old shed in 1892. It was built in stone with two roof pitches and was odd in being an extremely short building, each road capable of stabling only a single loco.

The branch workings from Keighley to Oxenhope, for which the shed was largely responsible were in the charge of 0—6—0Ts Nos. 1135-1138 from 1875/6 and Johnson '1F's Nos. 218, 219, 1397, 1398 and 1399 of 1883 (1725-1729 after 1907) were used for many years, specially built with enclosed cabs and vacuum brakes.

In Midland days Keighley was a sub-shed of Manningham, 29a, but after 1935 the four or five locos were supplied from a new parent depot, Skipton, following the introduction of push/pull working with 0—4—4Ts. These were succeeded in the 1950s by Ivatt '2MT' 2—6—2Ts which continued until DMUs were introduced in 1960. Keighley was restored to its parent shed of old on transfer to the North Eastern Region in May 1957, but Manningham continued to supply ex-LMS locomotives. In July 1951 engines outstationed had been '1F' tank No. 41820, '3F' 0—6—0 No. 43295 and ex-MR 0—4—4Ts Nos. 58075 and 58077, but by 1959 the shed housed only a single steam locomotive, a '3F' 0—6—0. The yard pilot duties, formerly carried out by a '1F' tank, had been taken over by 0—6—0 diesel No. D3656, which was stabled in the goods yard. Half of the shed's roof had been removed in 1958 and by early 1960, with six DMU drivers attached, closure was imminent. The shed housed only the Oxenhope goods engine, usually No. 43784, (followed by No. 43586) and on withdrawal of freight facilities from the branch, closed on 18th June 1962. It was demolished shortly afterwards.

The shed was peculiarly short and accommodation was further reduced in 1958 when BR removed half the roof. The loco here is '3F' 0—6—0 No. 43586, the Oxenhope goods engine and the last to stable regularly at the shed.

W. T. Stubbs

Keighley in happier days.

T. J. Edgington

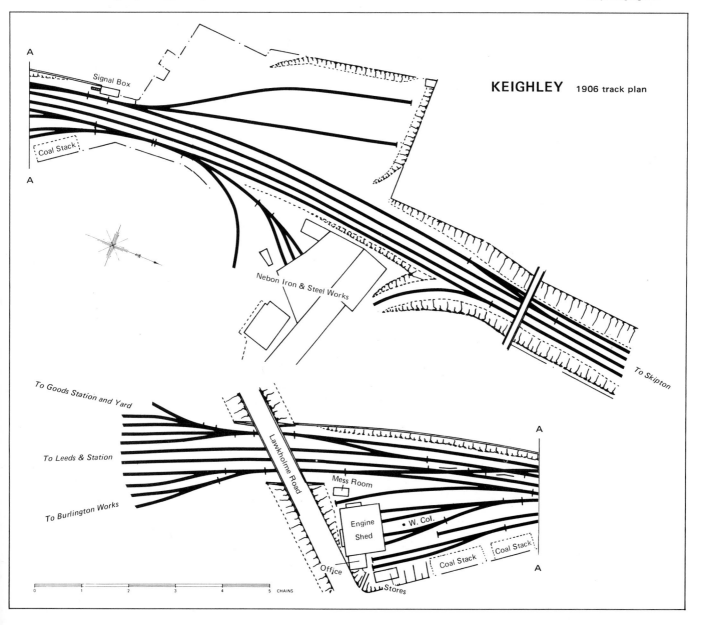

A

Signal Box

Coal Stack

A

KEIGHLEY 1906 track plan

Nebon Iron & Steel Works

To Skipton

To Goods Station and Yard

To Leeds & Station

To Burlington Works

Lawkholme Road

Mess Room

A

Engine Shed

• W. Col.

Office

Coal Stack

Coal Stack

A

Stores

0   1   2   3   4   5 CHAINS

Inside one of the better preserved roundhouses, circa 1949. The preponderance of tank engines suggests the scene is 'No. 1' shed, or the 'Metro' as it was known. This building was the last to be re-roofed, in the late 1950s.

W. Potter

KENTISH TOWN

Kentish Town was the Midland's London depot and opened along with the extension to the capital in 1867/8. Two adjacent sheds were built, each with 42 ft turntables, a four road fitting shop was erected at the rear and a coaling shed placed centrally in the yard. The roundhouse nearest to the main line was designated 'No. 1' shed, its companion 'No. 2', and this arrangement sufficed until the late 1890s. The main line required widening about and connections and sidings laid at the rear of the depot made it necessary for 'No. 1' shed and the fitting shop to be demolished. The south west corner of 'No. 2' shed also needed to be cut back. Replacement accommodation was obviously required and Messrs. E. Wood had been awarded a contract for two further roundhouses at a cost of £36,850. 9s. 4d. on 4th August 1898. These were sited to the north of the original building, alongside but offset. The two new buildings were completed in 1899 and a large fitting shop, served by a traverser, was finished shortly afterwards with the transfer of much of the old equipment and machinery. The surviving original roundhouse now became 'No. 1' shed and its companions Nos. '2' and '3' respectively. They were equipped with 55 ft turntables from the outset, from Messrs. Eastwood Limited and 'No. 1' shed's old 42 ft table was enlarged to a similar size in 1900, at a cost of £1,670. Included in the extensive rearrangement of the depot was a large 'double' coal stage and a greatly expanded loco yard, the depot remaining in this form until modernisation work by the LMS in the 1930s.

The facilities at Kentish Town were extensive and in Midland days, prior to Granet's reorganisation, the District Locomotive Superintendent ranked second only to the CME. Until it closed in 1932, the fitting (or rather erecting) shop was probably the most comprehensive outside Derby and was in two bays, each served by an overhead crane of about forty tons capacity. The machine shop was at the end, remote from the shed, the subsequent LMS facilities (including a combination lathe) occupying the former smithy. There was also a paint shop prior to about 1930, on the opposite side of the traverser. Although only the 'B' shed of the district, it was always the major London depot and the administrative headquarters and the District Loco Superintendent were always located there.

Kentish Town was MR shed No. 16 with an allocation swiftly rising to over seventy locos, including all the express types employed by the company. These included the various 2—4—0s, the most celebrated being Nos. 800 to 811 of the '800' class, built 1870-1 and stationed there for over ten years. They were succeeded by 4—4—0s of all the various types although some of the last 2—4—0s, Nos. 1475-86 built 1879-1881 were sent to Kentish Town (known as 'London' before the opening of Cricklewood) before Johnson finally decided on the 4—4—0 arrangement for express passenger work. An interesting break from the long series of 4—4—0s supplied throughout the remaining Midland period were the famous 4—2—2 'Spinners'. A return to older principles, they were considered 'undoubtedly amongst the finest single express engines ever constructed' and were an enormous success on the Leicester expresses. Successive enlargements of these engines, built

The great roof pitches impart a brooding atmosphere to this view of June 1935.   *W. Potter*

from 1887, arrived at Kentish Town, culminating in the ten 'Princess of Wales' examples in 1900. A number remained at the shed after their express days were over and were to be seen on local passenger work until the early 1920s. They were followed by the Belpaire 4—4—0s of 1900 (numbered 700-779 in 1907) and then some of the famous Compounds. Nos. 1031-1044 were at Kentish Town for many years and some were still active, on semi-fasts and locals, well into the 1950s. As the main shed for St. Pancras of course, express locomotives from other major depots, Leicester, Nottingham, Derby, etc. were serviced at Kentish Town on a daily basis, although simple turning and watering was carried out in a yard just north of the terminus.

The shed also housed a number of tank engines, particularly for the City traffic over the Metropolitan and these condenser fitted engines formed an important feature of the locomotive stock in the London district. They were engaged on passenger services on the main line and to Moorgate and Victoria, as well as the chequered Acton branch workings, which took them for a brief period to Earls Court on passenger trains. Goods traffic was worked

via the widened lines to the LCDR and the MR's own goods and coal depots in South London and via Acton Wells to Kensington. Kirtley designed ten 2—4—0Ts, Nos. 230-239, for the opening of the line to Moorgate but their long rigid wheelbase rendered them unacceptable to the Metropolitan Railway Engineer. Six standard Metropolitan 4—4—0Ts on order were thus diverted to the Midland, for use at Kentish Town, and became Nos. 204-209. The 2—4—0Ts were rebuilt to tender engines in 1869-70 and two were still at St. Albans in 1892. Kirtley next introduced two series of slightly different 0—4—4 'back tanks' with condensing gear, comprising eventually twenty-six engines, numbered 1200-1225 in 1907. Ten 0—6—0Ts with cut down boiler mountings, Nos. 880-889 (1610-1619 in 1907) were provided in 1871 for workings to the East London goods depots and remained on these duties until withdrawn in 1924-27. Standard Johnson tanks of 1874 and 1878 arrived in turn for local shunting and goods work and a further forty-one condensing 0—4—4Ts were added in the period up to 1895. No goods tanks were condenser fitted and these passenger tanks worked freights through the tunnels until 1899, when the '2441' 0—6—0Ts,

Delightful Midland well tank with more modern counterpart in LMS days. Such machines have long followed 'Dogs Head' beers into oblivion.

W. Potter

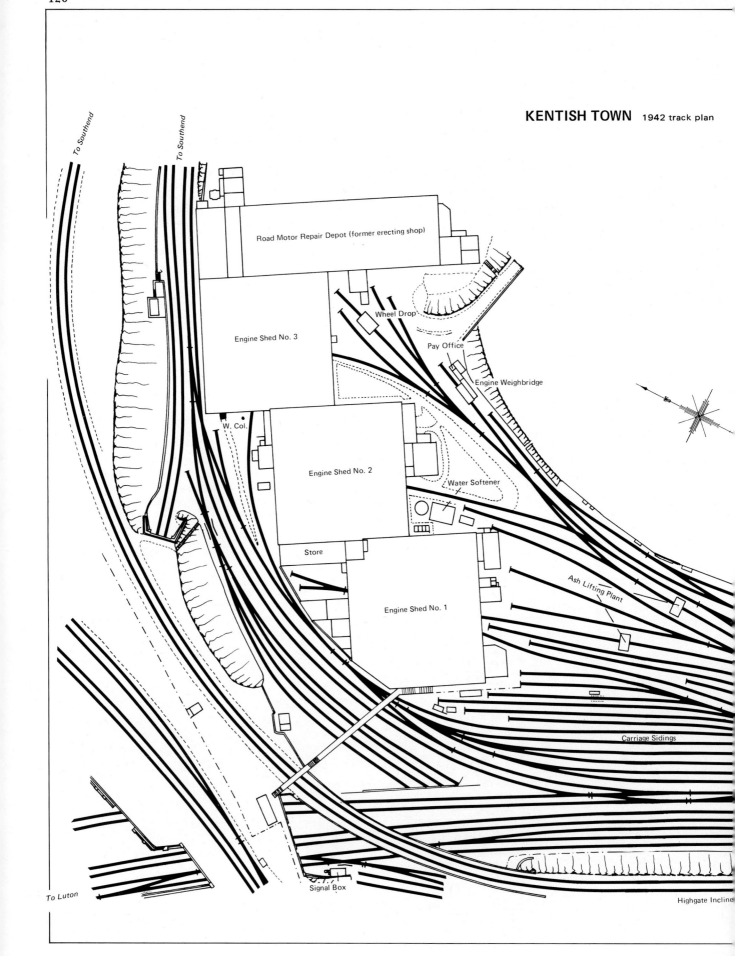

KENTISH TOWN 1942 track plan

To Southend

To Southend

Road Motor Repair Depot (former erecting shop)

Engine Shed No. 3

Wheel Drop

Pay Office

Engine Weighbridge

W. Col.

Engine Shed No. 2

Water Softener

Store

Engine Shed No. 1

Ash Lifting Plant

Carriage Sidings

To Luton

Signal Box

Highgate Incline

The imposing 'double' coal stage at Kentish Town in June 1935. It was swept away during modernisation work in 1939/40.

W. Potter

the first thirty of which were condenser fitted, became available. Whilst most of the passenger tanks were concentrated at Kentish Town or the St. Albans sub-shed, the goods tanks came mainly to operate from Cricklewood.

Over 120 locos were allocated in the mid-1930s when Kentish Town became 14B, officially a 'garage' of Cricklewood. '2P' and '3P' 4—4—0s and '4P' compounds were still very much in evidence, the shortage of large passenger engines having been partly solved by the provision of a number of ex-LNWR 'Claughton' 4—6—0s. Nos. 5955, 5964, 5973, 5974, 5978 and 6012, all in rather poor condition, were supplied by the Western Division in 1930, replaced as they were withdrawn by new 'Patriot' 4—6—0s. By September 1933 examples of this latter type at Kentish Town included No. 5905 *Lord Rathmore*, 5916 *E. Tootal Broadhurst*, 5933, 5954, 5958, 5971 *Croxteth*, 5973 and 5982. These were displaced in turn by new 'Jubilee' 4—6—0s as soon as they became generally available, from 1935. They became the staple express power until the end of steam, assisted by 'Black 5's and, in BR days, some 'Royal Scots' and standard types. Eleven 'Crab' 2—6—0s were allocated for fast freights in the 1930s. After trials with L & YR 2—4—2T No. 10621 and ex-Caledonian 0—4—4T No. 15264 in 1926/27, and the use of five Deeley 0—6—4Ts in 1928, new 2—6—4Ts and 2—6—2Ts largely displaced the old MR 0—4—4Ts. Eleven still remained by September 1933 (including 1211, 1219 and 1220, Kirtley double framed 0—4—4 well tanks) and

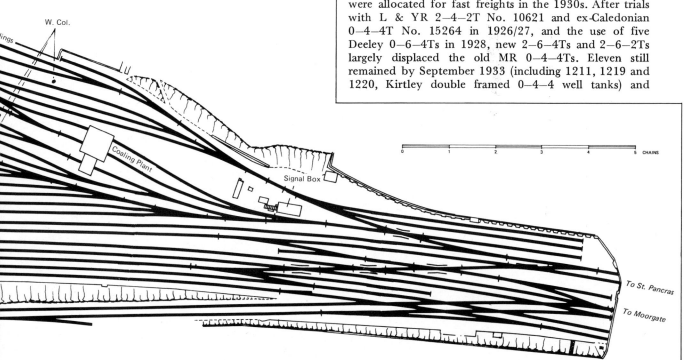

The Midland roundhouses were relatively clean and orderly places. Neatly stabled on 31st May 1924 are 4—4—0s Nos. 762, 758 and 742 and a 'single', No. 668.

H. C. Casserley

A stern warning at Kentish Town in 1922.

Courtesy Derby Museum

Condenser fitted locos for the 'widened lines' etc. were a feature of the shed for many years. The edict 'engines must condense' was officially 'rigidly adhered to' but in truth the apparatus seldom even functioned correctly! The rodding etc. required was poorly designed and regarded as a nuisance by the fitting staff. The picture of engines busily and dutifully condensing was largely an illusion for official consumption.

W. Potter

0–6–0 tanks, including LMS-built examples, totalled thirty. By the end of the Second World War only four of the old passenger tanks remained.

The old coal stage was replaced by modern concrete coal and ash apparatus in 1939/1940. Following bomb damage in the war, the roofs were also gradually replaced, in steel and glass, 'No. 3' shed being dealt with first, followed by Nos. '1' and '2'. 'No. 1' shed was always referred to as 'the Metro', being reserved for tank engines and the stores at the back as the 'Coronation Stores', having been brought into use at the time of King Edward VII's coronation. Many depots had such named facilities with origins often much more obscure than Kentish Town's stores. Sidings etc. at many engine sheds were often called 'Jubilee', 'Klondyke', 'Spike', etc., the latter having some connection with convict labour! ('Abba', or 'Abyssinia',

one of the LNWR sheds at Crewe, was described in Volume One, when its origin was not clear. It is one of the most exotic and derives from the Abyssinian campaign of 1868. That country's emperor, Theodorus, had arrested British missionaries in 1864 and it was four years before an expedition could capture Magdala and rescue them. The wretched Theodorus shot himself). Kentish Town, naturally, was provided from the first with a lodging house, a 'barracks', which possessed an interesting and possibly unique feature. Anxious not to miss any opportunity to educate the staff, the MR had gradient profiles (London-Manchester and London-Carlisle) painted on the walls of the recreation room and these 'murals' survived through LMS days.

Kentish Town still had ninety-nine engines in 1954 including new BR tanks Nos. 80047, 80048, 80059 and 80062, three '1F' survivors Nos. 41671, 41713 and 41724

0–6–0T No. 7103 and 0–4–4T No. 1382 by the coal stage in June 1935.

W. Potter

The ferro-concrete ash plant erected at Kentish Town in the late 1930s. These were far more substantial than the girder-built examples employed extensively elsewhere on the system. General arrangements, drawings, etc. of these feature in the introductory notes of Volume 1.

Photomatic

and thirteen 'Jubilee' 4—6—0s. Dieselisation on the Midland main line, especially the provision of DMUs on the commuter services, rendered the shed redundant relatively early and by November 1962 its remaining steam allocation, '3MT' 2—6—2Ts Nos. 40022 and 40031, 'Jubilees' Nos. 45622 *Nyasaland* and 45628 *Somaliland* and '2MT' 2—6—2Ts Nos. 84005, 84008 and 84029, were in store with numbers of other 'dead' locos awaiting disposal. Diesels, particularly Derby Sulzer type '2's based at Cricklewood, were still being operated by Kentish Town men, however, and servicing facilities were still available for visiting steam locomotives. The depot finally closed in the early months of 1963 and was afterwards sold for private use.

Work on the new roof of 'No. 1' shed approaching completion.

British Railways

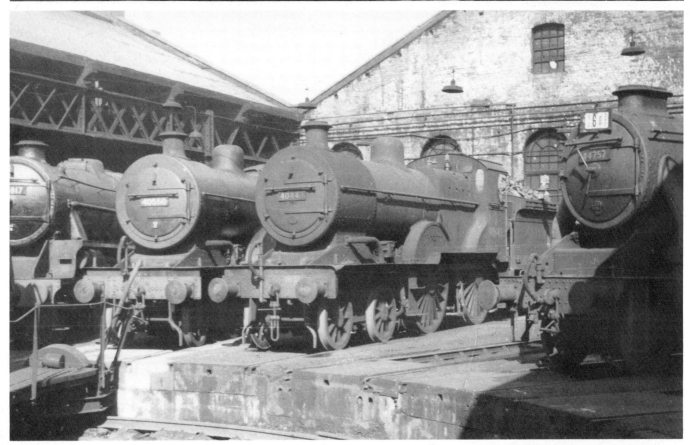

Two views in the 1950s.

Lens of Sutton and B. Hilton

Kettering on a rainy day in 1935.

Photomatic

KETTERING

On 20th June 1865 it was ordered 'That a steam shed for two Engines with Turntable be provided at Kettering, and that Mr. Crossley be instructed to communicate with Mr. Furtherway as to the additional land required'. This was presumably built, as various small improvements followed over the years, a new sand furnace in 1870 and additional machinery and shear-legs in 1871. In 1870 the Locomotive Committee had also requested 'that a permanent coal stage be erected at Kettering' and a new shed appeared in 1876, when gas was laid on 'to Kettering new Engine Shed', at £118.11s.0d. A small standard coal stage was provided in the same year. An estimate of £10,550 had been submitted for 'a new engine shed and sidings' as

early as 1872 and Messrs. C. Deakin had won the contract 'for the erection of an engine shed at Kettering' with a tender of £7,488.14s.9d. in 1875. It stood to the north of the station on the east side of the line, with the turntable originally sited between the station and the shed. It was removed in December 1896 to allow for extension of the platforms and a new 50 ft turntable, from Messrs. Eastwood Ltd., was provided on specially built-up ground in the north of the yard. An extra water column was supplied alongside.

The shed was similar to a number of others erected in the period, with decorative brick surrounding the windows and arched entrances. It remained in this form, with the original pitched roof until closure, but there were a few minor alterations carried out by the LMS. A water softener

The shed's arches with modern locomotives resulted in a cramped appearance, though the building was spacious enough inside.

R. J. Essery

'G3' 0—8—0s were the largest freight locos at Kettering until the war years when '8F' 2—8—0s took over. Two of the Fowler engines accompany earlier 0—6—0s in June 1936.
W. Potter

was installed, a 60 ft turntable with extra approach road (proposed in 1938) replaced the old Eastwood unit, the offices and mess were improved and the old shear-legs, on a siding by the turntable, were removed. Kettering was MR shed number 12 with a small sub-shed at Cambridge, closed following the Grouping. Its forty or so locos consisted mainly of 0—6—0s or 2—4—0s in the early years, with a few tanks for local work. Several of the 2—4—0s built in 1867, Nos. 193, 194, 198 etc., went there around 1880 and in later years Nos. 234-238, formerly 2—4—0Ts,

were stationed at Kettering. A fourth engine, No. 239, was the usual locomotive kept at Cambridge. In the early 1930s 2—4—0s still made up a quarter of the allocation, most of the remainder being '2F' or '3F' 0—6—0s. Kirtley 2—4—0 No. 20012 remained throughout the Second World War until withdrawn in 1945 and Johnson 2—4—0 No. 20216 survived in fact until 1949, shunting at Kettering and spending long periods out of use until transferred to Gloucester in March. It finished its days as Cheltenham Spa (Lansdown) station pilot.

Kettering shed and yard.
R. J. Essery

Scenes around the depot in its last years, with '9F' 2–10–0s much in evidence. The ornate lamp stood near to the turntable and can also be seen in the bottom photograph. The Ransomes & Rapier 60 ft turntable replaced a former 50 ft Eastwood unit.

R. J. Essery

After 1950 Cambridge ex-LNER shed took over a number of the Kettering workings and ex-Great Eastern engines particularly 'J15' 0—6—0s, became regular visitors. In December 1955 a notable engine paid a call, 'E4' 2—4—0 No. 62786 on the 4.55 p.m. from Cambridge, deputising for a failed Ivatt '2MT' Mogul. The 2—6—0s had largely taken over the Cambridge line by 1947, Kettering receiving some of the first of these locos, No. 6404 at first, followed by Nos. 6400-6403. '8F' 2—8—0s had arrived during the war for the main line freights replacing the 'G3' 0—8—0s previously employed on this work. Only four of these locos, Nos. 9501, 9572, 9580 and 9583, remained by 1946. '9F's were also used in the last years, rebuilt Crosti loco No. 92025 finding regular employment in 1961. Three diesel shunters were also at the shed by this time, acting as 'up' and 'down' yard pilots with a third shunting at Corby. Coded 15B since 1935 and 15C from September 1963, Kettering closed on 14th June 1965 and was afterwards demolished, the site inevitably becoming a car park.

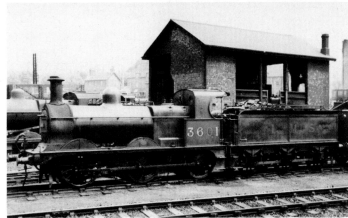

Top: A busy day at Kettering, 19th April 1959. The small coal stage was virtually rebuilt to give adequate clearance. *Above:* '2F' 0—6—0 No. 3601 stands at Kettering in June 1936.

W. Potter

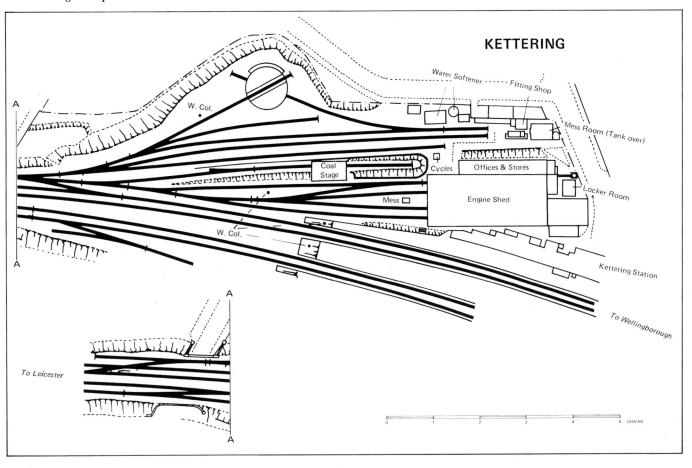

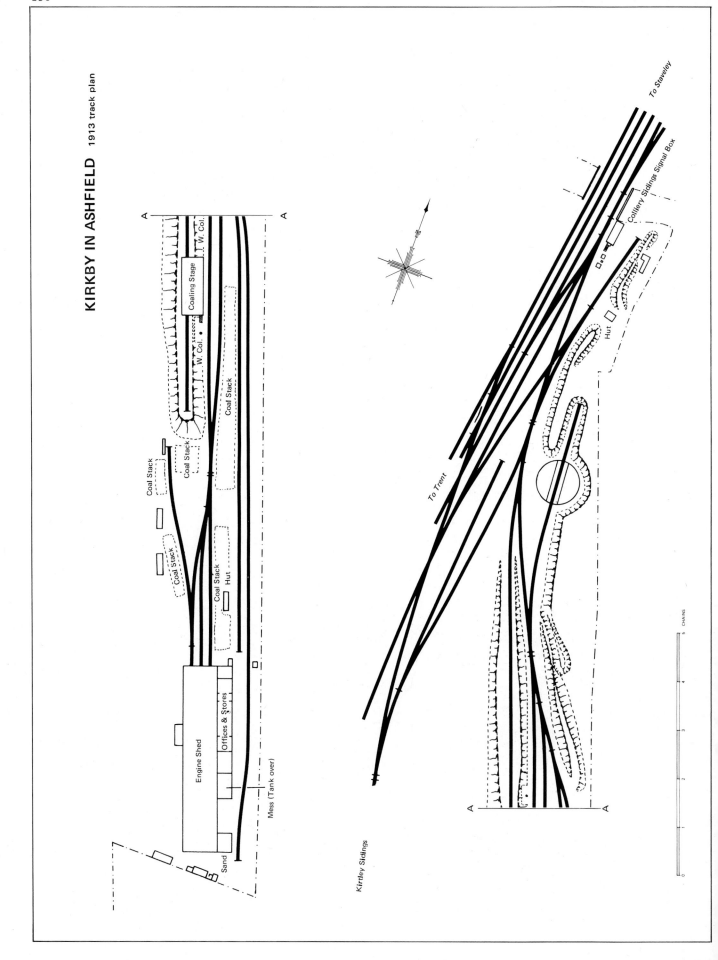

KIRKBY IN ASHFIELD 1913 track plan

Coaling Stage

W. Col.

W. Col.

Coal Stack

Coal Stack

Coal Stack

Coal Stack

Coal Stack

Coal Stack

Hut

Engine Shed

Offices & Stores

Mess (Tank over)

Sand

Kirtley Sidings

To Trent

To Staveley

Colliery Sidings Signal Box

Hut

A

A

5 CHAINS

Kirkby in Ashfield in July 1946. The occasion of an RCTS visit enables a fairly detailed listing of the locomotives on view. The 2—8—0 behind the telegraph pole is No. 8027 and (from left to right) three further members of the class occupy the front of the shed, Nos. 8269, 8100 and 8696. Two standard '4F's, Nos. 4140 (nearest) and 4474, occupy the right hand siding, and ex-MR 0—6—0 No. 22946 lurks behind '8F' No. 8269.

G. S. Lloyd

KIRKBY IN ASHFIELD

Kirkby shed and the extensive yards nearby were quite new developments carried out at the turn of the century. Coal gave birth to the Midland, nurturing it over the years, and as new areas of production opened up, the company was always there to provide the necessary transport facilities. This was the case concerning the district around Kirkby in Ashfield, part of a larger field destined to entirely usurp the traditional areas of South Wales, the North East, etc. in terms of production and profitability.

Plans and estimates were ordered on 6th October 1899 and on 14th December were forwarded to the Finance and General Purposes Committee. At £27,838 the cost was considered too high and the design was cancelled by the senior committee on 6th April 1900. The Way and Works Committee duly returned to their labours, but were only able to increase the estimate to over £28000; a dim view was taken of this and the proposal was 'mothballed' for the next year or so. At that sort of price, and intended to 'house 24 locos', the original proposals obviously envisaged a roundhouse and the disagreement centred on whether traffic would require the number of engines suited to this form of accommodation. It soon did but nevertheless the company decided that a three road straight shed would suffice and Messrs. J. Walker's tender of £7,106.12s.9d. was accepted on 7th August 1902. Equipped with shear-legs, a coal stage and 60 ft turntable, the brick built shed eventually opened in late 1903, its duties of course concerned almost exclusively with coal, forty or so 0—6—0s hauling endless train loads destined mainly for London.

Kirkby was a sub-shed of Nottingham, coded 18b and in 1935 it became 16C, a Nottingham 'garage'. The coal trade grew apace and the number of 0—6—0s steadily

The long overdue addition provided by BR in the late 1950s. Two of the shed's '8F' fleet, Nos. 48219 and 48405, outside the 'new extension' on 9th August 1964.

W. Potter

Kirkby after modernisation, on 7th April 1963. The ramp in the foreground is part of the disused MR coal stage. Diesels, mainly Brush Type '4's, 'Peaks', Sulzer Type '2's, and EE Type '1's, operated from Kirkby until 1970, although traffic declined drastically after the closure of Kirkby Colliery in 1968. The original part of the shed was de-roofed and the tracks lifted in April 1968 and diesels were housed in the 'new extension'. All traces have now finally disappeared and a trading estate now occupies the site.

Collection S. Summerson.

increased throughout LMS days, but little was done in the way of improvement; the turntable was fitted with a vacuum tractor in 1946 but the shed could still only house twelve to fifteen locos. Despite this apparent neglect the shed's traffic was of such value that numbers of new '8F' 2—8—0s were sent there during the late 1930s, their numbers reaching nearly forty by 1945. Apart from this there were twenty or so 0—6—0s, mainly LMS built '4F's, and accommodation was ludicrously inadequate. Complete modernisation involving new turntable, coal and ash plants and extension of the building was proposed in 1947, but these overdue measures were lost in the general reordering of priorities following nationalisation. It was over ten years before BR was able to turn its corporate mind to the problem.

In 1958 the 'first stage' began with the erection of coal and ash plants, closely followed by the 'second stage', a two road extension in brick, roofed with corrugated sheeting, on the west side of the shed. Welcome as it was, it was still barely adequate for an allocation of sixty-three locomotives. This number increased when Mansfield closed in April 1960, its remaining locos and men transferring to Kirkby. The depot's engines were still used almost exclusively on coal work and despite receiving its first '9F' 2—10—0s, Nos. 92080, 92110 and 92111 in 1964, Kirkby was destined to be one of the more ironic victims of the diesel programme. It closed as 16E on 3rd October 1966 (having been 16B from October 1955 to September 1963) with its new facilities something less than eight years old. Although the two road addition remained in use for diesels for a few more years, the entire shed was eventually demolished, the men transferring to Shirebrook Eastern Region depot.

The modern yard in the early 'sixties. The mechanical units had given barely eight years service when taken out of use in 1966.

R. J. Essery

Lancaster shed in August 1900.

Collection A. G. Ellis

LANCASTER

It is not clear precisely when the shed at Lancaster Green Ayre opened. The line from Skipton, with a loop to the LNWR station at Lancaster Castle, was completed in 1850 and it appears that the first shed was a small brick building near to the station. It remained standing until the 1930s and its small pit was still in use in the 1950s, primarily for brake adjustments to the tank engines engaged on the Green Ayre—Castle trains during the suspension of the electric service. By 1857 the Midland resolved 'That the North Western Company (presumably the 'little North Western') be applied to and requested to supply and put down a Turntable of sufficient strength for the use of Engines now required to work the Traffic'. The Committee read, on July 14th 1857, a riposte 'suggesting' that the MR was liable to replace the turntable and it is likely that the decision to construct the shed was taken shortly afterwards.

In the event, Green Ayre shed had four roads with a single bay workshop (chimney and boiler foundations were constructed as early as 1863). A new sand furnace was approved on 6th June 1871 and a set of shear-legs at £105.1s.10d. the following year. Nine engines were allocated by 1879, four 0—6—0s, four 2—4—0s and a solitary

The unrebuilt shed on 10th August 1926. The engines are 2—4—0 No. 216 and 0—6—0 No. 2728.

J. E. Kite

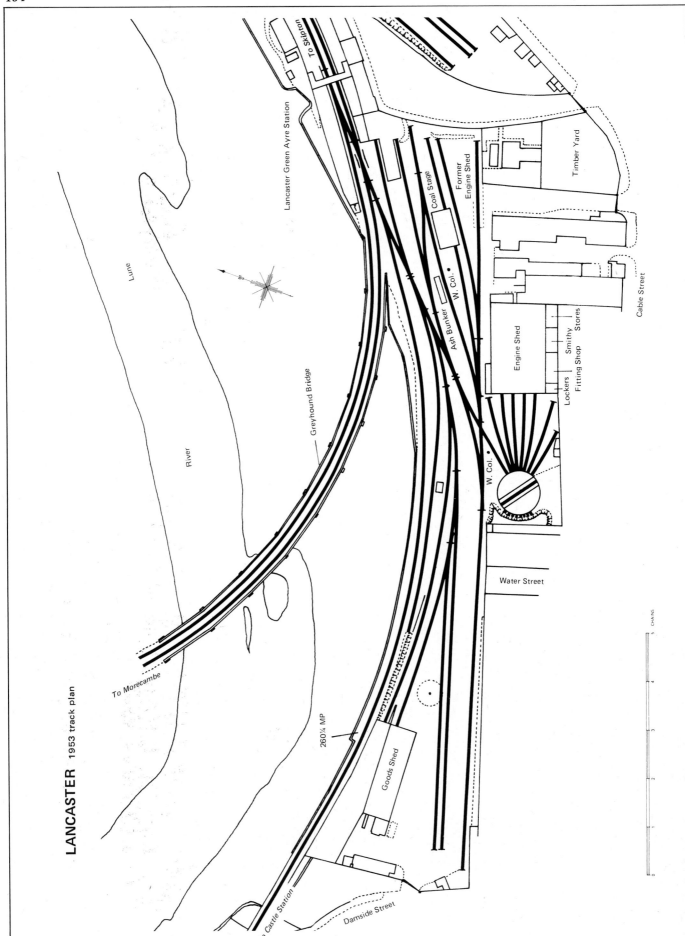

LANCASTER 1953 track plan

To Morecambe

River

Lune

Greyhound Bridge

Lancaster Green Ayre Station

To Skipton

Coal Stage

Former
Engine Shed

Timber Yard

Ash Bunker

W. Col.

Engine Shed

Cable Street

Lockers
Smithy
Fitting Shop
Stores

W. Col.

Water Street

260¼ MP

Goods Shed

To Castle Station

Damside Street

0   1   2   3   4   5   CHAINS

The shed had been rebuilt when this photograph was taken in 1947. The old repair shop (on the right) had long been put out of use.

L & GRP

Kirtley 2—2—2. Passenger work to Skipton and Leeds formed the shed's most important turns, handled until the First World War mainly by 2—4—0s of the '890' class, and several of Johnson's 2—4—0s of 1879 were still at Lancaster in 1920. The last to go was No. 213, a Johnson engine, in 1933, 4—4—0s afterwards having exclusive charge of the passenger work. There were less than thirty engines at the shed throughout LMS days but by 1953 there was a complement of nearly forty. Standard '3F' tanks had arrived for the varied shunting turns in the shape of Nos. 16551-16554, new from the Vulcan Foundry in 1928. There were six of them by 1945 and a single '8F' 2—8—0, the shed having by now acquired a number of workings on the ex-LNW main line to Crewe. Lancaster was notable in that it provided a 'last home' for a number of Compounds retained for the Leeds passenger trains. No. 41101 was the final example, withdrawn in 1959. By

1952 Ivatt Moguls, class '4' and '2', 2—6—4Ts and 'Crabs' were working from the shed which, although scheduled for modernisation in 1934, still retained its old coal stage. The roof had been renewed in 1933, the fitting shop being abandoned in the process, and in 1937 a new 60 ft vacuum operated turntable had been provided.

Lancaster had been Midland shed No. 32 and as M32 of the Midland Division in 1934, took over the workings of the closed LNW Lancaster shed. It became 11C under the ex-LNW shed at Carnforth in 1935, but was transferred back to the Midland Division in 1936 as 20H in the Leeds district. In 1950 it became 23C under Skipton but on this district being disbanded was recoded 11E, once more under Carnforth, in September 1951. It became 24J under Accrington in March 1957 and finally 10J in September 1963, keeping this designation until closure on 18th April 1966.

Lancaster in its last years.

C. I. K. Field

LEEDS HOLBECK

Bridge Road

Engine Shed No. 2

Engine Shed No. 1

Mess Room

Stores

Offices

Fitting Shop

Electing Shop

W. Col.

Ash Plant Single Skip Hoist

Ash Plant Single Skip Hoist

Coal Stack

W. Col.

W. Col.

W. Col.

Signal Box

Coaling Plant
2 x 150 T Bunkers

Weighing Machine

Lodging House

Coal Stack

Nineveh Road

To Normanton

Lines from Leeds

To Farnley

Central Division
To Leeds

CHAINS

0 1 2 3 4 5

Holbeck presents itself for the official photographer in July 1939.

National Railway Museum

LEEDS HOLBECK

The North Midland Railway opened its line into Leeds Hunslet Lane station on 1st July 1840, providing an engine shed nearby. Passenger services were transferred to the more convenient terminus at Wellington station following its opening by the Leeds and Bradford Railway in 1846 and a circular shed of the smaller sixteen road type was built in 1848 at a cost of £7,134. A two road workshop and tank house were erected alongside and a coke shed provided in the yard. The Midland's two depots could now accommodate some thirty-six engines, but with projected extensions to Carlisle and London it was obvious that Leeds would require greatly increased locomotive facilities. There were agreements with three companies, the North Eastern, the London and North Western and the Lancashire and Yorkshire for them to make use of the Wellington roundhouse, but the extent to which the rights were exercised is not clear; all three had acquired sheds of their own in the city, the L & YR previously finding accommodation at Hunslet Lane. It was vacated by 1857 when a Mr. Barlow of the Midland was 'authorised to purchase the Old Engine Shed belonging to the Lancashire and Yorkshire Company, maximum price £3,000.' The Hunslet Lane shed eventually went out of use following the opening of Holbeck.

The circular shed at Wellington stood in the way of new work connected with the NER/LNWR joint New Station and as early as 1864 the Midland agreed to vacate the building. In December of that year plans were prepared for an engine shed at Holbeck to house forty-eight engines. It was over a year later, in January 1866, that the various

tenders were examined and Messrs. Neill were successful with a quotation of £20,312.11s.5d. 'Butler R. & Pitts' were awarded the contract for the ironwork at a cost of £5,996.9s.0d. There followed a lengthy delay, apparently connected with the Midland's somewhat strained financial position and new contractors, Messrs. Nicholson & Son, took over when construction was well advanced in June 1868 'on the same terms as were given to James Neill'. The old Wellington shed had been handed over to the Joint Committee overseeing the building of the new station on 9th May, so the situation for the few remaining months while arrangements were completed at Holbeck, must have been somewhat hectic.

One of the earliest 'square sheds', Holbeck was equipped with two 42 ft turntables and a centrally placed 'coal shed' to serve both roundhouses. An eight road fitting shop (the 'engine repairing works') was provided on the west side of the site, adjoining Ninevah Road, physically separate from the main shed and equipped with many items from the old repair shops. A large new 'double' coal stage was built in Johnson's time, (in 1882/3), and the turntable in 'No. 1' shed was enlarged to 55 ft, then to 60 ft in 1902 and 1938 respectively.

Traffic to the Midlands and London ensured that from the outset Holbeck was one of the company's premier depots. The opening of the Carlisle route in 1876 provided further important through workings and Holbeck, coded 28, remained (and still remains) a major locomotive centre. There were rather less than fifty locos allocated when the shed opened, many of them Kirtley 0—6—0s. In the 1870s, 2—2—2s (including Nos. 11-20) and subsequently 2—4—0s (including Nos. 811-819 of the '800' class) worked the

New ash plants under construction in 1935, photographed from the growing framework of the coaler. *British Railways*

main passenger turns. A number of the latter engines were still at Holbeck around 1920, while other 2—4—0s at the shed for many years included Nos. 1502-1526, of the final 1879-81 batch. 4—4—0s dominated the express work by the turn of the century and of course the various enlarged 0—6—0s continued in service on the principal goods turns.

The opening of the Settle and Carlisle in particular demanded the introduction of goods engines of increased power and a large proportion of the 0—6—0s built in

1875/76 were divided between Leeds and Carlisle, (Nos. 1222-1251) working the 'Scotch Express Goods' traffic in its entirety for nearly thirty years. The 0—6—0s were assisted in the decade or so after 1899 by ten of the USA-built Baldwin locos, thirty of which were purchased by the Midland. Holbeck gained a sub-shed, 28a Stourton, in 1893 and many of the freight and shunting engines came to be concentrated there. A year or so before the sheds were divided in 1935 into 'concentration' and

1939, with all the new equipment operational, including the coal slaker to combat dust. *British Railways*

The vantage point for the two previous photographs, Holbeck's huge 'No. 1' type coaler. It held 300 tons, in two bunkers, and was eventually demolished in 1970 with the aid of explosives, an event warranting detailed coverage in the local press.

National Railway Museum

'2P' 4—4—0 No. 40323 rests inside Holbeck on 26th August 1955. The shed retained its original roof until the end and its ageing beams and variable covering inspired many photographers in the last years of steam. York (ex-NER) and Holbeck were favourites of the 'light and shade' photographers whose work brought a different dimension to railway photography in the 'sixties.

B. Morrison

Gloom at Holbeck, on an appalling August day in 1950.   *B. Hilton*

'garage' depots (Holbeck as 20A and Stourton as 20B respectively) the combined allocation stood at 172, 109 of them at the main shed. Holbeck's total included twenty 4—4—0s and fifty-four 0—6—0s, twenty of them '4F's of LMS parentage. Fowler 0—8—0s and 'Crabs' had arrived, but the most interesting development had been the introduction of ex-LNWR 'Claughton' 4—6—0s displaced by 'Royal Scots' from the west coast main line around 1928. In 1930 twelve of the class were present, working north to Carlisle and south to Leicester. They were gradually withdrawn over the next five years and were replaced by new 'Patriots'. Thus by September 1933 there were five 'Claughtons' at Holbeck, Nos. 5912, 5955, 5968, 5984 and 6025, and seven 'Patriots', Nos. 5902, 5935, 5963, 5983, 5997, 6000 and 6011. These in turn gave way to 'Jubilees', which became Holbeck's staple express power, to the very end of steam operation. Three 'Patriots', Nos. 5534, 5535, and 5538, remained, however, until postwar years and in 1943 the first rebuilt 'Royal Scots' arrived, Nos. 6103, 6108, 6109 and 6117. They handled the heaviest turns to Carlisle and Glasgow and were not withdrawn until the end of 1962. 'Crab' 2—6—0s, Nos. 13050-13054 (in red livery) appeared in 1927, joined three years later by Nos. 13130-13135. Stanier 2—6—0s were also tried at Holbeck early in 1934 but proved unpopular with the men particularly on the Ais Gill road and were eventually exchanged for five 'Crabs', Nos. 13071, 13084, 13116, 13150 and 13193. '8F' 2—8—0s and class '5' 4—6—0s succeeded the 0—6—0s and 'Crabs' on freight and secondary work.

The LMS had provided coal and ash plants in 1935 and the roofs were extensively repaired in 1937 and 1942. Nationalisation saw the allocation fall somewhat, to about ninety engines by 1954, with the final elimination of the Johnson '1F' 0—6—0Ts and '1P' 0—4—4Ts, due in great part to the introduction of Ivatt locos, class '2' and '4' Moguls and 2—6—2Ts. Two BR class '5's, Nos. 73010 and

73045, had joined the ranks of the 'Black Fives' and there were now eight 'Royal Scots' at the depot, powering, together with nearly twenty 'Jubilees', the principal London and Carlisle trains. The turntable in 'No. 1' shed was once again renewed in March 1956 and this is presumably the 'table referred to by M. F. Higson in his book *London Midland Fireman*. It was electrically driven and a source of wonder to the men, 'the wonderful machine was equipped with a smart control panel, little light and a host of button gadgets'. Electric 'tables were more exact than the vacuum operated units generally in use and stopping the turntable involved less of a 'crash'. The coaling plant was also out of action while the new turntable was being installed, engines going to Neville Hill (ex-NER) and Stourton for coaling. As a temporary measure a small crane was also installed at Holbeck.

The depot, along with its 'garages' was transferred to the North Eastern Region in January 1957 as 55A, a code it retained until closure as a steam shed. The repair shop had been one of the last in operation, engaged in selective service repairs only in the final years and eventually closed in early BR days. The last two 4—4—0s were transferred away in 1960 and by 1962 diesels were well in evidence, BR/Sulzer 'Peaks' having completely ousted the 'Scots'. Four years after transfer, the shed had received its first ex-LNER locos, two 'A3' Pacifics, put to work on the Carlisle trains. Their brief sojourn was of course soon terminated by the onward rush of dieselisation. Much photographed in its last months and a popular subject for the new 'light and shade' band of photographers, the shed closed to steam on 30th September 1967, having absorbed duties and men from three other Leeds sheds as steam disappeared — Copley Hill (ex-Great Northern) in September 1964, Farnley Junction (ex-LNWR) in November 1966 and Stourton (closed to steam a year previously) in January 1967, The buildings were demolished in 1970 and a diesel servicing depot erected on the site.

The cluttered yard in June 1938.   *H. A. Gamble*

LEICESTER

Leicester, somewhat unfortunately perhaps for the men working there, was something of a 'living museum', retaining its original Midland circular sheds through to the last years of the LMS. The first roundhouse, an early sixteen road building, opened soon after the Midland Counties line through Leicester in 1840. It stood to the north of the main station and later, on widening of the main line, was cut back somewhat, reducing its capacity still further. A second circular shed, a larger twenty-four road version, appeared in due course, probably in the mid-1850s and in 1868 a large new coke shed was built to serve both

sheds. A 42 ft turntable was installed outside in the yard in the same year but the old roundhouses survived the nineteenth century wave of new construction. The outside turntable was enlarged, first to 50 ft and then to 60 ft and a new shed, 'No. 3', was provided in 1893, a standard three road building erected in the yard near to 'No. 2' roundhouse. Estimates of over £3,000 had been obtained for this shed, 'to hold 9 Bogie Passenger Engines' in August 1892 and C. W. Hardy was awarded the contract the following November, with a tender of £2,455.

From the outset, Leicester was one of the principal passenger engine depots on the Midland main line and continued to be an important engine changing point even after the opening of the Extension from Bedford to

Leicester yard, apparently in early LMS days. The antiquated roundhouses were far too small for requirements even then and the shear-legs perforce were sited outside.

A. Wainwright

Three locomotive views taken at Leicester in 1933. The '2P' 4–4–0 at the top is parked alongside the three road straight shed and the 'Crab', No. 13171, is on the turntable siding.

G. Coltas

Outside 'No. 1' shed in 1933.   *G. Coltas*

London. The practice continued until after the Grouping and nearly every passenger type was present at Leicester over the years, from Kirtley 2—2—2s and 2—4—0s, through to the Johnson and Deeley compounds. Nos. 60-66 and 165-169, (28-34 and 23-27 in 1907) of the celebrated '800' class 2—4—0s were there from new after 1870, with many retained on local work until the early 1920s. 4—4—0s Nos. 161-164 (1907 Nos. 459-462) of 1894 were sent to Leicester on their construction and 'ran chiefly to London and Leeds and also frequently to Manchester'.

By 1880 the allocation totalled fifty-seven locos including thirty-three 2—4—0s and twenty-two 0—6—0s, the total rising to about one hundred by 1892. Leicester itself was MR No. 10 and had in its care smaller establishments at 10a, Stockingford (closed November 1932), 10b Coalville (retained and recoded 17C under Derby in 1935) and 10c West Bridge (originally the terminus of the Leicester and Swannington Railway and closed in June 1926). Six-coupled engines comprised well over half the allocation (many of them at Coalville) by the mid-1930s and main passenger traffic was handled entirely by 4—4—0s. 2—6—4Ts Nos. 2330-2335 had arrived for local work by March 1929 providing welcome assistance for the surviving Deeley 0—6—4Ts, Nos. 2005, 2006, 2011 and 2013, and 'Crab' 2—6—0s Nos. 13091, 13092 and 13201-13204 were at work by 1930. '8F' 2—8—0s had appeared by the end of the Second World War when 4—4—0s were still working most of the major passenger duties. Compounds in fact continued to work St. Pancras semi-fasts right up to 1957. 'Black Fives' later became familiar engines at Leicester and their numbers boosted by new BR class '5's Nos. 73003, 73004, 73046 and 73049.

Leicester was long overdue for modernisation in 1900, let alone the 1930s, but circumstances contrived to delay it until the mid-forties, by which time the ramshackle conglomeration of buildings gave every sign of having received the attention of the Luftwaffe! The first detailed proposals surfaced in 1938, at first for a ten road straight shed, with prolonged consideration being given to the site restrictions. It was calculated that the new depot could stable:

'Inside 30 locos
Outside 78 locos
Total 108 locos
Coal wagons 82'

An alternative was also drawn up, a single large round-house to replace the existing pair but war intervened and the old sheds were reprieved for a while, construction not

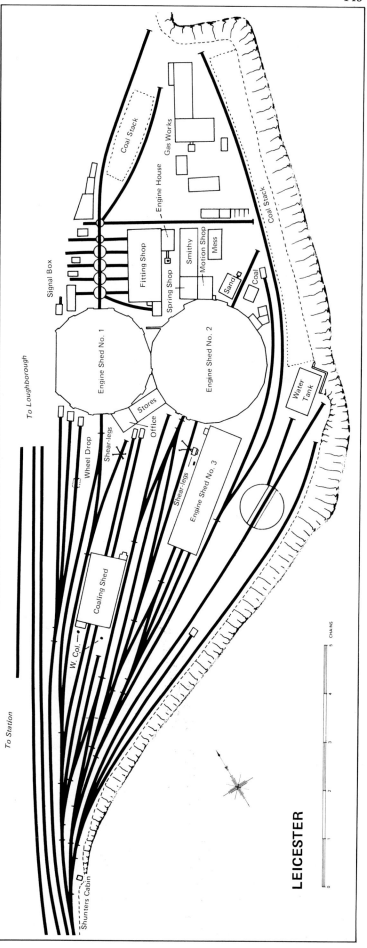

LEICESTER

144

One of a series of aerial photographs commissioned by the contractors on completion of the building in 1945. Some of the pits of 'No. 2' shed, in use until the end, are still visible and a standard wheeldrop has replaced the two sets of shear-legs. The second stage of the reconstruction, involving coal and ash plants, was in the hands of a separate contractor and was yet to begin.

Courtesy Leicester Museum

The completed depot in 1959.

Collection R. J. Essery

getting underway until about 1944. Further proposals appeared in 1945, including this time a water treatment plant, and work was more or less complete by 1946, the closed roundhouse at Wigston, outside the city, having been brought temporarily into use. It eased the congestion at Leicester itself and at one time had a daily roster of ten turns. The fine new polygonal building, however, had an effective life of only some twenty years. The shed had been 15C since 1935 and replaced Wellingborough as the 'A' shed of the district in September 1963. By this time it was also responsible for Leicester ex-Great Central Railway shed, an odd circumstance considering engines at first had to travel to Nottingham (a spur was later put in by BR) to gain access to ex-GC metals. Heavier spare parts for the diesel shunter at the old GC shed travelled by special van miles up the line whilst fitters simply walked or took a bus. Leicester closed to steam along with Wellingborough on 13th June 1966 and stood empty for some time, the preserved Midland locos being housed there as late as 1968. By the mid-1970s, however, it had largely disappeared, only the machine shop with its wheeldrop remained, forming a diesel servicing depot.

The old MR turntable, retained as a potentially useful 'spare'.

British Railways

Lincoln shed on 23rd August 1936. Various traders used the adjacent yard and indeed proposals did emerge at one time for a proper goods loading stage, with canopy, etc.

W. A. Camwell

LINCOLN

A small loco shed had been provided here from the opening of the line in August 1846 and by 1850 repairs were necessary 'to the floor and roof'. Little was done apparently, for the following year the Engineer was 'ordered to inspect and report on the condition of the roof of the Engine Shed at Lincoln Station'. A new engine turntable was ordered at 'Lincoln Station' in April 1858 and shortly before this the coke stage was re-roofed and repaired. It seems that the Midland's habit of accepting only the very lowest tender had begun to show its drawbacks fairly early in the company's history and in the event by 1866 a replacement shed was being considered. On 20th February that year, 'it being reported that the present shed was required for traffic purposes, it was ordered that the officers be requested to consider a report to this committee on the best means of supplying the necessary Engine accommodation at Lincoln'.

The new shed apparently opened the following year. A small coal stage was later erected outside, presumably a replacement, the drawings bearing the following note from the contractor, one William Duke: 'this is one of the drawings mentioned and referred to in my tender dated October 15th 1877'. The shed was equipped with a 42 ft turntable, enlarged in 1893 to 50 ft by Messrs. Lansdown, the building itself requiring repairs in October 1880. Lincoln was a sub-shed of Nottingham in Midland days and throughout subsequent LMS ownership, eventually passing to the Eastern Region as a sub-shed of the larger ex-LNER depot in the city in the early 1950s. As with most of these early inter-regional transfers, the shed

2–4–0 No. 20216 outside the rebuilt shed in July 1947.

H. C. Casserley

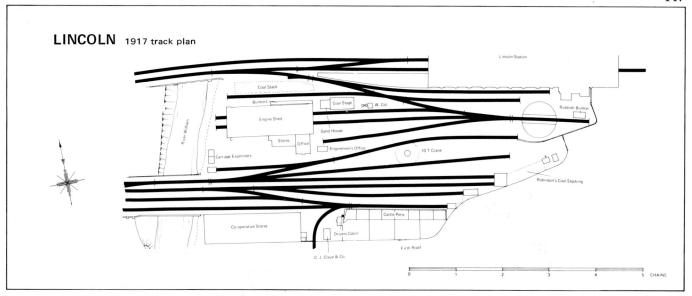

LINCOLN 1917 track plan

continued to operate its stud of ex-LMS locos, although ex-LNER types became increasingly commonplace.

Lincoln had been of far greater importance in its early years and in 1876 for instance, Nos. 25-29, part of the last batch of MR 2—2—2s turned out by Derby in 1863-66, were at the shed 'principally for the Derby trains and as far as Tamworth with the evening mail train'. Nearly sixty years later the shed still had charge of the Tamworth Mail's successor but the remaining duties comprised only a few local turns.

Developments at the shed over the years were hardly stirring, its set of shear-legs being taken away for use at Mansfield in 1909 and the coal crane receiving the benefits of electrical power in 1931. Re-roofing appears to have been carried out around 1943, at any rate during the war. Known as Lincoln St. Marks after absorption into the

Eastern Region in May 1953, the shed at first retained its LMS complement, MR '2P' 4—4—0 No. 40419, LMS '4P' 4—4—0 No. 41060, MR '1F' 0—6—0T No. 41686 and LMS '4F' 0—6—0 No. 44247. Repairs and washouts were to be carried out at the main shed, which would provide substitute power in the form of ex-LNER types (particularly welcome on one occasion in 1958 when the loco intended for the 2.52 service from St. Marks was derailed at the shed yard blocking the exit/entrance!) Familiar ex-LNER types used by Lincoln were Gresley 'J39' 0—6—0s (seldom seen beyond Newark), Robinson 'A5' 4—6—2Ts and ex-GER 'D16' 4—4—0s, both of the latter two classes working regularly to Nottingham and through to Derby Midland. The closeness of the LNER depot heralded a bleak future for the small shed, however, and it closed in January 1959.

The shed backed onto the River Witham and a watery fate awaited those who applied the brake in too lax a fashion! The occasion of this particular photograph is 9th September 1951. The new roof was applied during the war years, in the 'louvre' style adopted as a standard by the LMS.

B. K. B. Green

148

Ex-LNER 'J39' 0—6—0s were the most common 'interlopers' following Nationalisation and No. 64725 is making use of the shed here in 1950. The old 'pedestal' coal stage has been re-roofed by this time, and a drawing of this structure appears in the Introduction.

L & GRP

A conveyor belt was eventually required to facilitate coaling but in this view of 14th July 1947 looks in rather worse condition than the coal stage it was designed to replace.

H. C. Casserley

Manningham and its ancient 'coal shed' on 9th April 1967, '8F' 2—8—0 alongside.   *W. Potter*

MANNINGHAM

Manningham was the MR's Bradford depot and for many years was known by that name. Thomas Tilney's tender of £2,550.10s.0d. was accepted 'for a new Engine Shed, Bradford' during the period 1851 to 1853, the building presumably standing by the main station. The first depot established for working engines dated from September 1846 and was carrying out repairs by March 1847. Space was restricted at the shed and a new roundhouse with 'coal shed' and 42 ft turntable opened on a site just north of Manningham station, on the northern outskirts of the city, in 1872. The main passenger station was some distance to the south and engine facilities remained available there (a new 50 ft turntable and seven water columns were amongst the items ordered in 1890 on the construction of the new Bradford station). On 6th May 1887 plans and estimates were read for an 'additional Engine Shed (in wood) and Sidings, Manningham' and Messrs. William Brown and Sons' tender for its construction, of £3,927 was accepted on 29th July. It was of somewhat odd appearance, for the Midland at least, having a slated north-light pattern roof and being devoid of windows.

'Bradford' was coded 29 in MR days with Keighley and Ilkley as sub-sheds. Its allocation stood at forty-two engines in 1879 including Nos. 27 to 31, five of the last batch of 2—4—0s, and several of the 2—2—2s numbered between 136 and 149, turned out by Derby in 1854/7. The '156' 2—4—0s were the mainstay of the Bradford passenger engine stock for many years and Ahrons in 1919 has some interesting comments on their use at the shed:

No. 156, the first of the class, put in an almost unparalleled record of service at one locomotive station — Bradford. It was stationed there early in 1873, and may have been there even

before that date. In that year it was fitted with the Westing-house brake — which was about to be tried on the Midland — and was one of the first engines in this country to be so supplied. For some years it ran a Westinghouse fitted train between Bradford and Leeds. About 1881, No. 156 left Bradford for Mansfield but after remaining at the latter place for about three years, returned to Bradford in 1884 and was there until two years ago. No. 156 is the oldest passenger engine on the Midland, but has changed its original number (in 1907) and is now No. 1. A few years ago it was quartered at the North Eastern shed at Starbeck (Harrogate), under the Bradford district, to run the Midland trains between Harrogate and Leeds, Bradford has always had a large number of the '156' class, which used to form the 'backbone' of the tender passenger engines at this shed.

Tanks for local passenger work, mainly outstationed at Keighley or Ilkley were also a feature at Manningham, from the Johnson 0—4—4Ts to the Stanier 0—4—4s and eventually the 2—6—4 and 2—6—2Ts. This was not always the case, however, and Ahrons, discussing Midland tank engine policy after about 1875, is very illuminating:

There were, however, a good many other centres badly in need of passenger tank engines and chief amongst these was the Bradford district. For many years I heard it frequently — and, I believe, truly, stated that more passengers were booked at Bradford than at any other station on the Midland line. The local trains, of which there were a large number, were, until 1876, worked entirely by tender engines of the 2—2—2 and 2—4—0 types, but in 1875-6 Messrs. Neilson & Co. built thirty 0—4—4 side tank engines, Nos. 1252 to 1281 (1236-1265 in 1907). Of these, 20 were immediately sent down to Bradford, their appearance there having been heralded by the London condensing tank engine No. 147 (later 1235) of the No. 6 class which was tried at Bradford for a short time.

Bradford was also the earliest recipient of some of the newer freight locos, Nos. 1357-1371 (3020-3034 in 1907), virtually all of the 'express goods' 0—6—0s produced by

The Manningham 'coal shed', in use until the end of steam.

W. Potter

Dubs & Co., going to the shed new in 1878, where 'they put in more mileage than any other goods engine on the line'. Four of them ran through (two in each direction) to London during this period on the MR's fastest goods turns. By way of a close on nineteenth century events at Bradford, the shed's pilot engine was for a number of years, until being broken up in 1903, No. 2069A, a Hunslet 0—6—0ST of 1880. In the mid-1880s it had been seized by the company in lieu of debts owed to the railway by a Midlands iron foundry!

Reorganisation in 1935 saw the shed recoded 20E under Leeds, retaining Ilkley but losing Keighley to Skipton. This left Manningham with around thirty engines, the shed having lost many of its through passenger and freight turns. 0—4—4Ts Nos. 6402, 6403 and 6404 (renumbered 1902, 1903 and 1904 in 1946) went new to Manningham in 1932 and were later joined by Nos. 6400 and 6401 (1946 Nos. 1900 and 1901); L & YR 'Radial' 2—4—2Ts also appeared and both types were often operated from the sub-shed at Ilkley. No. 204, the last surviving Johnson 7′ 2—4—0 was at Bradford in 1934 along with No. 219, one of the last 6′ 6″ engines. 2—6—4Ts and '3MT' 2—6—2Ts together with the odd 'Crab' and '2MT' Mogul had ousted the old Midland tanks and many of the 0—6—0s by the mid 'fifties. Two ex-Caledonian 0—4—4Ts, Nos. 15169 and 15227 were also at Manningham, from April 1947 to July 1948.

The depot retained its original 'coal shed' and although no modern coal or ash handling apparatus was erected, a new 60 ft vacuum operated turntable appeared in 1938. The wooden shed went out of use and was completely demolished by the mid-1940s though its roads remained in use. Manningham became 55F from January 1957 with transfer to the North Eastern Region, but ex-LMS types, particularly '8F's, remained predominant, along with 'WD' 2—8—0s. Dieselisation had begun in 1959 with railcars on the Ilkley services and increasing numbers of 'Type 2' locomotives were to be found at the shed. It finally closed on 30th April 1967.

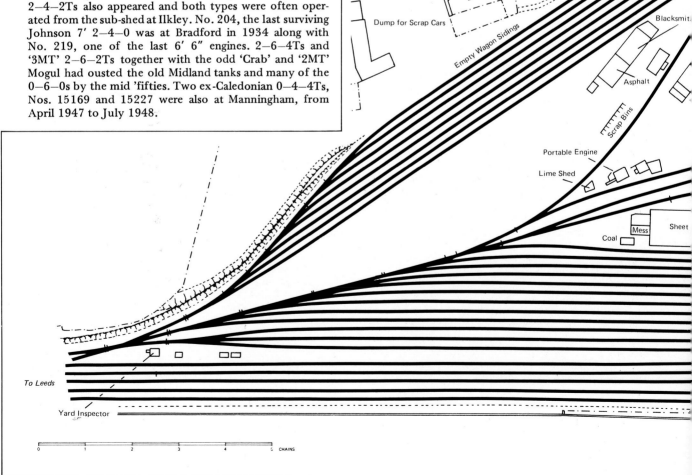

Garage
Chicken Run
Dump for Scrap Cars
Empty Wagon Sidings
Blacksmit
Asphalt
Scrap Bins
Portable Engine
Lime Shed
Mess
Sheet
Coal
To Leeds
Yard Inspector
0 1 2 3 4 5 CHAINS

One of the few views to have been discovered of the wooden straight shed at Manningham, erected in 1887. It had disappeared, at least by 1945 and probably quite a while prior to that. The roads and pits remained in use for engine stabling for many years.

Collection O. Carter

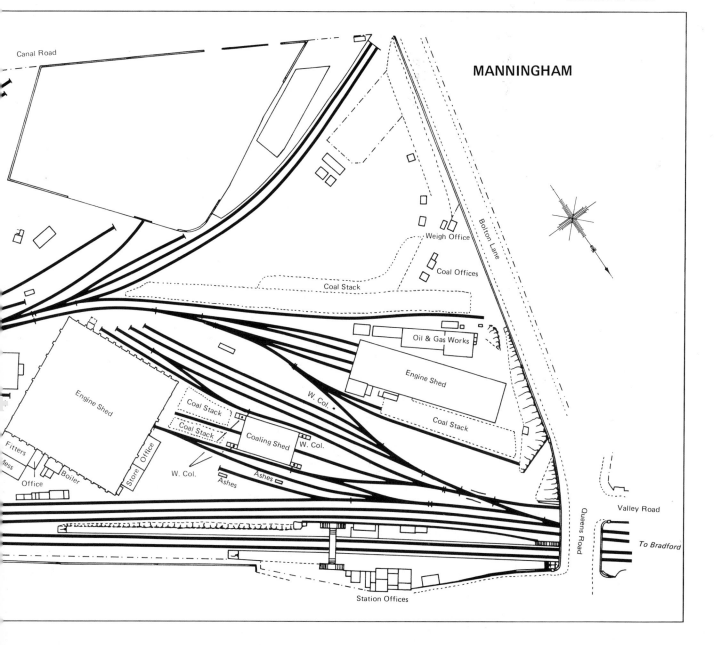

MANNINGHAM

Canal Road

Bolton Lane

Weigh Office

Coal Offices

Coal Stack

Oil & Gas Works

Engine Shed

Coal Stack

Engine Shed

W. Col.

Coal Stack

Coal Stack

Coaling Shed

W. Col.

Store Office

Fitters

Mess

Boiler

Office

W. Col.

Ashes

Ashes

Queens Road

Valley Road

To Bradford

Station Offices

Mansfield shed on 30th August 1936.

W. A. Camwell

MANSFIELD

A four road standard building with twin pitched roofs, Mansfield replaced an earlier single road shed sited nearer to the station. The original building had a water column and small coal stage directly outside with a 42 ft turntable located some distance away. An extra siding had been added and the mess room repaired in May 1871 but the little shed was far too small for the growing number of engines required in the area. William Parkes' tender of £4,730 was accordingly accepted on 2nd May 1881, for a shed to house twelve engines, 'with water tank, mess room, stores and sand furnace'. The shed, in brick with four roads, opened the following year in the triangle formed by the Southwell, Mansfield Town and Nottingham lines south of the station. The estimates for the new shed, together with the nearby sidings and including the cost of the required land, totalled £10,900 and had originally been obtained in 1877/78, the vendor being the Duke of Portland. In 1891 the shed was ordered to be extended, Messrs. Walker & Sons carrying out the work at a cost of about £2,800, the alterations appearing to have taken the form of an extension at the rear. Locos frequently made use of the triangle for turning purposes and the turntable remained some distance away by the station, even after its enlargement to 55 ft in 1900.

Mansfield was coded 18a, a sub-shed of Nottingham, and was principally concerned with passenger work, handled until post-Grouping days by some twenty Johnson 0—4—4Ts. Their 'intricate workings' took them all over the network of branches and secondary lines in Notting-

hamshire and Derbyshire, 'over some 182 miles of railways and about 20 different train services', including the following, described by Ahrons in 1919:

> The Mansfield-Sheffield route, via the Lancashire, Derbyshire and East Coast (now Great Central) Railway was not introduced until 1905. There used also to be a service of three Midland trains daily to Retford over the Great Central line, but at the end of the nineteenth century this had been reduced to one each way, and this solitary survivor has since been discontinued, as also have the Mansfield and Ollerton direct trains more recently. Truly, the Mansfield drivers get plenty of variation and have to learn a good many roads.

The locomotive scene at Mansfield would have been different indeed if the 1934 trials had been successful with LMS-built Caledonian Railway 0—4—4T No. 15266, on local passenger work, a favourite job being the Mansfield-Nottingham 'express' leaving just after 4.00 p.m. and arriving at Nottingham around 4.34. Facilities were modest to say the least but shear-legs were finally provided in 1909, a secondhand set from Lincoln, 'now very seldom used'. The cost was estimated at £52, 'with a view to saving light running Mansfield-Nottingham when engines require lifting for periodical examination'.

Later in LMS days the roof was to be renewed, at a cost of £2,055, but this idea was abandoned and the shed retained its Midland roof to the end. The layout would have been drastically altered if 1947 proposals regarding coal and ash plants, etc. had been acted upon but these too were eventually shelved. The most interesting developments regarding the locomotives came in the later LMS period, when 4—4—2Ts of LTSR (and LMS) construction, displaced from their home territory by new three-cylinder

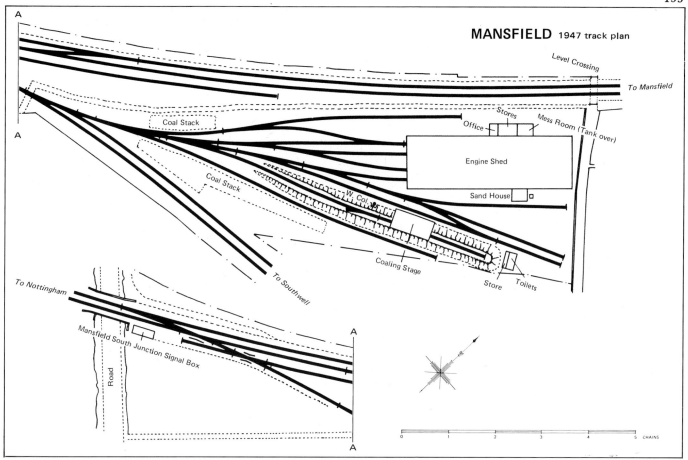

MANSFIELD 1947 track plan

2—6—4Ts, replaced many of the old 0—4—4Ts on local passenger work. By the end of the Second World War they included '2P's Nos. 2093 and 2098 of 1900/03 and '3P' engines Nos. 2122, 2125, 2129, 2140, 2143 and 2144. '8F' 2—8—0s had also arrived by now in the shape of Ashford-built No. 8622 and Brighton engine No. 8643. This was a presage of things to come and within ten years '8F's formed over a third of the 32 locos at Mansfield, supplanting to some extent the '3F' and '4F' 0—6—0s of earlier years. A single '1F' tank, No. 41885 remained,

along with three 4—4—2Ts, Nos. 41940, 41943 and 41947. The 'Tilburys' were withdrawn in 1956, with the exception of No. 41947, which went to Toton.

A 'garage' of Nottingham since 1935, the shed's code had altered from 16D to 16C in October 1955. It was to cease operations on 1st February 1960 but in the event this was postponed and closure did not finally come until 11th April 1960. The locos and men transferred to Kirkby in Ashfield and the building was subsequently sold for private use.

The shed in April 1954. The 0—6—0, No. 3634, was at Mansfield for many years and indeed was inside the shed on the occasion of the previous photograph.

W. Potter

A splendid series of official photographs taken at Millhouses have thankfully survived and this one, taken to show the coal stage, is one of the finest.

National Railway Museum

A posed study in 1938.   *British Railways*

MILLHOUSES

Referred to at first as 'Eccleshall', this was the largest of the straight sheds built by the Midland, with eight roads and a large 'double' coal stage. It stood by Millhouses and Eccleshall station and opened in 1901 as part of 'contract No. 2' of the line widening between Heeley and Dore and Totley stations in the south of Sheffield. An expenditure of £30 was subsequently necessary, in 1906, for the lowering of the coal stage line, 'to accommodate the larger locos.'

Coded 25a, a sub-shed of Grimesthorpe, the new shed primarily housed the passenger locos required for the Sheffield area. There were about eight 0—4—4Ts engaged on local passenger duties but only two or three 0—6—0s available for freight work. A stud of more than twenty 4—4—0s completed the allocation. Millhouses was elevated to 'garage' status, as 19B, under the 1935 arrangements and began to receive new Stanier types in place of its 4—4—0s in the late 1930s, eight 'Jubilees' having appeared by 1945. Indeed the shed was always fortunate when it came to the acquisition of modern types and its allocation of 30th January 1954 demonstrates this well. Of thirty-

A postcard view across the little River Sheaf, taken at some time prior to August 1909.   *Collection B. Hilton*

Another in the official series taken in 1910. The shear-legs were removed in later years.   *National Railway Museum*

nine engines only four were of pre-Grouping design, '2P' No. 40538, 0—4—4Ts Nos. 58077 and 58080 and a '2F' 0—6—0 No. 58209 (this engine shunted Queens Road goods depot, just south of Sheffield Midland station, and was at Millhouses for many years. Its LMS number had been 3071). There were several 4—4—0s of LMS construction and the 'Jubilee' stud had grown to ten: 45576 *Bombay*, 45590 *Travancore*, 45594 *Bhopal*, 45607 *Fiji*, 45609 *Gilbert and Ellice Islands*, 45654 *Hood*, 45656 *Cochrane*, 45664 *Nelson*, 45683 *Hogue* and 45725 *Repulse*. New Ivatt 2—6—2Ts and '2MT' Moguls were also at the shed, together with six 'Black Fives' Nos. 44830, 44848, 44851, 44964, 44986 and 45264, the latter a 'regular' for years. Some of the latest BR standard locomotives, recently introduced and still in process of delivery

were also available, in the shape of class '5's Nos. 73011, 73016, 73047 and 73048.

Along with the rest of the Midland's former Sheffield area, Millhouses was transferred to the Eastern Region in February 1958, as 41C under Darnall. Resources began to be concentrated on the former LNER routes in Sheffield in the 1960s and as a consequence the old Midland facilities were run down. Grimesthorpe had closed in September 1961 and closure was scheduled for Millhouses on 6th November the same year. It eventually closed on 1st January 1962 with its locos and duties transferred to Canklow, including several 'Royal Scots' acquired in its last years. After this the building was sold off to a private firm and still survives today.

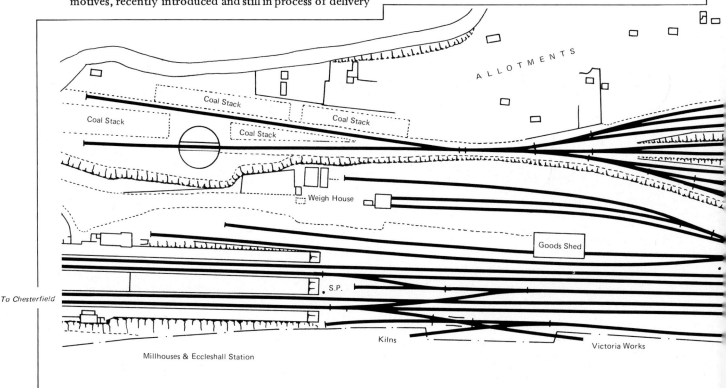

Millhouses on 14th September 1958 with locos (left to right) '4F' No. 44547, 'Jubilee' No. 45675 *Hardy*, BR '4MT' No. 76089 and '4F' No. 44408. The entrances were widened at some time by the judicious removal of the doors and some brickwork.

P. J. Kelley

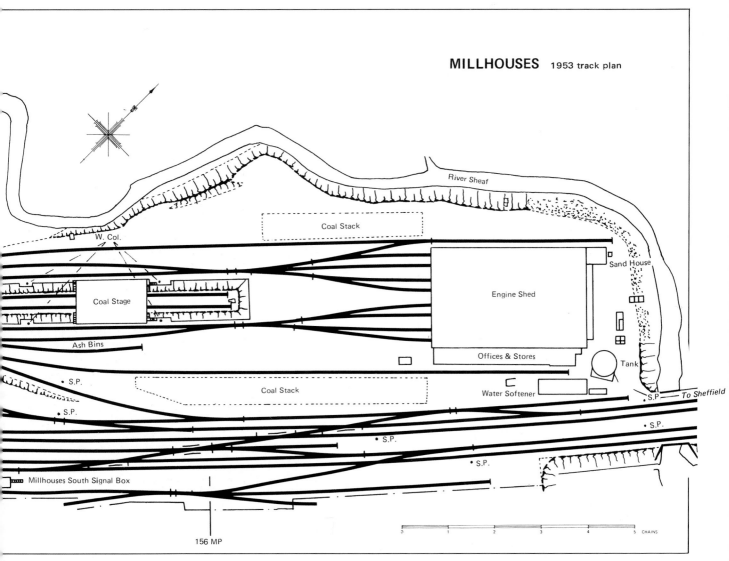

MILLHOUSES 1953 track plan

River Sheaf

Coal Stack

W. Col.

Sand House

Coal Stage

Engine Shed

Ash Bins

Offices & Stores

Tank

• S.P.

Coal Stack

Water Softener

• S.P.

To Sheffield

• S.P.

• S.P.

• S.P.

• S.P.

Millhouses South Signal Box

156 MP

0 1 2 3 4 5 CHAINS

Normanton in 1936, with LNER loco No. 2458 to the fore.

L & GRP

NORMANTON

Normanton was the 'frontier town' where traffic was exchanged between the North Midland and the York & North Midland Railway and in 1850 the station Joint Committee decided to erect a shed, for the use of both companies. This soon proved inadequate and the tender for a new shed, a twenty-four road polygonal roundhouse, was accepted in February 1866. It was of MR construction and the NER eventually stabled only half a dozen or so locos, compared to the Midland's total of nearly thirty. The building opened in 1867, the last of the MR circular sheds and shear-legs were provided two years later. The relative locomotive stocks had doubled by 1900 and Lancashire and Yorkshire engines were also dealt with at the depot from 1884. The Midland erected a five road straight shed for their use, with separate coal stage and turntable in that year, but this barely kept pace with the increasing locomotive numbers. The new shed for the L & Y was of straightforward Midland design but the coal stage was executed in the former company's own style. This situation, where joint interests resulted in a shed of MR design and facilities by a second company was exactly paralleled at Overseal, a shed built in conjunction with the LNWR and described in Volume 1 of this series. On 13th July 1882 the MR had read Joint Committee minutes authorising the purchase of land and thirty-one tenders ('a very high number') were invited for the new shed's construction, Messrs. R. Leake being successful with a price of £10,553.8s.9d.

The Midland stationed around sixty locos at Normanton (shed number 26) in 1921, the great majority of them 0—6—0s engaged on coal and mineral traffic. Passenger engines included seven Kirtley and Johnson 2—4—0s, a

Some details at Normanton in later years.

R. J. Essery

Normanton in August 1950.

B. Hilton

The L & Y-built 'coal hole', its design antecedents in marked contrast to the 'L & Y' shed provided by the Midland authorities.

R. J. Essery

pair of 'Spinners', Nos. 606 and 676 and three 0—6—4Ts. The L & Y shed and the Midland roundhouse were brought together under Midland Division control in November 1927 and from 1st October 1938 the LNER ceased to have a 'joint' interest, simply paying rent for any of its locos using the shed. With the forty or so L & YR engines Normanton's allocation in 1933 stood at nearly 120 locos, including new 2—6—4Ts Nos. 2310, 2311 and 2312 and a dozen Fowler 0—8—0s. LMS '4F' 0—6—0s also replaced many of the old Kirtley and Johnson six-coupled engines. The former L & YR locos were also engaged principally on coal traffic and comprised in the main Aspinall-designed '3F' 0—6—0s built between 1889 and 1917. Apart from twelve of these engines there were nine 'Radial' 2—4—2Ts, an Aspinall 0—6—0T, No. 11536, and six Aspinall 0—8—0s. New standard '3F's had largely replaced the old Barton Wright and Johnson shunting tanks by 1933. Ex-Caledonian 0—6—0s, Nos. 17250,

The shed on 25th May 1952. The two tanks on the right were amongst the last ex-LNER engines to make regular use of the shed.

W. Potter

The coal and ash plants erected by the LMS (seen here in September 1965) unfortunately obliterated the old Midland circular shed. The units were built in 1936/37 but the older shed would have seen relatively little use by then, especially since the amalgamation of both 'depots' officially into the Midland Division from 1927.

Collection S. Summerson

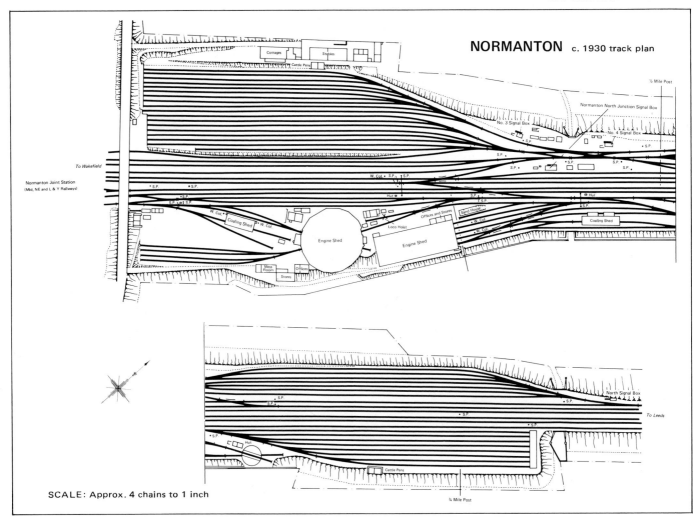

NORMANTON c. 1930 track plan

SCALE: Approx. 4 chains to 1 inch

A 'Jubilee' and an '8F' share the yard on 17th September 1961.
W. T. Stubbs

The Midland's water tank, an obvious contrast to the L & Y example. The building underneath was a store, and is labelled accordingly on the plan.

R. J. Essery

17290, 17331, 17383, and 17391 arrived in late 1939 and returned north at the end of 1941.

The Joint Committee had awarded the contract for 'the erection of a new 60 ft outside turntable' to the 'MR Derby Works' in 1909 and the Midland remained the major user of the depot and its facilities. Coal and ash plants were added by the LMS in 1936/37. MR and LMS 0—6—0s remained the predominant engine type but a large fleet of '8F' 2—8—0s had been allocated by 1945. Ex-L & Y engines continued to be allocated until the end of 1952 and only three ex-LNER engines remained in regular use at the shed by 1954, 'J71' 0—6—0Ts Nos. 68238, 68292 and 68294. The shed was incorporated into the North Eastern Region as 55E from January 1957, having been 20D since the 1935 rearrangement. The old Midland circular shed had disappeared long before to make way for the new coal and ash plants and only the 'L & Y shed', the five road straight building, remained in use. Normanton survived to be the last ER depot servicing steam locomotives, but it finally closed on 2nd October 1967, remaining available to service visiting steam engines until 1st January 1968.

'WD' 2—8—0s, most underrated and unsung workhorses, became increasingly common at Normanton. Two of them are clanking around the yard in this view taken in the shed's last years.

R. J. Essery

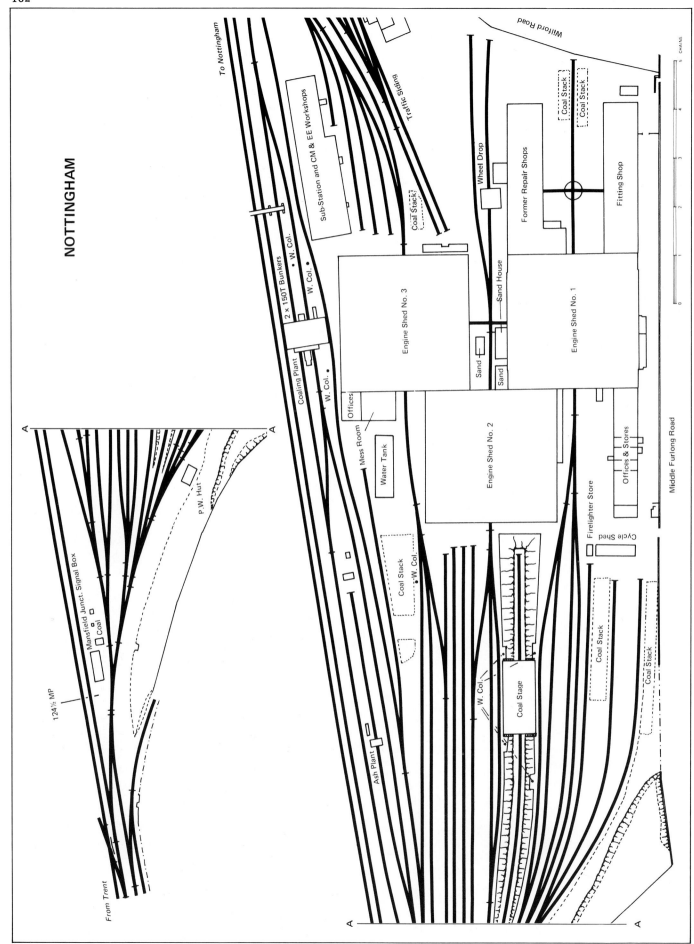

NOTTINGHAM

To Nottingham

Wilford Road

Sub-Station and CM & EE Workshops

Traffic Siding

2 x 150T Bunkers

Coaling Plant

W. Col.

W. Col.

W. Col.

Coal Stack

Wheel Drop

Coal Stack

Coal Stack

Former Repair Shops

Fitting Shop

Sand House

Engine Shed No. 3

Engine Shed No. 1

Sand

Sand

Offices

Mess Room

Engine Shed No. 2

Water Tank

Offices & Stores

Firelighter Store

Cycle Shed

Middle Furlong Road

Coal Stack

W. Col.

Ash Plant

Coal Stage

W. Col.

Coal Stack

Coal Stack

A

A

Mansfield Junct. Signal Box

P.W. Hut

Coal

124½ MP

From Trent

A

A

0 1 2 3 4 5 CHAINS

'2P' 4—4—0 No. 416 outside 'No. 2' engine shed in 1932.

G. Coltas

NOTTINGHAM

From inauspicious beginnings, Nottingham rose to become the Midland's largest and most important locomotive depot. The Midland Counties Railway opened from Derby to Nottingham on 4th June 1839 and erected a small straight shed similar to the brick building provided at the Derby end of the line. This was rapidly overwhelmed by the number of engines requiring servicing and a plan for a new shed was prepared in 1850. It was for 16 engines, indicating a circular design in keeping with the new

Midland company's usual practice. A tender of £3,300 from Messrs. Niel and Wilson Ltd. was accepted the following year and the shed opened a few months later. Most unusually, it was of the semi-roundhouse arrangement, with eleven roads and was erected at the eastern end of the station.

Only ten years later the company ordered 'that three ventilators be placed in the roof of the Nottingham Engine Shed as quickly as possible, complaints having been made by the Sanatory (*sic*) Commissioners'. From what we know of the subsequent indifference of the authorities

The same roundhouse, little the worse for wear, after a further thirty years use.

R. J. Essery

The shed yard and surviving coal stage on 28th April 1957.   *W. Potter*

towards engine shed working conditions the situation
must have been little short of atrocious!

The measures taken were short term, however, and the
following year plans and estimates were requested for a
new shed, 'the officers instructed to agree on a site for
. . . . 12 engines at Nottingham'. Further loco sidings at
Nottingham station were approved the following year, 'in
lieu' of the 'site for 12 engines' and the condition of the
surviving accommodation by this time is probably best
left to the imagination!

In July 1866, it was finally ordered that one of the
new roundhouses, to hold 24 locos, be provided and
tenders were accepted the following year. Messrs. E. Hall
were to construct the shed, at a cost of £12,622. 15s. 2d.
with Messrs. Harrop Summerville providing the ironwork
at £3,136. 15s. 7d. The new shed opened in 1868 in an
area of open fields known as 'the Meadows', tenders afterwards being invited for the admirable task of converting
the old shed into an 'ale store', a fit retirement for any
aged building! A second shed, logically enough referred
to as 'No. 2', was added at the north-west corner of the
first building in 1877 and a seven road fitting shop with

Mansfield Junction box, which
controlled movements to and
from the shed.

R. J. Essery

The main offices and stores block,
added to the original 'No. 1' shed.
R. J. Essery

The first of Nottingham's two 'high level coal stages', erected in 1877. A separate stage was erected to serve 'No. 3' shed, opened in 1893, but its demolition was necessary on modernisation in the 1930s.   *R. J. Essery*

the usual turntable arrangement was also provided, at the rear of 'No. 1' shed. A large new coaling stage was built to serve both roundhouses, the new building having a 46 ft turntable, larger than its companion's 42 ft example. A third shed, 'No. 3', provided with a 50 ft turntable and a separate coal stage was completed in 1893. A second fitting shop, opposite the original, followed in 1899 but both were closed by the early 1920s. All three turntables were gradually enlarged, beginning with the 'No. 3' shed example in 1912, when a new 60 ft table costing £610. 10s. 9d. was installed, 55 ft units later appearing in the other two sheds. Shear-legs were provided in each roundhouse, those in 'No. 3' being electrically operated, and apart from some additional smoke funnels in 1907 'to carry away smoke from the large new engines' and extra ash pits, alterations were at a minimum until general rearrangements involving coal and ash plants, etc. were executed by the LMS in the mid-1930s.

To describe the locomotive allocation and workings at Nottingham would involve a short review of the operation of the Midland Railway itself, so great were the number and types involved. There were about 50 engines in the early 1870s but this rose inexorably as traffic, particularly freight, grew in the heartland of the Midland empire. By 1919 an observer in the *Railway Magazine* wrote: 'Nottingham is the largest locomotive depot on the Midland Railway and has always included in its stock almost every class of engine on the line. In addition to main line engines and workings an army of 2—4—0 engines run in all directions radiating from Nottingham. The most intricate locomotive working was, and is, that performed by some 30 to 35 0—4—4 bogie tank engines which work over the network of Nottinghamshire and Derbyshire branch lines, the majority of these engines are stabled at Nottingham'. Over thirty years later the following applied: 'Nottingham locos have steadily increased since 1923 until at present there are 88 passsenger and 165 goods locos. More have arrived in the last few weeks. There are three sub-sheds — Lincoln, Mansfield and Kirkby. (The writer neglected to mention the small shed at Southwell). The first two are chiefly passenger but Kirkby is goods only. Nottingham works turns to London, Leeds, Sheffield and Manchester and local traffic to Leicester, Derby, Mansfield, Melton Mowbray and Lincoln'.

Nottingham's 'double skip' ash hoist. Such structures became familiar all over the LMS.

R. J. Essery

Replacements for the shed's fleet of Midland and LMS 0—6—0s included 'G3' 0—8—0s, with Nos. 9504, 9560, 9561, 9562, and 9581 available by 1930, followed by Nos. 9631, 9632 and 9633 in 1932. 'Crab' 2—6—0s had also arrived by 1930, with Nos. 13123-13127 and 13149 (new Nos. 2823-27 and 2849) and in November of that year, over five successive weeks, the first five engines (one at a time and six nights a week) worked the 4.50 p.m. Nottingham-Bakewell passenger train, returning on a freight from Rowsley to Beeston Sidings. Fowler 2—6—4Ts Nos. 2306-2309 (in red livery) and 2336-2342 (black and lined out)

The rear of 'No. 3' shed.

Collection B. Mathews

had appeared at Nottingham in 1929 and the shed's first class '5's, in the shape of Nos. 5040, 5041 and 5187-5189 were sent there in 1935. The red tank engines departed for Willesden in 1932 and in 1934 the shed had for a time five of the 3-cylinder 2—6—4Ts intended for use on the LTS section. They were engaged principally on shorter distance passenger turns, to Derby, Leicester, etc. and also took over the working of the 'Tamworth Mail', the 8.00 p.m. ex-Lincoln St. Marks from Nottingham as far as Tamworth. In February/March 1936 new Stanier tanks, Nos. 2429-2434, arrived for this sort of work, replaced in July by a second batch fresh from the North British Company, Nos. 2549-2553.

The territory covered by Nottingham locos was extended in 1932 when the ex-LNWR shed at Netherfield and Colwick closed and its duties over the GN/LNW Joint

The monstrous 'No. 1' coaler erected in the mid-thirties.

R. J. Essery

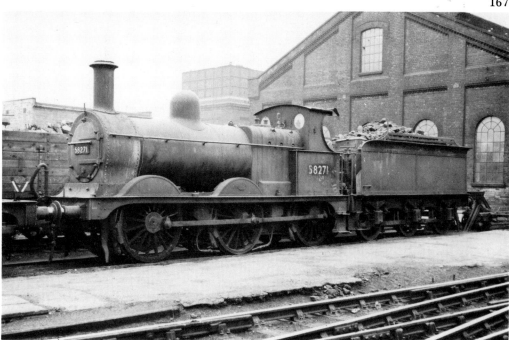

'2F' 0–6–0 No. 58271 outside Nottingham shed on 16th May 1954.

Hugh Ballantyne

Line to Market Harborough passed to the former Midland shed.

Coded 18 in Midland days, Nottingham naturally became a 'concentration' depot, 16A, in 1935. It retained its sub-shed at Lincoln, transferred to the Eastern Region in the early 1950s and Southwell (closed in 1955) whilst Mansfield and Kirkby acquired 'garage' status. Ivatt '4MT' and '2MT' 2–6–0s and 'Jubilees' added to the range of LMS designs but the only type allocated in any quantity were '8F' 2–8–0s, these engines totalling twenty-four by 1954. By November 1950 five 'Jubilees' and six class '5's formed the principal express power and from 1959 to 1964 various 'Royal Scots', released by dieselisation elsewhere, became available. No. 46100 *Royal Scot* and, appropriately, 46112 *Sherwood Forester* among others finished their days at Nottingham.

Toton was chosen as the area depot in the early 1960s and, although it was intended at one time to convert Nottingham for diesel servicing, declining and changing traffic patterns led to its complete closure. It had been coded 16D, Toton taking over as 16A in September 1963, and was closed completely in April 1965, remaining steam duties going to the former Great Northern Railway shed at Colwick.

Ex-Midland locos at Nottingham in July 1938, 0–6–0 No. 3424, 2–4–0 No. 20219, and 0–4–4T No. 1252.

W. Potter

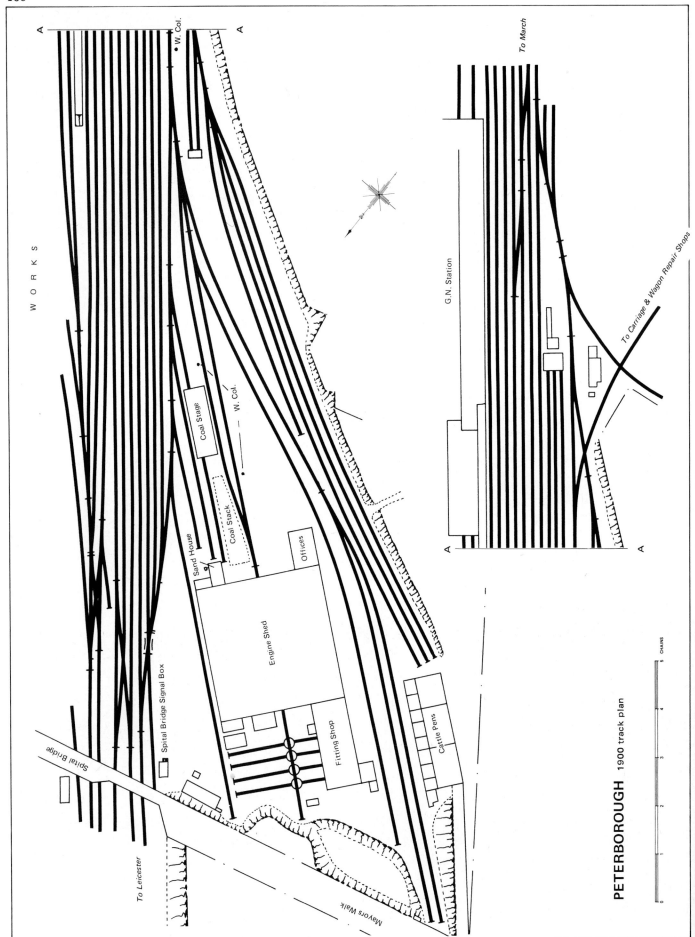

A

A

W. Col.

A

A

To March

W O R K S

G.N. Station

To Carriage & Wagon Repair Shops

Coal Stage

W. Col.

Sand House

Coal Stack

Offices

Engine Shed

Fitting Shop

Cattle Pens

Spital Bridge Signal Box

Spital Bridge

To Leicester

Mayors Walk

PETERBOROUGH 1900 track plan

CHAINS

0 1 2 3 4 5

'Spital Bridge' towards the end of its existence, on 19th April 1959.

W. Potter

PETERBOROUGH

The new shed at Peterborough opened in 1872 and was provided with a fitting shop arranged in the usual fashion. The new roundhouse replaced some earlier engine facilities (a depot had been established for MR engines from March 1848, and repairs to engines had been undertaken from shortly afterwards. A set of shear-legs was provided in 1866) and was sited by Spital Bridge, a little north of the main station. Its 42 ft turntable was replaced by a 50 ft example costing £1,420 in 1899.

Although at first the line to Peterborough was constructed to thwart the embryonic Great Northern, the shed's later importance was due in great part to traffic off the Midland and Great Northern Joint line straggling in from Norfolk. M & GN engines were dealt with at Spital Bridge (until 1936 when the LNER took over responsibility for them) and the line was worked effectively as a separate section until closure by BR. Ahrons, in his classic 'Train Working in the latter part of the 19th century' articles, threw some fascinating light on arrangements at Peterborough and is worth quoting at length:

Until 1893-94 Peterborough was a more important Midland locomotive centre than it now is, for the Midland then worked the present Midland and Great Northern joint line between Peterborough and Lynn. The line from Sutton Bridge to Bourne was worked by the Great Northern engines, except that the Midland ran one or two cattle trains over it. There were at this time 10 passenger engines at Peterborough, the 2—4—0 engines Nos. 1070 to 1079 (127-136 after 1907) of which two — usually Nos. 1071 and 1073 — were sub-stationed at Lynn. The Peterborough engines ran to Leicester, and with one turn they worked a train through to Birmingham, returning thence at 4.40 p.m. They also worked certain trains on the Lynn road. In 1914 there were only about five Peterborough passenger engines, which ran to Leicester. With one turn they went to Birmingham

and with another to Burton. These turns were recently usually worked by two of the 4—2—2 'singles', Nos. 600 and 602 (formerly Nos. 25 and 27) which were stationed at Peterborough, but there are about three of the old No. 1070 class remaining there, with more than 40 years' continuous service at one shed. One of these, No. 1072 (now No. 129), used in the 'seventies to be a thorn in the flesh of the Great Northern main line drivers. The Midland line runs parallel to the Great Northern for a distance of about 6 miles, and, starting northwards from Peterborough, No. 1072 frequently showed the Great Northern express engines a clean pair of heels.

But for long service at one locomotive shed, some of the Midland goods engines can give points and a beating to any locomotives with which I am acquainted. The Peterborough goods engines were Nos. 500 to 529, which were built in 1864-65 by Messrs. Stephenson. They went as new engines to Peterborough, and as Nos. 2416 to 2445 are still there, after more than 50 years; not one has been broken up. The longevity of the Midland double-framed goods engines is remarkable, and is due to two causes: in the first place, they were strongly built, with very solid frames; and secondly, they were thoroughly well looked after both by Mr. Kirtley and Mr. Johnson.

Lynn of course was really an M & GN concern and Bourne (actually built by the GNR and used by both MR and GN engines) was the official sub-shed. Peterborough was Midland number 9 and its repair shop had gone out of use before the Grouping. In 1935 the shed was recoded 16B in the Nottingham District. Coaling and ash disposal plants, by Messrs. Henry Lees and Babcock & Wilcox respectively, were provided around 1936. However, it found itself increasingly on the periphery of affairs and the loco stock remained very 'Midland' in nature. There were forty-six engines allocated in June 1933, twenty-eight of them built by the Midland, the remainder being LMS-built '4F' 0—6—0s and a single '3F' tank No. 7100. The Midland locos are worth listing in full and included the following: Kirtley double-framed 2—4—0 No. 21, Johnson 2—4—0s Nos. 77, 132, 181, 215 and 227, 0—4—4Ts Nos.

Elderly Midland engines figured prominently in Peterborough's allocation throughout much of the LMS period, lending the shed a definite 'Midland air' in the 1930s. No. 311, one of the last Johnson 7 ft 4—4—0s, emerges into the evening sunlight in September 1933. *Photomatic*

The almost statutory stored 4—4—2T No. 41969 (buffer beam of a second, 41975, just visible on the left) accompanies 'B1' 4—6—0 No. 61348 and '8F' No. 48266 on 24th May 1959. Quite why so many of these passenger tanks were retained, 'laid-up' at various ex-MR sheds for such prolonged periods, is not really that clear and few, if any, seem to have been returned to traffic. *P. J. Kelley*

LMS engines declined at Peterborough in the last years, giving way to ex-LNER 4—6—0s, 0—6—0s, 'WD's and, of course, Ivatt-designed moguls from the M & GN section.

A. V. Fincham courtesy V. Forster

1422, 1423 and 1424, '1F' 0—6—0Ts Nos. 1726, 1814, 1847 and 1884, '3F' 0—6—0T No. 1943, Kirtley double-framed '1F' 0—6—0 No. 2828 and thirteen Johnson 0—6—0s. Many of these locos disappeared in the next decade. The shed took over the locomotives from the ex-LNW Water End shed when it closed in 1932 and by July 1946 its passenger complement stood at twelve 4—4—0s; eight '2P's, two '3P's, Nos. 756 and 767, and two Compounds, Nos. 1015 and 1055.

Peterborough itself passed to 'foreign' administration in August 1950, becoming 35C under New England. Ex-LNER engines, 'D16' 4—4—0s, etc. took over many of the duties and began working to Rugby, etc. on LMR turns. The shed was recoded 31F in the Cambridge District in February 1958, but with New England shed so close it was surprising that the shed had lasted even this long. Closure of the M & GN section meant the shed's days were numbered and the last '4F's were replaced by redundant Ivatt Moguls from the old joint line. Spital Bridge finally closed on 1st February 1960 and was demolished the same year. The remaining men were subsequently accommodated in a signing on point at Peterborough East station, and relieved trains between Whitemoor (March) and the Rugby and Nottingham areas of the LMR.

End of the day's work at Peterborough in 1950.

L & GRP

Looking north up the East Coast main line in 1958. The 'down' passenger train is about to pass under 'Spital Bridge' itself.

A. V. Fincham, courtesy V. Forster

The shed yard on the same occasion. The photograph is interesting in many respects, not least for the view it provides of the roof detail.

A. V. Fincham, courtesy V. Forster

Redditch in 1935, in original condition.

R. J. Buckley

REDDITCH

The small engine shed at Redditch opened, on a site about half a mile north of the station, in 1872/3. An estimate of £3,800 had been prepared in January 1872, but as early as June 1869 discussions had been held regarding the 'proposed exchange of land with Mr. Ballard for an engine shed at Redditch'. The new shed had a single road and measured 118 ft by 23 ft with a 42 ft turntable placed directly outside. A short stub siding was also provided off the 'table, which had been removed by 1903. Half a dozen

locos were supplied by Saltley, with the little shed designated 3c, the practice continuing even in later years when Redditch officially became a sub-shed of Bournville. The engines, 2—4—0s at first, worked passenger trains to Birmingham, Ashchurch and Leicester as well as shunting at Redditch itself. There were four 0—6—0s in 1880, replaced ten years later by a similar number of 0—4—4Ts.

Deeley 0—6—4Ts took over the passenger services following their introduction and joined a single 0—6—0 normally engaged on freights to Alcester and Evesham. By 1957 the *Railway Observer* had the following to report: 'Redditch is nominally sub to Bournville (21B) but locos

The shed around 1938. A 42 ft turntable was originally provided outside, on the site occupied here by Stanier 2—6—2T No. 91.

W. H. Whitworth

Redditch coal stage in the early 1960s, a timber built concern bravely resisting the passage of time.   *R. J. Essery*

are supplied from Saltley (21A), a new shed road has recently been completed along with a new concrete ash pit. The allocation consists of 40115, 43046 and 43223 (21A) and 42186 (21B).'

DMU services began between Birmingham and Redditch on 25th April 1960, but the shed, 'sub' to 85F Bromsgrove since incorporation into the Western Region in February 1958, remained open 'to house two locos, either a 2–6–4T or 2–6–0 tender engine for one passenger turn and parcels duty and an LMR '3F' tank or WR 0–6–0PT for the Redditch yard pilot'. The ex-GWR engine was normally a pannier of the 84XX series, but after closure on 1st June 1964 its pilot duties fell into the hands of a diesel shunter.

Left & bottom right: Coal stage details. *Top right:* Redditch also had a neat little office with a store alongside for the minimal paperwork and servicing required at the depot.

R. J. Essery

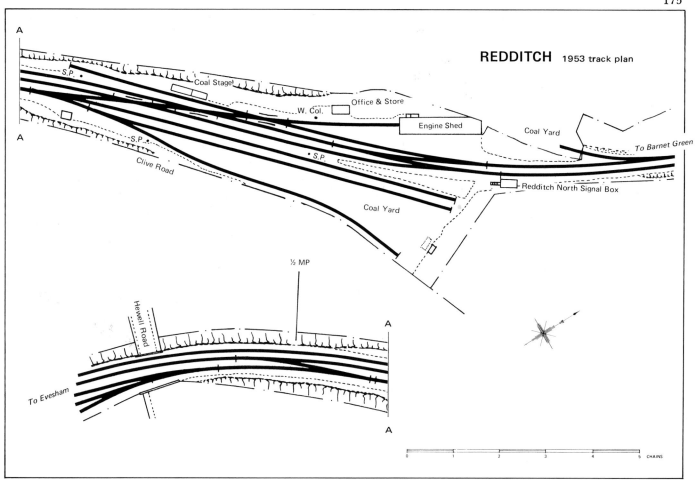

REDDITCH 1953 track plan

Coal Stage!

S.P.

Office & Store

W. Col.

Engine Shed

Coal Yard

To Barnet Green

Clive Road

S.P.

S.P.

Redditch North Signal Box

Coal Yard

½ MP

Hewell Road

To Evesham

A

A

0 1 2 3 4 5 CHAINS

The shed was re-roofed, apparently around 1938/39, utilising the 'single pitch' design normally employed at much larger sheds. When applied to small buildings (as at Coniston, on the ex-Furnesss Railway system, to be described in a subsequent volume) the result was unattractive in the extreme.

R. J. Essery

Bitter protests were voiced in the nineteenth century when the railway first penetrated the Derbyshire valleys and indeed the yards did little to enhance the view at Rowsley. Although little real trace now exists, the area remains a brick-strewn wasteland and has not been returned to productive use. This photograph was taken in happier times on 10th September 1950.
B. Hilton

The original Manchester, Buxton, Matlock and Midland Junction Railway terminus at Rowsley, circa 1870, the single road shed in the middle distance.

Collection B. Mathews

ROWSLEY

There was a small one road shed here with entry from a turntable sited immediately outside. It was built in 1849 when the Manchester, Buxton, Matlock & Midland Junction Railway completed its line from Ambergate to a terminus at Rowsley. On the opening of the new line to Buxton, curving away westwards to follow the Wye Valley, a new station was opened and a larger, four road shed replaced the original building, the old terminus subsequently forming a goods yard. It opened in late 1879/1880, Messrs. E. Wood's tender of £2,561 having been accepted in 1878. It was an odd structure vaguely reminiscent of the buildings at Bromsgrove and one road at least may have been intended for coaching stock. The roof

pitch on the station side covered two roads in conventional manner whilst a second pitch, of equal size, spanned only one road. The remaining space was occupied by a boiler house and chimney in the front and sand furnace, stores, etc. inside. A third, much smaller roof section covered the fourth road on the eastern side. A coal shed was provided and a new turntable and pit appeared in the yards to the south in 1882. In 1887 it was ordered 'that a well be sunk at Rowsley to provide an increased water supply for the Company's Locomotives'.

The shed increased rapidly in importance; extensive yards had grown up between Rowsley and the next station to the south, Darley Dale, and after 1877 banking duties (for the climb up to Peak Forest) and shunting turns increased steadily. The shed had acquired a dozen 0—6—0s by 1892, most freights changing engines at Rowsley

Rowsley on 19th September 1948.

H. C. Casserley

Rowsley, circa 1948.

Real Photographs

The curious 'hybrid' Rowsley coaler, in April 1958. It combined design elements from Bowen-Cooke's LNWR 'elevator' units with a concrete bunker and the LMS steel-framed 'skip hoist' principle.

W. Potter

'3F' tank No. 47679 shunts the coaling plant road in 1949.

Real Photographs

between remarshalling, etc. Within twenty years it had become far too small for the numbers of engines involved and in November 1899 the land necessary for a new shed was ordered to be purchased. Plans and estimates totalling £28,938 were obtained in May 1900 and referred to the General Purposes Committee for consideration and approval. The senior committee were not keen on the expense involved and in October 1902 alternative proposals, reduced to £22,030, for 'shed, coal stage, office, etc.' were being put forward to the G.P.C., probably more in hope than in expectation.

The Finance men did not relent until after the First World War and by 1919 space had been cleared for a new four road shed, on the 'down' side, in the yards to the south. The building was to be in brick and the original MR plans provided for a 'coal bunker' to cover one pair of tracks with room for a conveyor belt 'for future use' to serve the remaining pair. Provision was also made for the shed to be doubled in size, 'the future extension' to be erected on the office side of the shed, leaving them oddly in the centre of the building. The 'coal bunker' would have been the Midland's first mechanical coaling plant but in the event the task of completing the shed and its facilities fell to the LMS. 'MR' detail drawings were still being issued on 23rd January 1923 and the main building work was more or less complete late that year.

Rowsley was officially a sub-shed of Buxton in MR days, coded 20a. It became 17D, a 'garage' of Derby in 1935, with many of the former parent shed's duties and locos transferring to Buxton ex-LNWR depot. Rowsley was also made responsible for the Cromford and High Peak locos from this time and ex-North London tanks now joined the allocation of fifty or so Kirtley and John-son 0—6—0s and '1F' tanks. 'Crab' 2—6—0s later appeared, along with '3MT' 2—6—2Ts and standard '3F' tanks, and for many years there was also a small complement of 4—4—0s, including Compounds Nos. 40929 and 41077, on passenger work to Buxton, Derby, Nottingham, etc. Stanier types were not really much in evidence until the late 1950s and declining traffic, followed by diversion of what remained on the Midland's Manchester main line, heralded a bleak future for the remote shed. It was recoded 17C in April 1958 and 16J from September 1963, but closed on 27th April the following year. It remained available for servicing visiting engines and closed completely about the end of 1964. The shed was demolished along with the station and yards, the whole site today bearing little evidence of its great railway past.

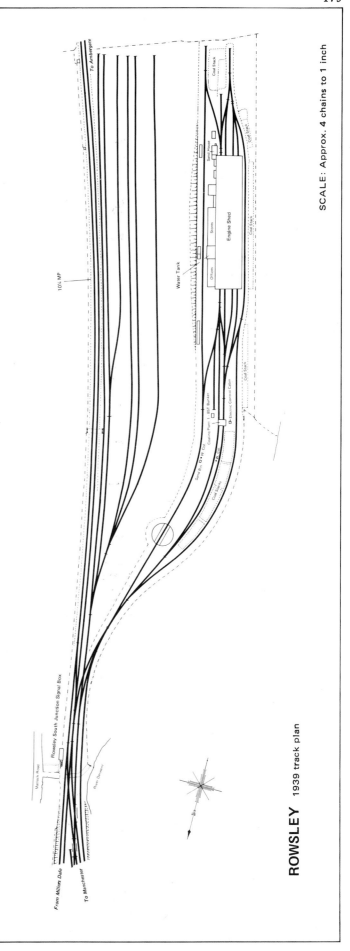

SCALE: Approx. 4 chains to 1 inch

ROWSLEY 1939 track plan

Midland days at St. Albans.   *L & GRP*

ST. ALBANS

The small two road shed at St. Albans opened on a site south of the station in 1868 to house engines working the local services on the new London main line. Built in brick to a rather attractive design employed at one or two other small depots during this period, it was provided with a small coaling shed and a 42 ft turntable. It remained unaltered save for the provision of a water softener and a 'conveyor belt' coaling machine many years later. The coaling crane in the little shelter received the benefits of

electricity in 1931, but by the late 1940s had finally expired! Under Kentish Town for a period, St. Albans eventually became a sub-shed, 15a, of Cricklewood and most of its dozen or so locos were engaged on local passenger work to and from St. Pancras and Moorgate. Throughout most of Midland ownership pensioned-off express locos sufficed for the St. Pancras trains, various classes of 2—4—0 finding their way to St. Albans over the years. Beyer-Peacock locos dating from 1867 were used after rebuilding by Johnson in the early 1880s, Nos. 197-199 being there in 1892, together with two similar engines rebuilt from 2—4—0 tanks in 1869-70. These were followed

Condenser fitted Fowler 2—6—2Ts were the mainstay of the St. Pancras commuter trains from their appearance in the early 1930s virtually until the demise of steam. Two of them stand at the shed in July 1956.

K. Fairey

St. Albans in 1949.   *L & GRP*

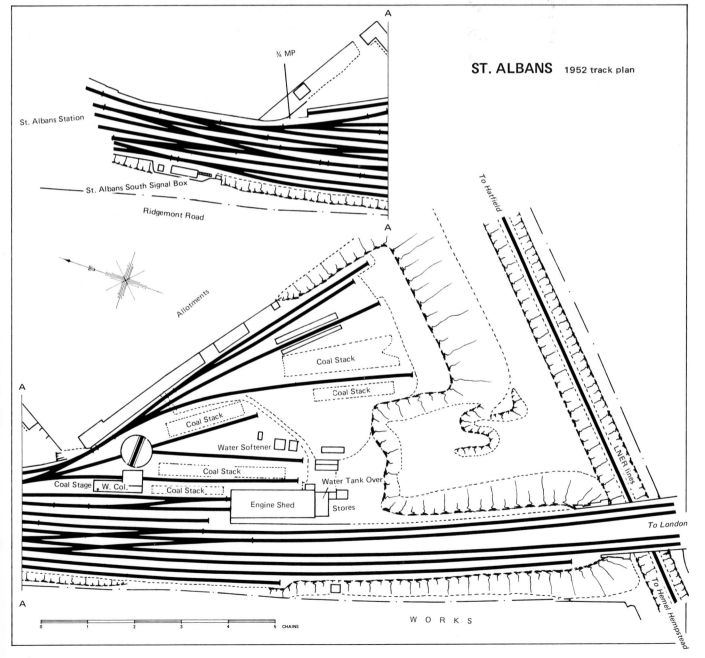

ST. ALBANS   1952 track plan

¾ MP

St. Albans Station

St. Albans South Signal Box

Ridgemont Road

A

A

Allotments

To Hatfield

LNER lines

Coal Stack

Coal Stack

Coal Stack

Water Softener

Coal Stack

Water Tank Over

Coal Stage

Coal Stack

W. Col.

Engine Shed

Stores

To London

To Hemel Hempstead

A

A

0   1   2   3   4   5 CHAINS

W O R K S

The shed itself altered little over the years, although the entrance was widened in 1922, the two arches giving way to a girder lintel. '1F' tank No. 41854 accompanies a Fowler 2—6—2T in this 1950 photograph.

T. J. Edgington

LMS '3F' 0—6—0T No. 7261 and Fowler 2—6—4T No. 42334 at the ageing St. Albans coal stage in 1949. A re-clad roof gave this building a new lease of life and rendered it the longest serving of its type.

L & GRP

Midland architectural style shown to advantage in 1949.

L & GRP

by members of the Kirtley '156' and '890' class, together with various Johnson 2—4—0s. In 1921 Nos. 35, 58, 59, 60, 115, 123, 169 and 170 were present and the 2—4—0s were not finally displaced until about 1927. Ex-LTSR Baltic tanks Nos. 2100-2107 had arrived in 1920 for local passenger duties and the last two survivors, by then renumbered 2196 and 2198, were withdrawn in 1933/34. The Moorgate trains continued to be worked by 0—4—4Ts until the arrival of condenser fitted 2—6—2Ts in 1931. The first three Fowler 2—6—4Ts came new to St. Albans in January 1928, providing urgently needed extra power, and Stanier and Fairburn engines of this wheel arrangement were at St. Albans until the end of steam in 1960. The Hemel Hempstead branch passenger service was worked for many years, up to 1930, by a vacuum fitted 0—6—0T, Nos. 1668 or 1669 being the usual engines in early LMS days.

There was also usually a couple of shunting tanks, a '1F' and a '3F' as well as '2F' or '3F' 0—6—0s for local goods work. Apart from the addition of one or two further 2—6—2 tanks, St. Albans retained this complement virtually until the end. Coded 14C since 1935, it closed on 11th January 1960 with dieselisation of the St. Pancras services. Several locos remained in store and a '3F' tank, usually No. 47554, continued to make use of the facilities for some months. Indeed the shed and yard were more or less intact, if much vandalised, as late as July 1967. The site now, however, is part of a large car park.

The shed's prominent water softener.   *L & GRP*

SALTLEY 1950 track plan

Inside Saltley in the early years.

L & GRP

SALTLEY

Some rudimentary engine accommodation was provided by the Birmingham and Derby Junction company from its completion in August 1839, but it was not large enough for the Midland's growing needs and by 1850 repairs were long overdue. Accordingly, instructions were issued that they be proceeded with 'forthwith' requiring somewhat menacingly 'that the cause of delay be explained'. 'The cause of delay' was probably that the building had virtually fallen down; for the next year the company's Engineer was 'asked to report on the most suitable site for an Engine

Shed at Birmingham'. Some difficulty seems to have ensued for it was 1854 before plans could be drawn up for a 'Round Engine Shed', with stores, smithy and three road fitting shop at the rear, the building having twenty-four roads grouped around a 39 ft turntable. Problems arose almost immediately, and the shed was ordered 'to be repaired at a cost of £5 due to the incompetence of a driver running his engine through the wall. He has been ordered to repay the money'.

A 42 ft turntable was later added in the yard outside and, although the shed was given an extensive refit in 1864, later in the same year the company's officers were once again searching for a new site. This was duly discov-

Some members of Saltley's vast 0—6—0 fleet in 1931.
G. Coltas

Saltley in September 1936. The great coaling plant was a variation on the 'No. 1' type, with a capacity of 300 tons. Roundhouse entrances were normally located in the gable side, but in 'No. 3' shed the opposite was the case, giving it a rather unusual appearance.

W. Potter

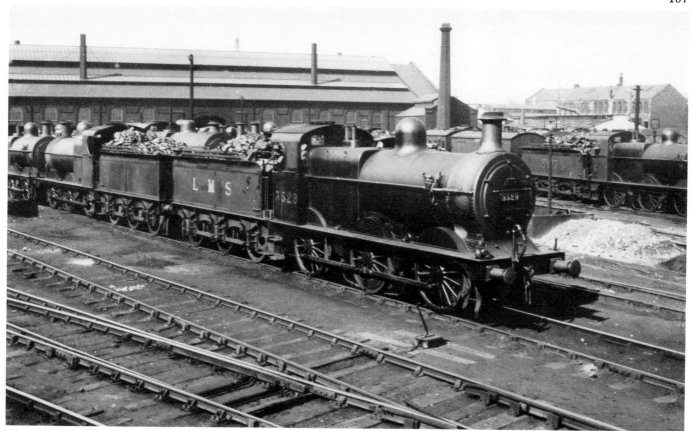

The yard and 'No. 3' shed in 1931.

G. Coltas

ered a little to the north on the opposite side of the main line, an area with plenty of scope for expansion. Messrs. Jeffrey Pritchard Ltd.'s tender of £14,622. 15s. 0d. was accepted on 16th April 1867 with Harrop Summerville Ltd. providing the ironwork for £3,024. 18s. 11d. The new 'square shed' opened the following year, but the old depot, particularly its fitting shop, remained in use for several years.

A second building, 'No. 2' shed, was erected alongside in 1876 and an eight road fitting shop was added at the rear of the original building, now 'No. 1' shed. It was intended to install a 42 ft turntable in the new shed, the same size as its companion, but the diameter was subsequently enlarged to 46 ft. The opening of the new fitting shop in 1877 meant the final abandonment of the old 'Round Shed' and the transfer of remaining usable equipment (valued at £431) to the new depot was completed later in the year.

Saltley was extended yet again with the construction of a third roundhouse unit in 1900. Rather larger than its predecessors, it contained a 60 ft turntable, purchased from Messrs. Eastwood for £1,057. 15s. 10d., the whole project having been originally planned in 1894 when a 50 ft turntable was envisaged. The opening of 'No. 3' shed brought Midland developments at Saltley to a close and in March 1900 the old circular building was ordered to be removed 'at once'!

When 'No. 2' shed opened in 1876, Saltley, with 72 locos, was the Midland's busiest depot after Derby. It was concerned mainly with freight but there were also some notable express turns, principally to Bristol on the West of England 'Scotch Expresses' and fast trains to the East Midlands. Prior to about 1870 Sharp Stewart 2—2—2s

(introduced in 1853) worked the Bristol trains, almost to the exclusion of other types, and Nos. 94, 97, 98 and 99 of the last 2—2—2 design, turned out from Derby in 1863/ 1866, were at Saltley for many years. They took over the most important passenger turns, principally the 2.15 p.m. from Birmingham right through to Peterborough and the 8.00 p.m. from Bristol (Scottish Express) between Birmingham and Derby (Birmingham was a major engine changing point for trains, passenger and goods, off the Bristol line). Most of the earliest coupled class, the '50' 2—4—0s, were at Birmingham from 1863 to the late 1870s and some of the best-liked of this type, the '800's, were still at the shed in the early 1920s. Nos. 2193-2197 (413-417 in 1907), Johnson's enlarged 4—4—0s, were at Saltley for many years following their introduction in the early 1890s and over twenty 4—4—0s remained almost the sole passenger stock as late as 1933. Several of Johnson's new singles were sent to Saltley on their construction in 1892 and were an immediate success on the Bristol trains.

By 1920 'Birmingham' was described by Ahrons as 'another centre for tank engines', referring to the 0—4—4Ts working the heavy 'roundabout' suburban service on the Kings Norton lines and the Walsall branch. They had also taken over Redditch trains formerly worked entirely by old '80' class tender engines before their withdrawal in the 1880s and 1890s. By 1933 most of the local duties had passed to a number of Deeley 0—6—4Ts, nearly half of the class being stationed at Saltley.

Goods work was handled by various ex-MR 0—6—0s with over 100 of this type operating in the mid-1930s, LMS-built engines supplied to Saltley by this time being a few '4F' 0—6—0s and a number of 'Crab' 2—6—0s, 13059- 13064 and 13139 (later Nos. 2759-2764 and 2839), new

Saltley in 1959, after rebuilding of all three roundhouses. The large numbers of 0—6—0s had been greatly diminished by this time and ex-LMS and BR standard types were much more in evidence.

Photomatic

in 1929 followed by Nos. 13195-13200 (1934 Nos. 2895-2900) in 1930. There were also a few 0—8—0s, for example Nos. 9672-9674. Even by the end of the Second World War Stanier types comprised only a few 'Black Fives' and 2—6—4Ts.

Coded 21A since the 1935 reorganisation, Saltley's MR code had been No. 3, the depot being known then simply as 'Birmingham'. The LMS had provided modern coal and ash plants by 1936 and various alterations were carried out to the motive power and control offices in the same year. Re-roofing came after the war and new designs were drawn up and contracts issued for Nos. '1' and '2' sheds during 1946/8. Work was delayed until after Nationalisation and was carried out using concrete, a contrast to the steel and glass example in turn applied to 'No. 3' shed. The turntable sizes had increased over the years, with 55 ft units eventually appearing in both 'No. 1' and 'No. 2' sheds. The old fitting shop had been closed by the LMS and by 1939 had been converted to road lorry maintenance.

In terms of number of engines, Saltley was the LMR's most important shed with 191 locos allocated in 1954. A number of LMS and BR-built 0—6—0 diesel shunters had arrived by 1952 and 'Crab' and Ivatt '4MT' Moguls had made inroads on the great fleet of MR and LMS 0—6—0s. Although still over 100 strong, their numbers had been further reduced since the war by fresh arrivals of standard Stanier types, which by 1954 included 23 class '5' 4—6—0s and 14 '8F' 2—8—0s. Further standard types of LMS and BR design (particularly '9F' 2—10—0s) followed in the 'fifties and the numbers of 0—6—0s steadily diminished. 2—6—4Ts were supplied from the 1930s onwards for

local passenger work and new BR standard No. 80063 joined the Fowler and Stanier engines in 1954. Saltley men were evidently less inclined to put up with design-inflicted discomfort (the 0—6—0s must have been bad enough!) and in 1960 six Fowler side-window cab 2—6—4Ts were exchanged for earlier engines without windows. The men had complained of severe draughts when working the early engines over the Evesham-Ashchurch lines. Notable visitors to Saltley in this period in the early 'sixties were 'V2' 2—6—2s from the North Eastern Region, usually returning to Newcastle on the 8.05 a.m. from New Street.

Saltley was though, overwhelmingly a freight depot and up to the Second World War had lodging turns 'around the clock', to Swansea, Liverpool, Manchester, Carlisle, Leeds, Bradford, Peterborough, London and Bristol. Many of these were lost during the war, but the Carlisle one was retained, the longest through freight in the country using a single crew. Bournville, Walsall and Redditch had been sub-sheds throughout Midland days, but Walsall closed in September 1925. Bournville became a 'garage' in 1935 and only Redditch remained, finally closing in the 1960s. Stratford-on-Avon was officially regarded as a 'garage' from 1935, as 21D, until its final closure in 1957. Saltley was re-coded 2E from September 1963, engines in the final years up to 1967 tending to consist almost entirely of Ivatt Moguls, '8F's, 'Black Fives' and '9F' 2—10—0s with 'Austerity' 2—8—0s also common. The shed closed to steam on 6th March 1967 and, although all three roundhouses were largely demolished, Saltley remains an important diesel depot.

At the rear of Grimesthorpe, on 14th September 1958.   *P. J. Kelley*

SHEFFIELD

The Sheffield and Rotherham Railway (amalgamated with the Midland in 1845) opened its line from the north into Sheffield to a terminus at Wicker Street on 1st November 1838 and erected a small two road engine shed nearby. This proved adequate for some twenty years, until in 1860 the Midland's Locomotive Committee requested that the Way and Works Committee 'examine Sheffield station with a view to selecting a site for a new Engine Shed'. Messrs. C. Humphreys' tender of £7,780 was duly accepted that year, for a circular shed to the north of the station, at Brightside. The new shed opened in 1861, the old building being pulled down in March of the following year.

Wicker Street ('the Wicker') was abandoned to the goods department when the new line from the south opened on 1st February 1870, with its new through station, but Brightside shed remained in use for several years. The inevitable replacement shed, once again a short distance to the north, opened in late 1877 surrounded by some of the darkest satanic mills this most industrialised district of Sheffield could offer. Giant factories like the 'Cyclops Works' added to the brooding atmosphere. The

shed stood by Grimesthorpe Junction where the Attercliffe goods spur joined the main line and was subsequently known as 'Grimesthorpe'. Within three years the allocation comprised seventeen 2—4—0s, thirty-eight 0—6—0s and four 0—4—0WTs.

An eight road fitting shop was approved on 15th September 1898 and was unusual in being physically separate from the main shed. Access to the shop was via a traverser and a separate two road paint shop was also provided. The new shed had a 46 ft turntable and in 1901 a 60 ft 'table (later enlarged to 65 ft) was provided outside, with a second coal stage erected alongside its new approach road. Brightside (Grimesthorpe was a name much more in keeping with the immediate surroundings!) had continued to see some use as far as engines were concerned, but appears to have finally been dispensed with when its shear-legs were taken 'across the road' to the new shed in 1901.

The next developments came with the installation of coal and ash plants by the LMS in 1936/37. Grimesthorpe became Midland shed No. 25 and as further depots were opened in Sheffield it gained Millhouses and Canklow as sub-sheds. There were one hundred and fifty locos officially allocated until the separate listings brought about under the 1935 scheme, the depot becoming 19A with about eighty locomotives. There were always a number of

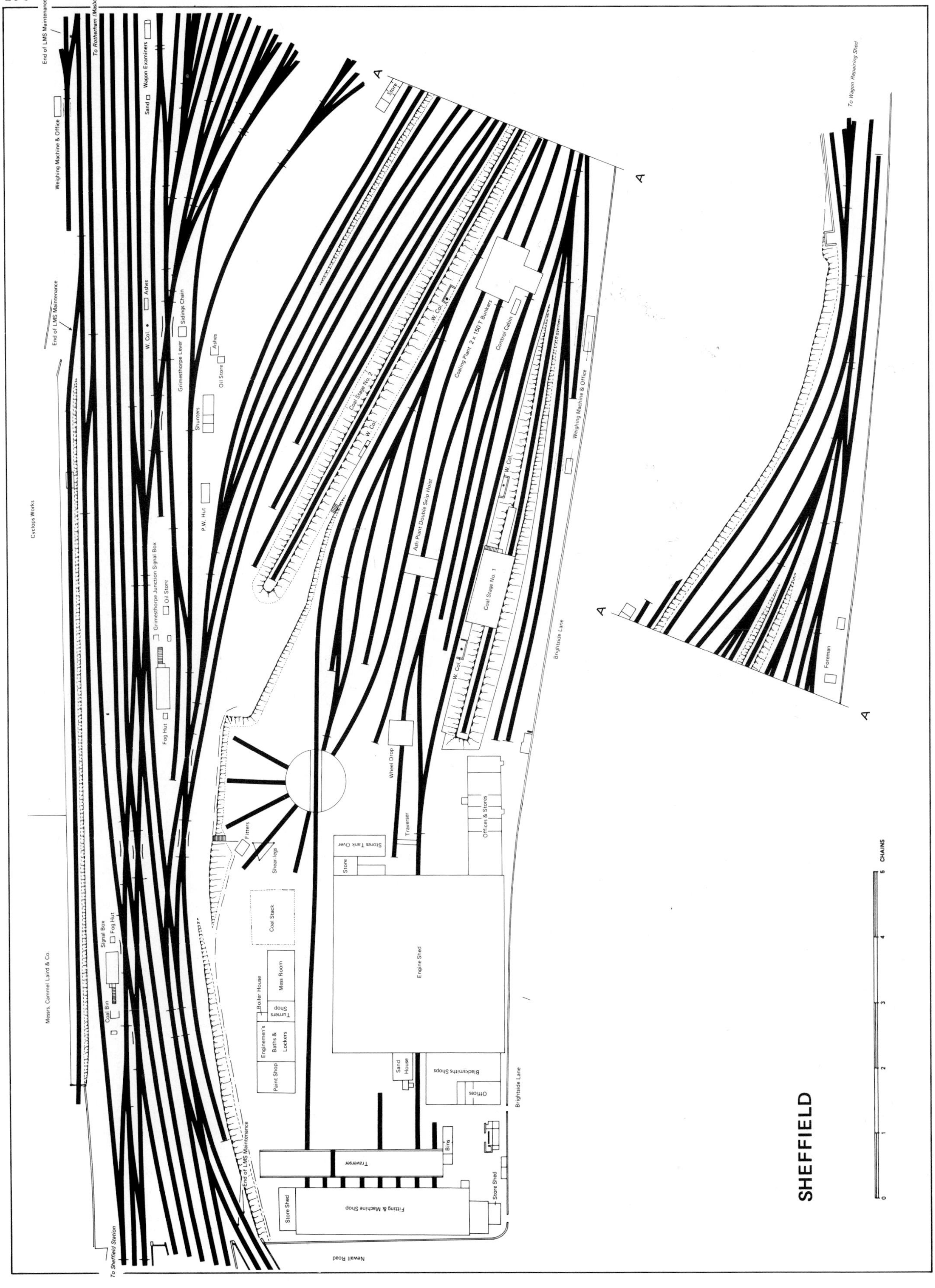

SHEFFIELD

Cyclops Works

End of LMS Maintenance

To Rotherham (Masborough)

Weighing Machine & Office

Sand

Wagon Examiners

Ashes

W. Col.

Grimesthorpe Lever

Sidings Chain

Ashes

Oil Store

Shunters

P.W. Hut

Grimesthorpe Junction Signal Box

Oil Store

Fog Hut

Coal Stage No. 2

W. Col.

W. Col.

Ash Plant Double Skip Hoist

Coaling Plant 2 x 150 T Bunkers

Control Cabin

Weighing Machine & Office

Store

Coal Stage No. 1

W. Col.

Brightside Lane

Wheel Drop

Traverser

Stores Tank Over

Store

Offices & Stores

Fitters

Shear-legs

Coal Stack

Engine Shed

Boiler House

Mess Room

Turners Shop

Enginemen's Baths & Lockers

Paint Shop

Sand House

Blacksmiths Shops

Offices

Brightside Lane

Signal Box

Fog Hut

Coal Bin

Messrs. Cammel Laird & Co.

To Sheffield Station

End of LMS Maintenance

Newall Road

Store Shed

Fitting & Machine Shop

Store Shed

Traverser

Bins

To Wagon Repairing Shed

Foreman

0 1 2 3 4 5 CHAINS

The Sheffield steam crane pressed into service on 14th July 1920, traverser servicing the 'outstation shop' in the foreground. It is not clear whether this method of lifting was the normal technique employed at Sheffield for running repairs, in addition to the shear-legs, at this time. It may only be that the travelling crane inside the shop was out of action at this time.

Collection B. J. Radford

passenger locos among predominently goods engines, notably in the last century Nos. 900-909 (78-87 in 1907), 2—4—0s of the '890' class introduced in 1871. The shed's seventeen 2—4—0s of 1880 increased by five over the succeeding decade, but 0—6—0s increased by nearly twenty, the four well tanks initially supplied giving way

Outside shear-legs were also provided at Grimesthorpe, on a spur off the 60 ft turntable provided in 1901. The siting of this table allowed the provision of a second roundhouse, which unfortunately never materialised.

Collection R. S. Carpenter

to eleven 0—6—0Ts by 1892. New 4—4—0s Nos. 2203-2212 were sent to 'Sheffield' for new Manchester/Liverpool expresses in 1893 and a further new service, local trains on the new direct Barnsley line, were handled by 0—4—4Ts, Nos. 2238-2247 (later 1391-1400). The usual fleet of 0—6—0s handled freight traffic of course, until 1929 when 'Crab' 2—6—0s (followed by 'G3' 0—8—0s) appeared. 'Black Five' 4—6—0s followed and the sixty or so 0—6—0s were reduced by half, their more onerous tasks handed over to '4MT' Moguls, '8F' 2—8—0s and so on. Sheffield was no stranger in fact to Mogul engines, ten of the thirty Baldwin locos having arrived from America in 1899. They were used along with the larger 0—6—0s on main line coal trains, but all had disappeared before the First World War. Grimesthorpe retained a number of 4—4—0s for local passenger and pilot work and in 1946 '2P's Nos. 324, 362 and 401 and '3P's Nos. 716, 728, 729, 731 and 765 were present. No. 40728 was one of the last of the clan and survived at Sheffield until 1952.

Diesel shunters arrived in 1956 and part of the old repair shops, (closed as a 'CME' shop in the 1930s and subsequently restricted to mileage examination) were converted for their use. The diesels shunted initially at 'the Wicker', Queens Road and Brightside yard.

The shed was incorporated into the Eastern Region as 41B in February 1958 under Darnall and it was the first major shed in the area to close. Its steam locos were transferred to Canklow on 11th September 1961 while its shunters went to Darnall.

0−6−0s by the Sheffield 'No. 1' coaler in August 1955.

B. Morrison

Inside Grimesthorpe in 1938. *British Railways*

Locomotives around the outside turntable in LMS days. In the background is Grimesthorpe Junction signal box. *Photographer unknown*

194

Skipton's wooden buildings on 11th October 1936.

W. A. Camwell

The sheds a year later. There is little sign yet of the accelerated decay which only fourteen years later earned Skipton the verdict: 'somewhat tumbledown . . . the roof being practically non-existent.' No record has come to light, but fire or some other catastrophe may have been visited on the depot.

L & GRP

SKIPTON

'The Tender of J. Tilney for an engine shed at Skipton, at £239' was accepted in 1850, a turntable having already been provided at the station. A 'new improved' 46 ft turntable from Cowans Sheldon was installed in 1877 and a new three road shed in wood was completed around the same time. A second, similar shed was added on the north side and a new coaling stage built in 1892. Once again the building was intended to house nine tender engines and it was constructed by Messrs. C. Murgatroyd, whose tender of £2,889. 3s. 7d. had been successful on 5th May 1890. The old turntable at the south end of the station remained in use for many years until replaced by a 60 ft

vacuum operated 'table in the late 1930s. This was sited immediately outside the earlier of the two sheds, access thereafter being effected directly off the turntable. Both buildings were in dire condition by the late 1940s and, although a new roof for the older portion was planned by the LMS, nothing was actually done. In 1951 the *Railway Observer* reported 'it is to be hoped that the somewhat tumble-down wooden shed at Skipton will be rebuilt in the near future, the roof being practically non-existent'. BR soon afterwards rebuilt the entire shed in brick with concrete and asbestos roof, new offices and so on.

There were normally forty or so locos based at Skipton, coded 30 in later Midland days. A further thirty or so locos were at the main sub-shed, Hellifield, with a handful

One of the rebuilt sheds, on 25th September 1965 with, left to right, 2-6-2T No. 84028 (behind is No. 41272), 4-6-0 No. 75059 and 0-6-0T No. 47602.

Hugh Ballantyne

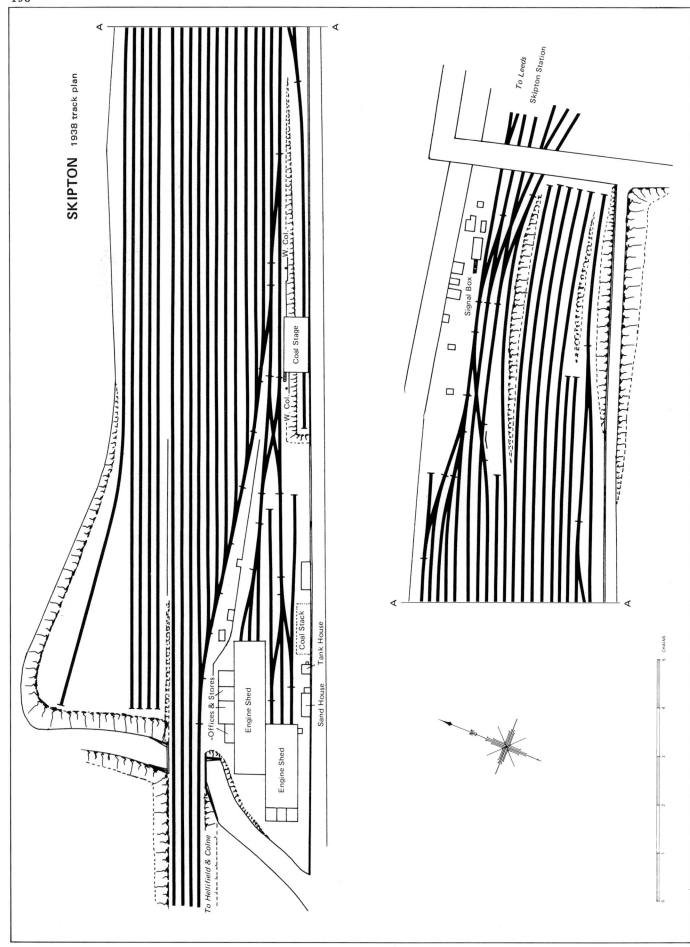

SKIPTON 1938 track plan

A

To Leeds
Skipton Station

Signal Box

A

A

To Hellifield & Colne

Offices & Stores

Engine Shed

Engine Shed

Coal Stack

Sand House

Tank House

Coal Stage

W. Col.

W. Col.

0 1 2 3 4 5 CHAINS

Skipton in BR days. Following the rebuilding, access to the smaller of the two sheds was from a turntable positioned outside. For many years locos had made use of a table at the far end of the station, some considerable distance away. Opportunity was thus taken during rebuilding to remedy this time-consuming and awkward procedure.

R. J. Essery

of engines at Colne and Barnoldswick. The shed became 20F in 1935 and achieved 'concentration' status, although it retained its old code, in 1946. More than half the allocation were goods types, all 0–6–0s, although by 1945 a solitary '8F', No. 8081 had found its way to the depot. 2–4–0s had been the mainstay of the passenger services in the 19th century, most of the 1876 batch with 6' 2½" coupled wheels going to Skipton for the Carlisle line. They were not successful on the fast expresses and after several incidents with broken crank axles they were transferred away. Nos. 55-59 with 6' 8" wheels were much more successful and were employed on the Morecambe, Leeds and Bradford trains. The first four of Johnson's 7' 2–4–0 engines, introduced in 1877, were also at Skipton for many years. Johnson's 0–4–4 and 0–6–0 tank designs were also common after the turn of the century, the former on local passenger work to Ilkley, etc. the latter employed in the not inconsiderable yards at Skipton.

Four of each of these engines survived the Second World War. For a time Aspinall 0–6–0s Nos. 12106, 12108 and 12109 joined the fleet of over twenty MR and LMS 0–6–0s. In the late 'twenties/early 'thirties the LMS fitted three '4F' 0–6–0s, Nos. 3893, 3999 and 4000, with tender cabs, in order to better protect crews on snowplough duties. This feature was retained on various engines right up to 1965, Skipton becoming one of the last sheds to operate this type. No less than twenty-one were withdrawn from the shed in the period 1964-65. During the 'fifties Ivatt's various standard designs, the '2MT', tender and tank versions, and the '4MT' Moguls increasingly replaced the old Midland engines. The shed was grouped under Accrington as 24G in March 1957 (having been 23A briefly in 1950-51) and under Carnforth as 10G from September 1963. It closed completely on 3rd April 1967 and has since seen further use by the local authority.

The old MR coal stage was retained at Skipton and engines were hand coaled until the end.
R. J. Essery

Southwell, a delightful country engine shed, with attendant paraphernalia on 14th July 1935. Tucked away inside on this occasion was '3F' 0—6—0 No. 3811 resting between goods turns.

W. A. Camwell

SOUTHWELL

The short line northwards from Rolleston Junction to a terminus at Southwell opened in July 1847 and from its size and style the shed would appear to date from around this time. The line was extended northwards in April 1871 but the first mention of the shed does not appear in the minutes until 19th June 1890, when the company deliberated on the 'purchase of land to ensure water supply for Engine Shed, Southwell'. On 16th April the following

year an additional siding and the coaling platforms were installed and after this Southwell fades back into obscurity.

It was coded 18d, a sub-shed of Nottingham, and normally housed one or two of the army of 0—4—4Ts working the branch traffic in the area. In earlier years 2—4—0s were used, No. 14 being stationed there in 1880. Nottingham remained the parent shed until Southwell's closure on 10th January 1955, the regular complement for some years having been two engines only, an ex-MR '1P' 0—4—4T for the branch passenger train to Rolleston Junction and a '3F' 0—6—0T for the Newark (Castle) pilot duty. Nos. 58077 and 47631 were working on the day of closure. Newark (GNR) shed took over the duties, No. 58077 being sent there with Nos. 58085 and 41779 from Nottingham. No. 58065 replaced 58077 at the end of 1955 and this engine and No. 58085 (MR Nos. 1367 and 1422) continued to work the branch from Newark and, briefly Lincoln, becoming the last active members of the class. No. 58085 was withdrawn in April 1959, closure of the branch following in June of that year. An interesting 0—4—4T working, both pre- and post-war, was the Monday mornings only empty stock train to Nottingham, the purpose being to change the single coach, if required, as well as the engine. The train ran non-stop from Rolleston Junction to Nottingham Carriage Sidings with the engine continuing through to the parent shed. By way of a footnote, both these 0—4—4Ts, Nos. 58065 and 58085 were fitted with special high coal rails, to allow longer periods between trips to Southwell shed for re-coaling.

The shed in June 1956. The building itself was out of use by this time and engines were not allowed to enter. Use was still made of the siding, however.

H. C. Casserley

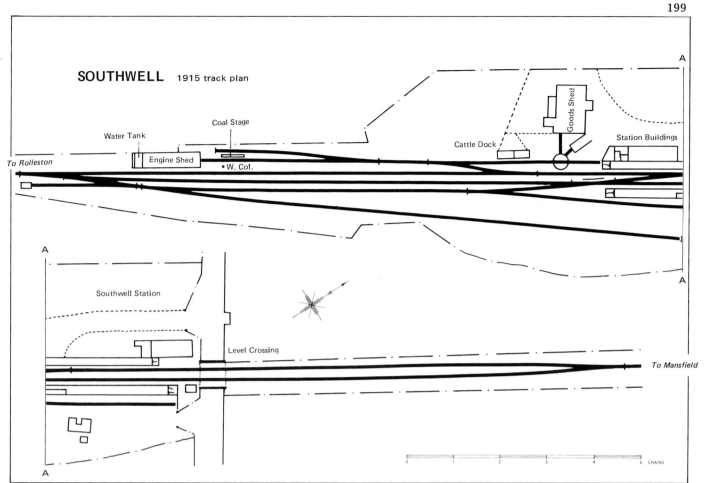

SOUTHWELL 1915 track plan

Water Tank
Coal Stage
Engine Shed
• W. Col.
To Rolleston

Cattle Dock
Goods Shed
Station Buildings

A
Southwell Station
Level Crossing
To Mansfield
A
A
A
A

0   1   2   3   4   5   CHAINS

Ex-MR 0—4—4T and coach retire to the shed together in BR days.

N. R. Knight

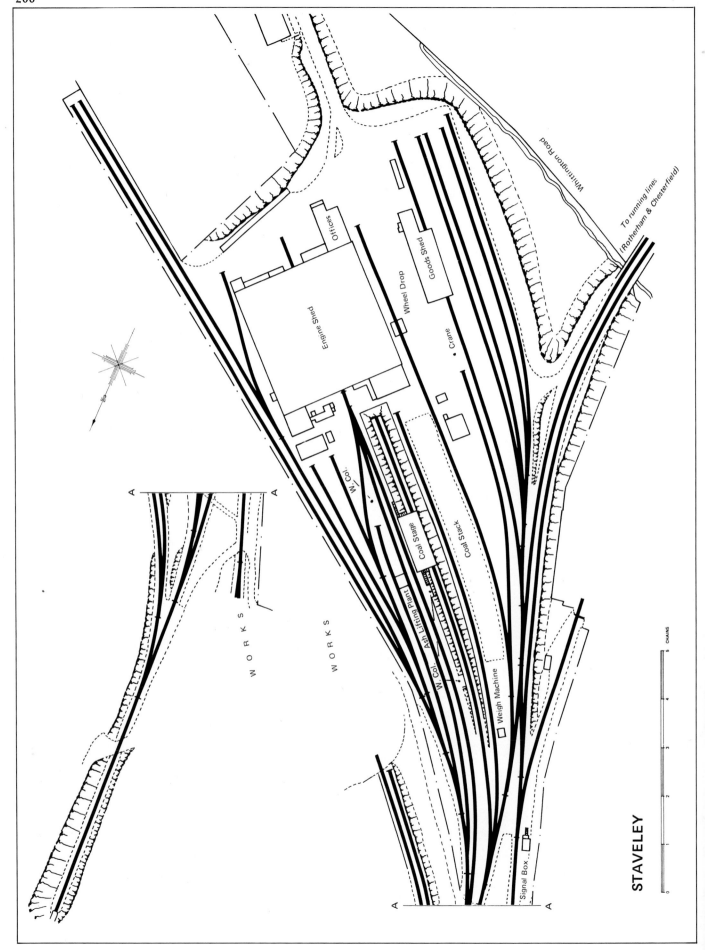

STAVELEY

Offices

Engine Shed

Wheel Drop

Goods Shed

Crane

W. Col.

Coal Stage

Ash Lifting Plant

Coal Stack

W. Col.

Weigh Machine

Signal Box.

W O R K S

W O R K S

A
A

A
A

Whittington Road

To running lines:
(Rotherham & Chesterfield)

0 1 2 3 4 5 CHAINS

'Barrow Hill' on 19th May 1957. It acquired this title on Nationalisation, to distinguish it from the ex-Great Central 'Staveley' shed close by.

W. Potter

STAVELEY

Staveley, a standard roundhouse, opened in late 1870 to house the increasing number of locos working the local iron and mineral traffic. Engine facilities prior to this comprised a 'new coke stage and Engine Turntable' installed in early 1862 by John Woods Ltd., at a cost of £735. The new shed's duties were predominantly freight in nature and until LMS days the allocation, which rose to a peak of some eighty locos in the 1930s, consisted in the main of 0−6−0s, together with shunting tanks for the nearby works and yards. Fowler 0−8−0s, including Nos. 9529-9535 on their construction in 1929, replaced some of the ageing Midland 0−6−0s and many others gave way

to LMS '4F' versions. '8F' 2−8−0s, eventually numbering over twenty locos, became the principal type in later years, supplemented by 'WD' engines. Staveley's most celebrated engine type, however, proved to be humble shunting tanks.

In May 1866 the Midland absorbed six small 0−4−0Ts and an 0−6−0 tank from the Staveley Coal and Iron Company and entered into a contract to provide shunting engines for the Works. Three more 0−6−0WTs were absorbed from the Sheepbridge Company in 1870. They survived over twenty years to be replaced by Johnson, later Deeley, 0−4−0Ts, assisted later by larger '1F' tanks. Nos. 1746-1754 were there by 1914, together with 0−4−0Ts Nos. 1518, 1520, 1521, 1525, 1526 and 1527 (Johnson) and Nos. 1528, 1529 and 1530 of Deeley design. The complement by 1946 had been reduced to

The shed on 4th July 1954, with its slightly exotic girder ash lifting gear.

W. Potter

The shed during roof alterations, on 13th April 1958.
W. Potter

0—6—0s parked by the side of the shed, 4th July 1954.

B. Hilton

The re-roofed shed, in which condition it survives today.

R. J. Essery

The old Midland coal stage was similarly treated, though of course was dispensed with on dieselisation. *R. J. Essery*

The box controlling movements to and from the shed.
R. J. Essery

four Deeley engines and ten '1F' 0—6—0Ts. A handful were retained until the end of steam working, in October 1965 and, in keeping with Midland tradition, a number had spent many years continuous service at Staveley. No. 1752 had put in over forty years at the shed when it was withdrawn in 1958 and several others achieved over thirty years service. The last survivors were Nos. 41528 and 41533, BR/Kitson 0—4—0STs Nos. 47001 and 47005 and '1F's Nos. 41708, 41734, 41763, 41804 and 41835 of which 1708 is now preserved, at the Midland Railway Centre, Butterley. The engines, on being put out of use, were stored initially at Staveley, then Canklow and finally at Holmes Curve, Masborough, until formally withdrawn in December 1966, on expiry of the Agreement.

As many as seventy engines remained at Staveley well into the 1950s, but the old Midland coal stage remained in use, supplemented by a rudimentary ash plant provided in 1928. The roof was reclad in asbestos sheeting in the late 'thirties, adequately serving the shed even after its conversion to diesel maintenance in the 1960s. Staveley was MR shed No. 24 and became 18D under Toton, a code it kept from 1935 until transfer to the Eastern Region as 41D in February 1958. Its small sub-sheds at Sheepbridge and in the Iron Works itself were really Works property and regarded as 'sub' mainly for operating purposes. Known now as 'Barrow Hill' to distinguish it from the neighbouring ex-Great Central straight shed, it was one of the last ER steam depots, with 39 locos still operational in March 1965. Diesels, Clayton type '1's and English Electric type '3's, had been increasingly in evidence for several years and steam was finally ousted on October 4th 1965. The remaining operational locos were transferred to Langwith (ex-LNER), but the depot continues to operate diesel locomotives to the present day.

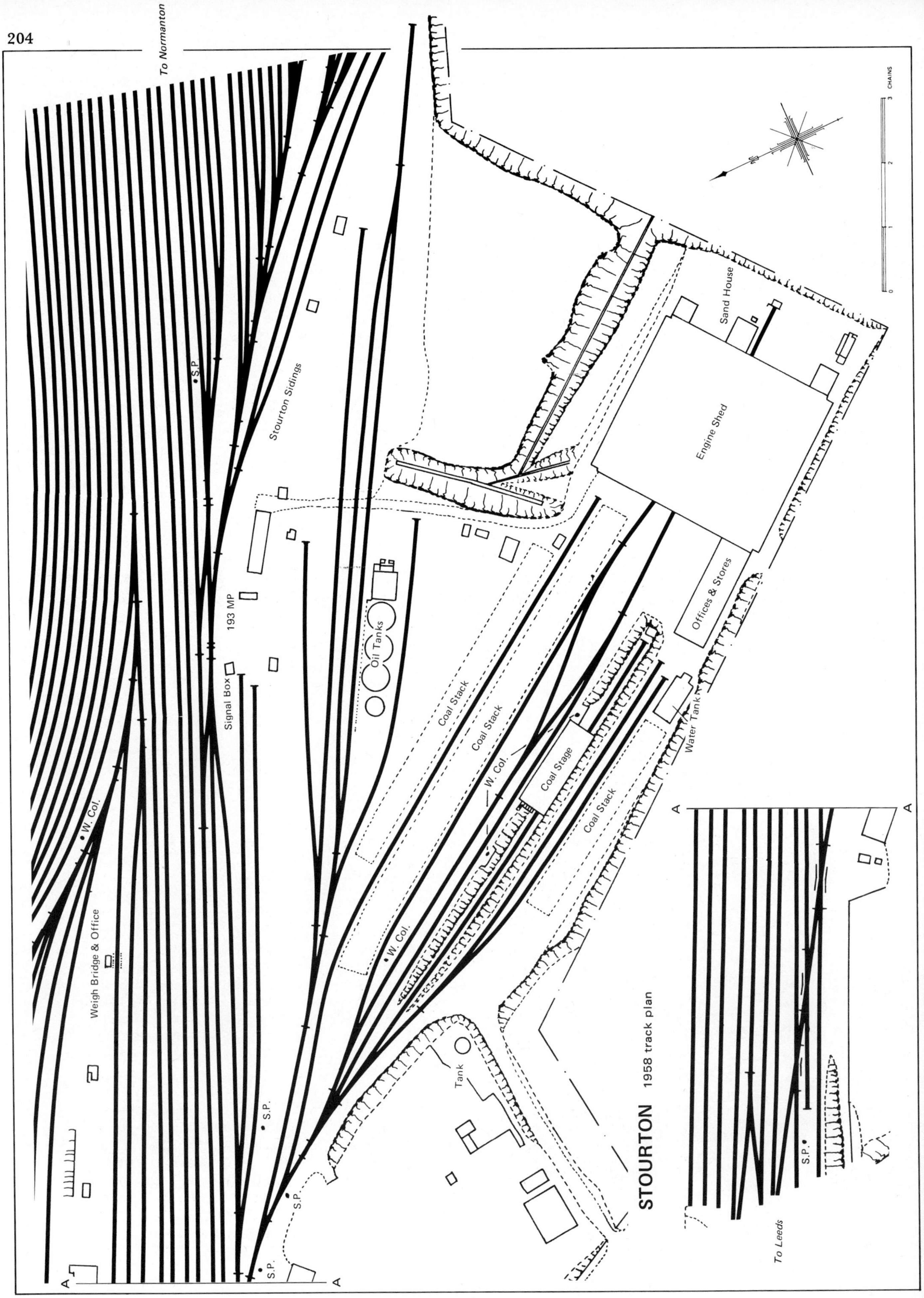

To Normanton

S.P.

Stourton Sidings

193 MP

Signal Box

W. Col.

Oil Tanks

Weigh Bridge & Office

S.P.

S.P.

S.P.

W. Col.

Coal Stack

Coal Stack

Coal Stack

W. Col.

Coal Stage

Coal Stack

W. Col.

Tank

Water Tank

Offices & Stores

Engine Shed

Sand House

3 CHAINS

2

1

0

STOURTON 1958 track plan

A

A

A

A

S.P.

To Leeds

Rebuilt shed and yard in early BR days, 25th May 1952.

W. Potter

STOURTON

Stourton shed was built to service locos working into the adjacent yards, 'Stourton Sidings', laid out to improve the Midland's freight operations in the Leeds area. The shed, housing a Cowans Sheldon 50 ft turntable, opened in 1893 with an allocation rising at times to over sixty locomotives. All of them were freight types, the complement at first consisting of 0–6–0s, with a few '1F' tanks for shunting.

The shed had an uneventful history, although it was re-roofed at last, in the early 1950s, in the same ugly style

as Cricklewood and Toton. The depot was coded 28a by the Midland, a sub-shed of Leeds Holbeck, becoming a 'garage', 20B, in 1935. It was an important freight engine depot and six '8F' 2–8–0s had arrived by 1945, the number doubling over the next few years. Three Fowler 0–8–0s had appeared by 1930 and two still remained at the end of the Second World War. In late 1939 ex-Caledonian 0–6–0 No. 17353 arrived at Stourton, followed the next year by Nos. 17242, 17280 and 17331, transferred from other Leeds area sheds. Further Scottish engines, ex-GSWR 0–6–2Ts Nos. 16919, 16923, 16924, 16925 and 16927 had also been present in the mid-1930s. All the latter had been withdrawn by 1938. The allocation

Earlier times. 0–6–0s Nos. 3130 and 3860 at Stourton, October 1934.

G. S. Lloyd

Although the depot was generally thought part of the Leeds area, it enjoyed a relatively isolated setting. This was the view on 17th September 1961.

W. Potter

fell to a total of something under fifty following the Second World War, Ivatt class '4' Moguls putting in an appearance for the first time, with Nos. 43014 and 43044. Stourton remained a stronghold of '1F' 0–6–0Ts until quite late and five were still at work in the sidings in the mid-1950s.

Diesel shunters eventually arrived and in 1956 numbers of them were being stored at Stourton prior to delivery to other sheds. In the same year during alterations at Holbeck, some of the main shed's locos were forced to travel to Stourton (as well as Neville Hill ex-NER shed) for coaling and turning. No mechanical coal or ash apparatus was supplied by the LMS and to supplement the old

Midland 'single' stage BR eventually provided a coaling crane and some rudimentary ash disposal apparatus.

The former Midland organisation in the Leeds and Bradford areas passed to the North Eastern Region in January 1957 but LMS designs remained well in evidence, despite the increasing numbers of 'WD' 2–8–0s. Stourton became 55B, but steam finally disappeared in January 1967. The story may have been very different if an early BR scheme for a large new marshalling yard nearby had come to fruition. Preparatory earthworks were completed but nothing further was done. If work had progressed some improved facilities would obviously have been required at the shed.

A fine portrait of LMS '3F' tank No. 47538, outside the rebuilt shed.

B. K. B. Green

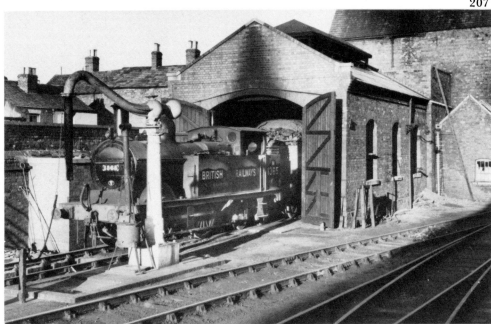

Tewkesbury shed on 10th September 1950, nestled in a corner alongside the 'Quay Branch'. The water tank lay at the rear of the shed, hidden by brickwork.
W. A. Camwell

TEWKESBURY

The short branch from Ashchurch to Tewkesbury Wharf on the River Avon opened with the Birmingham-Gloucester main line in 1840. A new station replaced the original somewhat rudimentary facilities when the line was extended through to Malvern in May 1864 but the goods shed etc. remained alongside the freight-only 'Quay Branch'.

The exact opening date of the brick-built engine shed is not clear but some kind of locomotive facilities would

of course have been necessary from the outset. Indeed in 1859 a new ashpit (cost: £3) was ordered at 'the Tewkesbury Station' and the likelihood is that the shed pre-dates the 1864 extension (the 'Tewkesbury and Malvern Railway', worked from the first by the Midland and officially absorbed in 1876).

0—4—4 tanks and 0—6—0s on local work stabled and coaled at the little shed, which backed onto a malthouse. It was a sub-shed of Gloucester, and could become surprisingly busy, especially with a high volume of freight to the wharf and on occasions (when excursions were run from

Tewkesbury in 1949. MR 0—4—4Ts were the regular engines for many years, their regime ending on the withdrawal of No. 58071 in 1956. Popular engines on the Evesham line after this and into the early 'sixties were Ivatt 4MT 2—6—0s, 'regulars' at Tewkesbury including Nos. 43013, 43017, 43033, 43036, 43046, 43047 and 43049.

L & GRP

The shed on 12th June 1937. Visiting engines imparting an improbably bustling atmosphere comprise 0–6–0s No. 3062, 4–4–0 No. 527 (both Gloucester engines), 2–6–4T No. 2372 (from Saltley) and 0–6–0 No. 3078 (again a Gloucester loco). Inside the shed is ex-MR 0–4–4T No. 1348, from Bournville shed.

W. A. Camwell

Overcrowding could become acute and locos often had to be stabled on the far side of Oldbury Road, '8F' 2–8–0 No. 48388 is thence consigned on 14th June 1953. This area was the site of the original terminus, opened in 1840, trains being horse-drawn until 1844 when the line was extended to the wharf.

B. Hilton

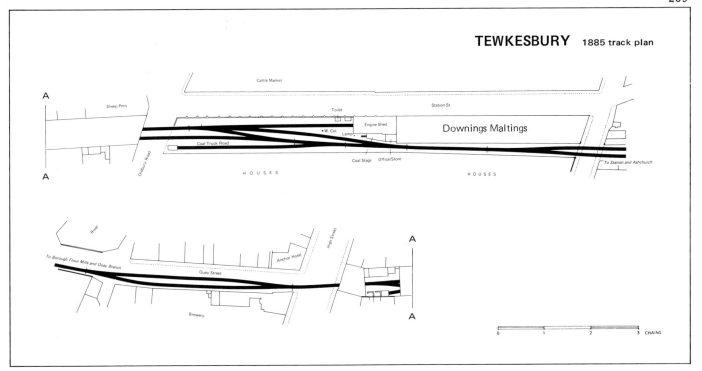

TEWKESBURY 1885 track plan

Birmingham for instance) locos were forced to stable further down the branch on the 'running lines'. Fishermen's trains to Ripple and Upton were also common and the shed also serviced engines off the Birmingham-Ashchurch trains. These were 0—6—4Ts until about 1935/36 when they were replaced by 2—6—2Ts and 2—6—4Ts.

The Johnson 0—4—4Ts went out of use around 1956, giving way to 2—6—4Ts (notably No. 42327), Stanier 0—4—4Ts (Nos. 41900, 41902 and 41903 were thus occupied in the 1950s), and ex-GWR pannier tanks of the

'57XX' type. Ivatt class '2' tanks had also seen regular use in the 'fifties. The pannier tanks were increasingly in evidence following the shed's transfer to the Western Region in February 1958.

The Ashchurch-Tewkesbury line had closed to passengers on 12th August 1961, but the shed was reprieved at the last moment and for a short time housed two locos, one for the daily goods train to Upton and the other for the Redditch line. It finally closed on 7th September 1962.

Ex-MR 0—4—4T No. 1353 and '3F' 0—6—0 No. 3754 stabled at Tewkesbury in 1948. The small coal stage and canopy were provided by the LMS, replacing a small stage at the side of the shed. The 0—6—0 was associated with Tewkesbury for many years, working (as No. 43754) the last Upton train. For a period its companion on regular goods work was Ivatt 2—6—0 No. 46401, which, although more comfortable when returning from Upton tender first, was nevertheless unpopular with the crews.
W. Potter

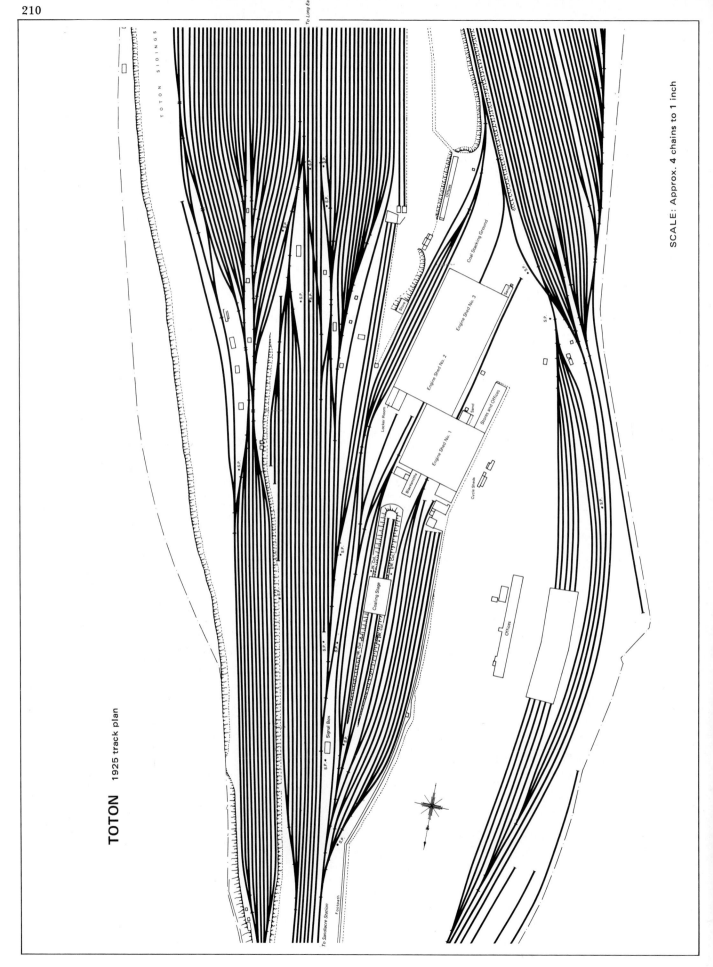

TOTON   1925 track plan

SCALE: Approx. **4 chains to 1 inch**

The Toton complex in BR days. Much of the vast output of the Nottinghamshire coal field was channelled through here and the facilities were accordingly extensive. Toton handled more coal than any other UK yard and contained probably the largest mechanised network in the country, after modernisation of the 'up' sidings in 1951. The roundhouses lie in the upper part of the photograph, the building in the foreground being one of two large wagon repair establishments.

Aerofilms

TOTON

Toton was a purely railway creation, its yards and complex junctions developing on open farmland near Long Eaton, more or less midway between Derby and Nottingham. Coal production from the Derbyshire and Nottinghamshire coalfields was increasing apace and much of it was dealt with at Toton, where the yards were eventually to extend for over one and a half miles. The first mention as far as the Locomotive Department is concerned arises in the minutes of 1855-1857: 'Sandiacre; resolved that the tender of G. Thompson be accepted for construction of a small engine shed and cottage at the new sidings there'. (The later shed and yards were situated between Stapleford & Sandiacre and Long Eaton stations).

Plans for the first roundhouse at Toton were ordered on 2nd March 1869 and were eventually to cost about £16,100. The existing accommodation had undergone

some improvements, however, a new coal stage having been ordered for the shed on 18th August 1868. The first shed, a standard twenty-four road building with a 42 ft turntable, was completed in 1870 and a second square unit 'No. 2' shed was built alongside three years later. The number of locos required at Toton continued to increase inexorably, and in 1899 plans were drawn up for a further two roundhouses. This would have made Toton the largest of the Midland locomotive depots, at least in terms of area under cover, but following doubts expressed by the Finance and General Purposes Committee (the ideas were cancelled and revised twice during 1899) the running department was forced to content themselves with only a single extra building. Messrs. J. Walker & Sons' tender of £17,256. 14s. 0d. was accepted for 'No. 3' shed on 14th December 1899 and it was ready for use in early 1901. The new building was equipped with a 55 ft turntable and shear-legs and an enlarged coal stage was also

Toton 'No. 1' shed in the early 1930s.   *Collection J. B. Radford*

The old Midland 'double' coal stage undergoing demolition on the shed's modernisation. There is a photograph of this building in operation in Volume 1, page 3.

Collection J. B. Radford

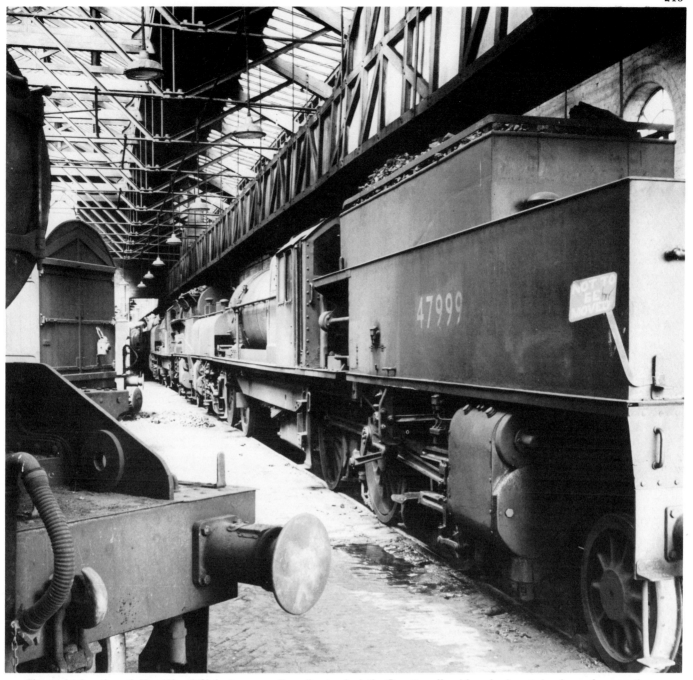

The road taken through Nos. '2' and '3' sheds was usually well-patronised; the Garratts suffered from inadequate bearing surfaces, partly the result of an ill-judged attempt at standardisation. They were thus, particularly in their latter years, frequently 'stopped', and a fine machine, well-received over large areas of the world, faded to an ignominious and unsung end in its country of birth. No. 47999 along with 47998 were the last two members of the class to retain the original square bunkers. The shed staff at Cricklewood disliked them because of this and they were rarely used on Brent trains, being mainly employed on freights to Birmingham.   *B. Morrison*

provided for the expanded depot. The 42 ft turntables in Nos. '1' and '2' sheds were replaced by 55 ft and 60 ft units respectively in 1926/27, at a cost of £6,622.

Coal trains, mainly to London and Birmingham, provided the great bulk of the duties and all the successive generations of goods engines were used at Toton, from Kirtley 0—6—0s to BR '9F's. In between came Johnson '2F' and '3F' locos, Fowler '4F's, '7F' 0—8—0s and Stanier '8F' 2—8—0s. Unusual freight engines were tried out at Toton at various times, from ten of the Baldwin Moguls purchased in 1899 to a stud of twenty Garratts

sent new in 1930. Other strange imports over the years included ex-LNW 19″ goods 4—6—0s, L & Y 0—6—0s and even Glasgow & South Western '3F' 0—6—2Ts. The Baldwins were only a transitory feature but the big 2—6—0/ 0—6—2s remained at Toton for over twenty years. Special accommodation was required and a new road was taken through the length of numbers '2' and '3' sheds, enabling some of the big locos to stable under cover. Twenty-six Fowler 0—8—0s had arrived by 1933 but of the 140 or so locos at the shed the great majority were still 0—6—0s. There were nearly eighty of them, including twenty-two

'No. 2' shed 'in between roofs' in 1948. The view illustrates the limitations on stabling room imposed by the 'Garratt Road'. Bomb damage in 1941 is reputed to be the root cause of the rebuilding work at Toton, but it has not been possible so far to confirm this. 'No. 2' was rebuilt during 1949 but 'No. 3' on the left was re-clad only.

Aerofilms

LMS '4F' engines and 'old timer' No. 2835, a Kirtley double-framed loco fitted with a class '2' boiler. A dozen or so tanks, including Johnson example No. 1856 shunted the surrounding yards, subsequently aided by several 0—6—0 diesels. The pioneer diesel shunter, in fact, No. 1831, rebuilt from a Johnson tank, carried out trials at Toton in 1934 and new diesel electric shunters became the regular hump engines after 1939.

The number of locos at the shed continued to increase, principally with the addition of more than fifty new '8F's during the war years; further LMS-built 0—6—0s arrived and even a couple of LNW 'Cauliflowers' Nos. 8512 and 8619 had found their way there by 1941.

Various repairs and alterations were carried out at Toton over the years, beginning with a £1,779 outlay by the Midland in 1903 for unspecified 'loco shed improvements'. Coal and ash plants were supplied in the early

1930s. Various repairs were carried out to the three roofs, but full scale renewals were eventually carried out in the late 1940s. The water supply came from some distance away, by the Top Lock of the Derby Canal and in 1956 a new supply was arranged from the nearer Erewash Canal. A diesel repair shop was proposed as early as 1944 but the increasing numbers of diesels, particularly shunters, came generally to be housed in No. '2' shed.

The 'up' sidings were modernised in 1951 (the 'down' side had been dealt with in 1939) leaving them amongst the largest mechanised yards in the country and in 1955 a reviewer in the *Railway World* had the following to say: 'The up yard handles the largest coal traffic in the country and the Motive Power Depot services about 154 locos including 18 Garratts and 11 diesel shunters. Others are mostly '8F's and various 0—6—0s. The Garratts work coal trains of about 1500 tons up to Cricklewood. They seem

Two views inside 'No. 2' roundhouse on 8th July 1948, with Garratt No. 47979 figuring prominently.   *H. C. Casserley*

Garratts again at Toton. *Top:* No. 47971 stands alongside 'No. 3' shed, on 24th July 1955. *Above:* No. 47987 on 29th June the following year.

B. Morrison and F. Dean

Toton's 'double skip' ash hoist was an interesting variation on the girder-built units found all over the LMS. The principle employed with all the steel-framed units was the same and the main difference between this type of equipment and the more familiar 'concrete tower' variety of ash disposal plant was the use of a storage bunker. In units like the one at Toton (and at Nottingham, for instance, illustrated in this volume) ashes etc. from the locomotive were 'paddled' into tubs which were raised when full and inverted, emptying the contents into a waiting wagon. In the concrete plants, ashes were lifted from ground level or from an underground pit and stored in a bunker until disposal via wagons was convenient. For drawings etc. and a more detailed account, see Volume 1.

British Railways

Toton's 300 ton 'No. 1' type coaler, with a coal 'slaker' visible alongside. This design was employed at Saltley among other places, but seemed to find greater favour on the LNER, where considerable modernisation work was also carried out during the 1930s.

British Railways

It is easy to over-emphasise the role of the Garratts at Toton but by far the largest proportion of the freight work was in the hands of more everyday locos, from 0—6—0s to '9F' 2—10—0s in BR days. Prominent for many years of course were Stanier '8F' 2—8—0s and two of them, Nos. 8182 and 8495, rest inside 'No. 2' roundhouse on 8th July 1948.

H. C. Casserley

to be very popular with the men because of their huge handling capacity and even more so with the introduction of rotary bunkers.' Despite the writer's assertion, the articulated locos were anything but popular with the crews and '9F' 2—10—0s entirely replaced them two years later.

Originally Midland shed No. 17, Toton had been 18A since 1935, a new adjacent diesel maintenance depot emerging as 16A in September 1963, eventually absorbing most of the work of all three locomotive districts in the East Midlands. The shed officially closed to steam in December 1965, the last engines being a single stored '8F' and a handful of BR '78000' Moguls. The three round-houses have now been demolished, the only portion to survive being part of the old water softening building, now used as a plant and machinery workshop.

'9F' 2—10—0 No. 92024, with Franco-Crosti boiler, at Toton on 29th June 1956.

F. Dean

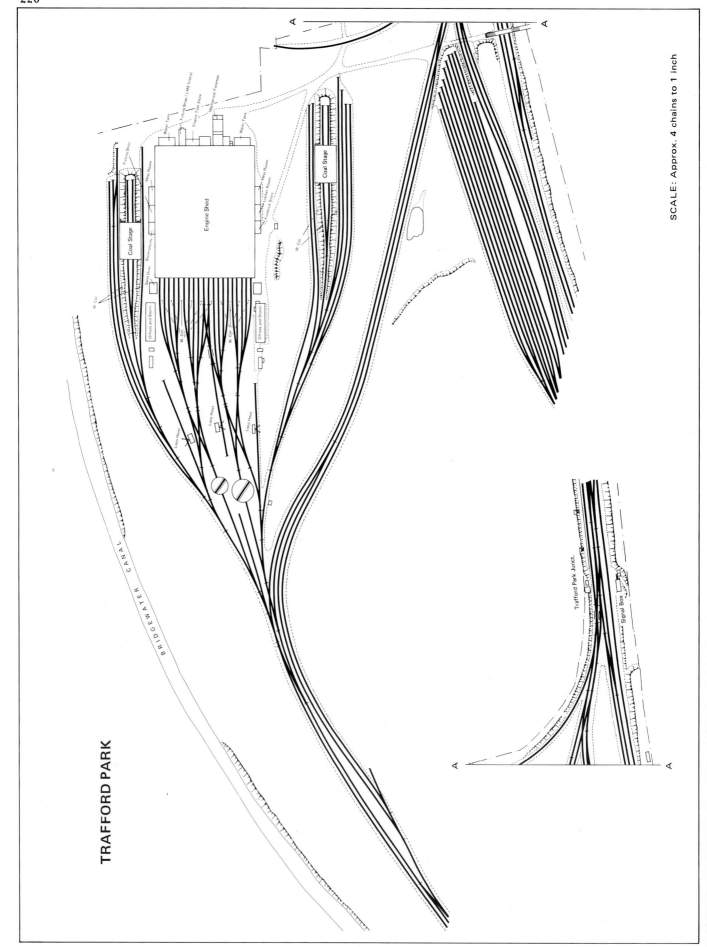

TRAFFORD PARK

BRIDGEWATER CANAL

Coal Stage

Fitting Shop

W Col

Water Tank

Fitting Shop (LMS tunes)

Engine Tool Store

Mechanical Foreman

Water Tank

Mess Room

Mess Room

Firebrick Store

Firebrick Locker Room

Engine Shed

Boilersmiths

Sand Drier

Coal Stage

W Col

Offices and Stores

W Col

W Col

Offices and Stores

Loco Hoist

Loco Hoist

Loco Hoist

Trafford Park Junct.

Signal Box

SCALE: Approx. 4 chains to 1 inch

A   A

A   A

Stanier 4—6—0 No. 5069 stands at Trafford Park in August 1936, ex-Great Central engines well in evidence in the LNER portion of the shed.

W. Potter

TRAFFORD PARK

The Midland's by no means inconsiderable share of traffic from Lancashire and Cheshire, to the continual chagrin of the LNWR, depended on a complex pattern of line sharing, working agreements and so forth with various other companies. The MR was able to tap Liverpool/Manchester-Scotland traffic by courtesy of the Lancashire and Yorkshire Railway and its entry to Manchester from the south was completed on Manchester, Sheffield and Lincolnshire metals. Its most lucrative penetration, however, was obtained by its involvement in the Cheshire Lines Com-

mittee, a third of whose directors were Midland men. The rest of the board seats were equally divided between the Great Northern and the MS & LR, the latter of course eventually to become the Great Central and the division of ownership led to a variety of joint arrangements.

The owning companies were anxious to partake in the increasing wealth of the varied industries (as well as the considerable passenger traffic) on the west side of Manchester and a large twenty road straight shed was erected on marshy ground alongside the Bridgewater Canal. A spur was laid from a point just west of Throstle Nest Junction, where the Midland's 'South District Line' left the

'Black Five' predecessor. MR 4—4—0 No. 726 at Trafford Park c. 1914.
Collection R. Carpenter

It was rarely possible to appreciate the great extent of the joint shed at Trafford Park. This photograph portrays it admirably in June 1933.

W. Potter

CLC main line and the shed, with exactly duplicated facilities, opened in March 1895. There had, in fact, been a shed in use prior to this, sited over a mile to the east, at the junction of the CLC and the Manchester South Junction and Altrincham company's line. Known as 'Corn-

brook', it was squeezed between the running lines and the Bridgewater Canal and its three roads (leading onto a turntable at the southern end) curved to accommodate the sweep of the canal at this point. The curious curved building, the towpath bordering its northern side, went out of use following the opening of Trafford Park.

At first the division was between the Great Central and the Midland only, the latter's offices, turntable and coal stage and ten roads occupying the southern side. Around 1898/99 the Great Northern gained entry, taking over five of the Midland's roads, and offices were provided for their use at the rear of the shed. Trafford Park was a sub-shed of Belle Vue, coded 21a (the Great Northern used the code number 7) and the twenty-five or so Midland engines stabled there were used primarily on passenger work as well as freight. Due to a shortage of 0—4—4 tanks ten of Johnson's large 0—6—0Ts built in 1902, Nos. 2761-2770 (1940-1949 after 1907) were sent new to Trafford Park for goods and local passenger work, remaining on the latter duties until the first of the Deeley 0—6—4Ts, Nos. 2000-2004 ,were sent there new in 1907. Four of the 0—6—0Ts remained in Manchester until 1917. A dozen or so 4—4—0s worked the longer distance passenger trains. Compounds were first allocated in 1909, Nos. 1011-1021 remaining there for many years. They were displaced from 'top link' duties before 1939 by class '5's and 'Jubilees' but still found use on CLC locals in the 1950s, in place of withdrawn ex-LNER 4—4—0s.

The Great Northern interest merged with the Great Central after 1923 and by the mid-1930s the Midland, or rather LMS, engines had moved over to occupy the centre roads of the shed. Their old quarters by 1943 were given over to stored ex-CLC Sentinel railcars, 'dead'

There were three loco hoists in the yard but the LNER, at least, saw fit to provide additional apparatus inside the shed. Ex-Great Central 4—4—2T is being attended to here in August 1936.

W. Potter

The great roof pitches did not well survive the rigours of wartime and only blackened timbers remained by 1952.　　*N. E. Preedy*

Robinson 2—8—0s 'and a general air of peace and quiet'. By this time the superintendent and foreman in over-all charge were LMS men.

The shed was covered by seven hipped roof sections, slated and, but for the central pitch, covering three roads apiece. The twenty roads were numbered upwards from north to south. By 1952 the roof cladding had all but disappeared, the LNER offices and MR coal stage were derelict and a start had been made on renewing the roof

in corrugated sheeting. The whole shed was afterwards severely cut back and the northernmost six roads were left open to the elements. A coal shelter and conveyor belt were subsequently provided in this area.

In 1935 the depot had become a 'garage', 19G, of Sheffield, but supervision came from Longsight ex-LNWR shed. In 1950 it acquired its own district, as 13A, with responsibility for the former MR and CLC sheds in the area. This was short lived and in May 1950 it was taken

Inside the LNER quarters in June 1933.　　*W. Potter*

BR reclad part of the shed in corrugated sheeting, providing some minimal shelter, at least.

D. Banks

properly 'into the fold', as 9E. Another ill-starred transfer occurred from January 1957 to April 1958 when it came under the Derby District as 17F, afterwards reverting to 9E. In 1954 there had been thirty-four locos of LMS design with thirty-eight ex-LNER types still remaining. Eight LMS 4—4—0s were still there for local passenger duties along with 2—6—2Ts and 2—6—4Ts. There were four 'Black Fives', four '8F's, and a stud of half a dozen 'Jubilees', Nos. 45618 *New Hebrides*, 45622 *Nyasaland*, 45628 *Somaliland*, 45629 *Straits Settlements*, 45652 *Hawke* and 45655 *Keith* for the St. Pancras expresses.

Ex-LNER locos included two of the last original 'Director' 4—4—0s, Nos. 62653 *Sir Edward Fraser* and No. 62658 *Prince George*, as well as four of the 'Large Directors'. Other engines in this ex-GC stud were mainly 'J10' 0—6—0s, together with 0—6—2Ts and 0—6—0Ts. The last of them appears to have gone around 1960 and the stud increasingly consisted of 'Black 5's, '8F's and 'WD's, restricted to freight work.

Trafford Park closed on 4th March 1968 as one of the last operational steam depots. The site is now obliterated by freightliner development.

'4F' 0—6—0 No. 44587 occupies the 'coaling area' provided in BR days. Both coal stages had fallen into dereliction and were replaced by this basic elevator and shelter, occupying the former LNER part of the shed.

R. J. Essery

'1F' 0–6–0Ts, including Nos. 1725, 1850 and 1860 rest at Upper Bank on a Sunday morning in June 1935. The photographer's notes describe the shed as 'isolated and ungetatable', making it a 'bête noire' among enthusiasts.

G. S. Lloyd

UPPER BANK

There was an engine shed at Swansea, presumably dating from the opening of the Swansea Vale Railway in 1860-61, a set of shear-legs having been provided in 1889. The new shed opened near Upper Bank station, a mile or so out of Swansea St. Thomas' in 1893, utilising much of the equipment from Swansea, including the shear-legs and an engine boiler. Messrs. Rowlands were the contractors, their tender of £5,696 having been accepted on 29th July the previous year. The 42 ft turntable provided was a redundant unit from Colne, in Lancashire. In 1899 the shear-legs pit was lengthened and in 1902 a shelter was provided over the coaling ramp. There had in fact been two earlier, but abandoned, proposals for a large new shed to serve Swansea. Both arose in 1874-5 with the commencement of MR operation and coincided with the construction of the 'new line' on the west side of the Tawe Valley via Morriston East and Clydach-on-Tawe. The old line via Llansamlet was retained, eventually for freight only and the two single track sections were joined at Upper Bank in the south and Glais Junction in the north. Plans and estimates for a large new shed at Llansamlet totalling £18,125 were superseded when a more convenient site was discovered at Upper Bank (this last suggestion arising in Johnson's appraisal of the SVR locomotive stock). The estimated cost was lower at £18,064 and indeed it was resolved that the necessary land be purchased. This second proposal also failed to come to fruition and nothing

further arose for the next twenty or so years. Both of these abortive projects envisaged roundhouses but the depot eventually constructed was on a much smaller scale.

Upper Bank was coded number 6 in MR days, with Gurnos as a sub-shed. It operated over thirty locomotives, nearly all '1F' tanks of successive designs, '3F' 0–6–0Ts in the shape of Nos. 1930 and 1931 arriving by 1914. Two 0–4–0STs, Nos. 1139A and 1140A (1523 and 1524 in 1907), came new to Upper Bank in 1903 and orders were issued the following year that backs be fitted to their cabs. They remained at the shed throughout Midland days but shortly after Grouping No. 1523 had been removed to Gloucester. About a third of the complement was based at Gurnos working the passenger service to Brynamman East and so on, but the principal duties of Upper Bank's engines were the through freights to Hereford. Stopping gratefully at every available water column on this lengthy journey the '1F's and '3F's remained on these improbable duties until they were abandoned in the 1930s. Nos. 1620-1639 had been sent new to Swansea in 1874/5 and six of them, Nos. 1632-36 and 1638, were still at the shed in the late 1920s. Of the later 1878 design Nos. 1775-1779, 1816-1819 and 1824 were sent to South Wales, all fitted with overall cabs. No. 1824 was vacuum fitted for passenger duties. Several Johnson 0–4–4Ts were also at Upper Bank for local passenger work until transferred away in 1928.

The former Midland sheds in South Wales had obtained Western 'A' Division codes by 1926, Upper Bank becoming A33 until 1930. It then became W33 until 1935, the

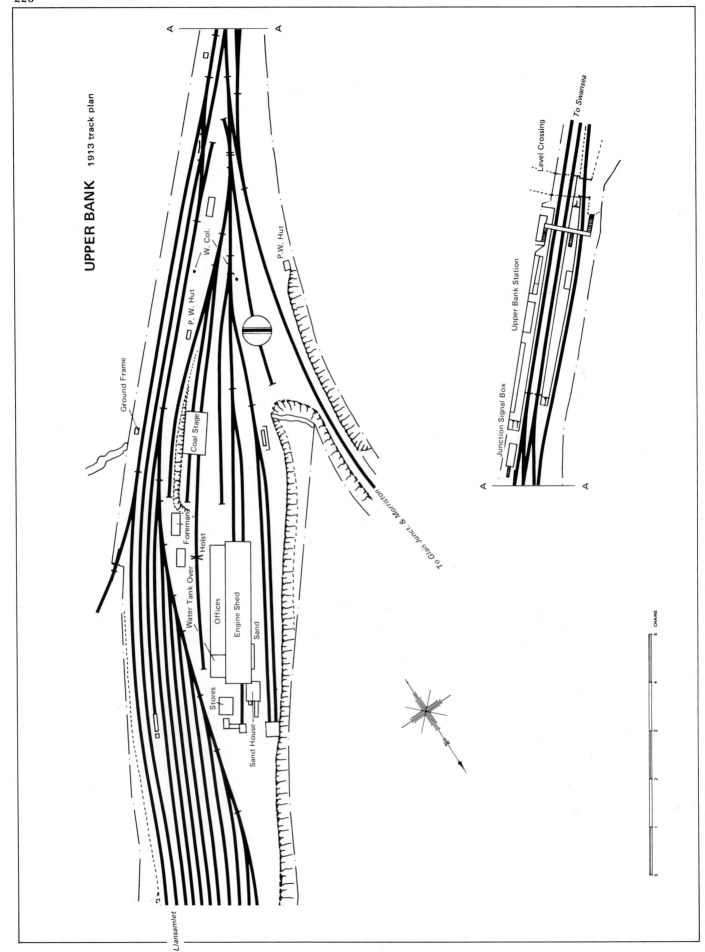

UPPER BANK 1913 track plan

Ground Frame

W. Col.

P. W. Hut

P.W. Hut

Coal Stage

Foreman

Water Tank Over

Hoist

Offices

Engine Shed

Sand

Stores

Sand House

To Glais Junct. & Morriston

To Llansamlet

Junction Signal Box

Upper Bank Station

Level Crossing

To Swansea

CHAINS

0 1 2 3 4 5

MR '3F' tank having its coal liberally doused on 27th August 1948. Both Upper Bank and Gurnos passed to the Western Division in 1926, becoming sub-sheds and carrying plates of Swansea ex-LNW. *H. C. Casserley.*

reorganisation of that year leaving it as 4C in the Shrewsbury District. The Western Region took over following Nationalisation and Upper Bank again became a sub-shed of Swansea ex-LNWR depot, now 87K. Swansea East Dock succeeded as parent on the closure of the old LNW shed in September 1959. By 1961 ex-GWR pannier tanks had taken over completely at Upper Bank (the last MR-built tanks having been transferred to the LMR in 1957) and at Whitsun that year the following examples were 'on shed' — Nos. 6700, 6738, 6741, 6755, 6762, 6764, 6765, 6767, 6777 and 6778. The sub-shed at Gurnos closed in April 1962 and its remaining engines and men transferred to its parent shed of MR days. Upper Bank itself closed on 4th February 1963.

Upper Bank on 9th July 1950. 'On shed' that day were '1F' tanks Nos. 41769, 41824 and 41860, MR '3F' tanks Nos. 47230, 47258, and 47259, and LMS '3F' engines Nos. 7481, 7681, 47478, 47479 and 47655.

T. J. Edgington

Wellingborough on 19th April 1959. The centre building was originally the 'coal shed' latterly becoming 'the Garratt Engine Shed' and also, evidently, housed a wheel drop. On the left is the store and smithy, the fitting shop of Midland days. The water softener adjacent stands on the site originally intended for a second roundhouse. 'No. 2' shed for some reason eventually appeared further to the south, where it survives in use today.

W. Potter

WELLINGBOROUGH

Wellingborough was a busy and important depot, tucked away amidst the Northamptonshire countryside. It was the centre of the scattered but highly developed Northamptonshire ironstone traffic and throughout most of the shed's existence its locos were concerned chiefly with the workings arising from the quarries, as well as vast quantities of coal from the East Midlands.

A new water tank, with pipes, etc. was provided for locomotive purposes in 1863, but it is not clear if a shed had already been built. In any event, improved facilities were much needed by 1867 when tenders were accepted for the construction of a new roundhouse, Messrs. Cox agreeing to construct the shed at a cost of £12,558.14s.10d. with Messrs. Swingler & Co. providing the ironwork for £3,036.14s.1d. Opened the following year, it stood on the east side of the line, with a four road fitting shop appearing in 1869. This last feature was set back a considerable distance to the rear of the shed to allow for the construction of a further roundhouse, the proposal eventually materialising as a separate 'square shed' sited some distance to the south, the reserved area remaining unused. This

Wellingborough from the footpath, 1st May 1960. Most notable engine present is ex-LNER 'B17' 4—6—0 No. 61660. This was the only known visit of this class to Wellingborough, arranged for the photographer's benefit.

K. Fairey

Two of Wellingborough's freight engines, outside 'No. 1' shed on 24th September 1955.

H. C. Casserley

left the fitting shop in a curiously 'marooned' position separate from both sheds. The new 'No. 2' opened in 1872, a tender of £10,119.4s.5d. having been accepted by the company in April of the previous year. A new 'double' coal stage serving both roundhouses replaced the old 'coal shed' in 1881 which fortunately survived to find a new lease of life from the 1930s, as a shelter for the huge Garratt engines.

LMS developments included new coal and ash plants in the 1930s, the reconditioning of 'No. 1' shed roof, the provision of a water softener and a 60 ft turntable in 'No. 1' shed. This last item required extensive rearrangement of the cast iron supporting columns and the table inside 'No. 2' shed remained 55 ft in diameter. 'No. 1' was afterwards used as the running shed, though some repairs and boiler washouts were undertaken whilst 'No. 2' served as the 'concentration' shed, where all the major mileage examinations and boiler cleaning were carried out.

Most of the shed's complement were 0−6−0s engaged on heavy freight work and, apart from ten of the Schenectady 2−6−0s at work in the 1900s, they remained in sole charge until the arrival of Fowler 0−8−0s in 1929 and Garratts in 1930. In 1921 the allocation comprised eighty 0−6−0s, five 0−6−0Ts for shunting, seven 2−4−0s for main line local passenger work, four 0−4−4Ts for the Higham Ferrers and Northampton branches and a trio of surviving Johnson singles, Nos. 603, 640 and 672. Four years earlier eight ex-LTSR Baltic tanks, Nos. 2100-2107 were at the shed as freight pilots, in an attempt to ease the wartime locomotive shortage. Ten of the articulated locos and five 0−8−0s were at work by June 1933 and all but thirteen of the remaining sixty locos were 0−6−0s, in the main '3F's and '4F's of MR and LMS origin. A single '1F' tank No. 1810 remained, with six LMS 0−6−0Ts and Johnson 2−4−0s, Nos. 127, 203 and 251 and 0−4−4Ts Nos. 1230, 1246 and 1259. These worked local passenger trains on the lines to Bedford, Leicester, Northampton, Kettering and Higham Ferrers. The Garratts disappeared before the end of the Second World War and the ranks of the 0−6−0s were drastically reduced by an influx of over thirty new Stanier '8F' 2−8−0s. Ex-LNWR locos were also present, in the shape of 0−8−0s Nos. 9438 and 9443. They had been provided for ironstone workings but spent most of their time 'on shed', being unpopular with the ex-Midland men. In any case their stay was only temporary after transfer of the LMS 'G3' engines to the Central Division.

A few 'Tilbury Tanks' including *Thundersley* itself were at the shed from 1947 to 1953 and No. 41922 on

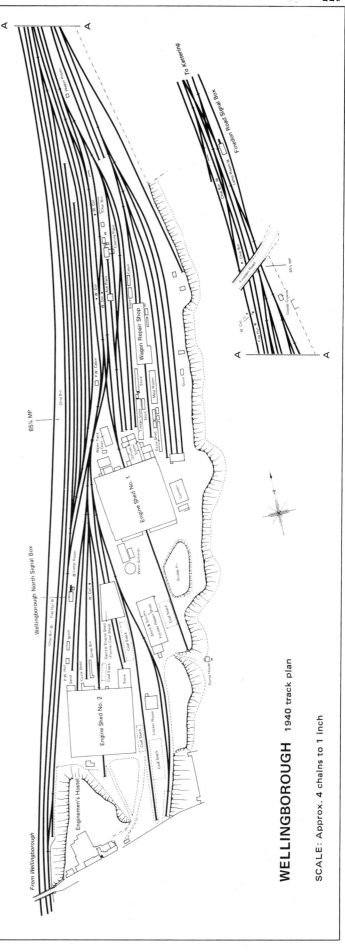

WELLINGBOROUGH 1940 track plan

SCALE: Approx. 4 chains to 1 inch

Wellingborough's 'elevator' type coaler on 5th May 1960, with '8F' 2–8–0 No. 48007. These units were conceived by C. J. Bowen-Cooke of the LNWR and were first introduced at Upperby (Carlisle) in 1919. One or two further units were provided at non-LNW sheds in the years immediately following Grouping.   *K. Fairey*

the Northampton trains in 1950 was probably the last of its class on passenger work. '9F' 2–10–0s including the ten Crosti-boilered examples came to Wellingborough in 1954. Various ex-LNER engines, principally 'V2' 2–6–2s, but also more rarely 'B1' 4–6–0s were to be found at the shed for repairs following the transfer of the Great Central main line to the London Midland Region. A 'J6' 0–6–0, in fact, No. 64256, managed to spend a few relaxing days on the Higham Ferrers goods in February 1959. The last 0–4–4T was transferred to Plaistow in 1954 and by 1956 an unlikely loco was 'spare engine' for the Higham Ferrers branch, ex-L & Y 2–4–2T No. 50650. '01' 2–8–0 No.

The former 'coal shed' and 'No. 2' roundhouse, 6th June 1959.   *T. Wright*

2–4–0 No. 20194 inside Wellingborough, June 1936. The turntable has been set to allow a Garratt entry to the roundhouse, either for shunting purposes or to allow the articulated loco to stable on the siding at the rear.

W. Potter

Inside 'No. 1' shed on 2nd June 1957, showing the rearranged supporting pillars and girders necessary on the installation of the new 60 ft turntable.

C. I. K. Field

Wellingborough on a hazy September evening in 1950.

B. Hilton

63742 was to be seen on the same duties on 25th May the same year.

As shed No. 13 under the Midland, with Northampton, 13a, as sub-shed, Wellingborough acquired 'concentration' depot status in 1935, becoming 15A. Diesel shunters had arrived in 1954 and in 1960, after a period of depressed activity, the depot's work had increased such that 'WD' 2—8—0s were being borrowed from other sheds. This was

a brief interregnum, however, and traffic continued to disappear. In September 1963 the shed became 15B under Leicester and the remaining steam engines were dispensed with on 13th June 1966. 'No. 1' shed had been demolished in July 1964 but the rest of the depot was adapted to service diesels, a function it still performs, although the 'No. 2' roundhouse itself is now occupied by a private concern.

An '8F' 2—8—0 stands vigil at the demolition of 'No. 1' shed on 2nd July 1964.

K. Fairey

Westhouses on Sunday, 8th July 1951. The majority of locos on view are '8F' 2—8—0s, Nos. 48057, 48060, 48118, 48136, 48333, 48353, and 48650, with 0—6—0s Nos. 43317, 43580, 43850, 58166 and 58196. Inside the shed were a further fifteen 0—6—0s, mainly '4F's, a standard '3F' tank and another half dozen '8F's.

B. K. B. Green

WESTHOUSES

Plans and estimates totalling £21,750 were considered on 1st March 1889 and 'Westhouses and Blackwell' engine shed came into use in the following year. Part of its title which soon disappeared was derived from the nearby 'Blackwell Branch'. It was a six road straight shed built in brick, and equipped with a 'single' coal stage and a 50 ft turntable from Eastwood Ltd. Like a number of sheds opened by the Midland in Nottinghamshire and Derby-shire, Westhouses, Midland shed number 22, existed largely to serve the local coal industry and by 1921 housed four 2—4—0s, five '1F' tanks, twenty-nine Kirtley double-framed 0—6—0s, eighteen Johnson 0—6—0s and five '4F' locos. The shed was virtually closed for a period in the 1930s as a result of the Depression, being used as a stabling and booking on point only. Maintenance and washing out was performed at Toton during this time and was not resumed at Westhouses until 1939. At the end of the LMS's existence the complement stood at something over fifty, the old Midland engines being replaced at first by

Westhouses on 9th August 1964. The steep descent to the shed yard from the Blackwell Branch is evident in this photograph. *W. Potter*

234

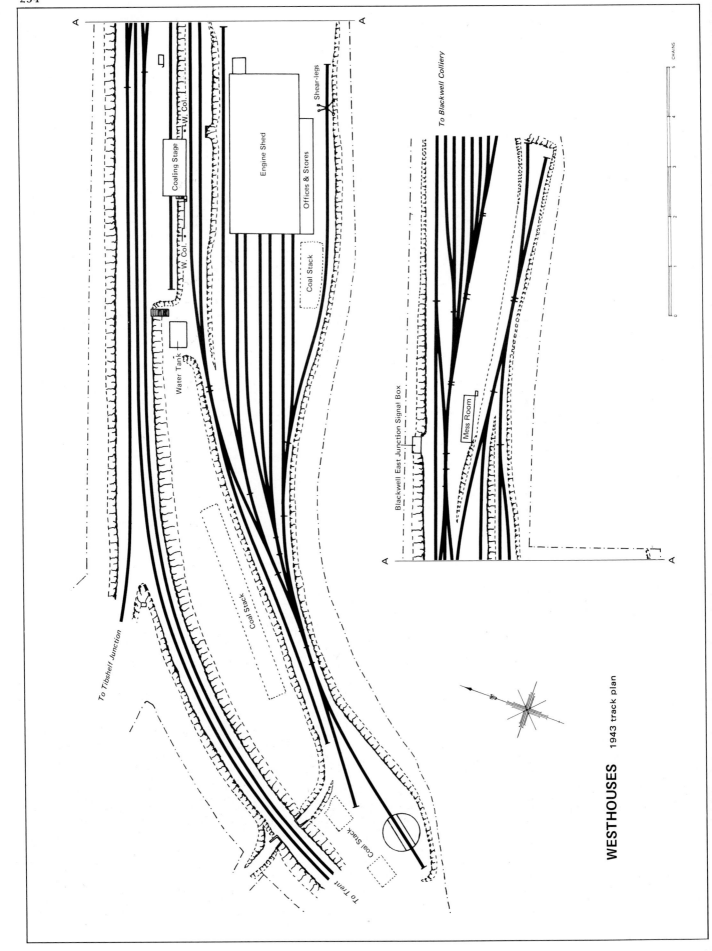

To Tibshelf Junction

To Trent

Coal Stack

Coal Stack

Water Tank

Coaling Stage

S. W. Col.

N. W. Col.

Engine Shed

Offices & Stores

Coal Stack

Shear-legs

To Blackwell Colliery

Blackwell East Junction Signal Box

Mess Room

A

A

A

A

WESTHOUSES   1943 track plan

0   1   2   3   4   5   CHAINS

Shed and yard on 7th September 1958.   *B. Hilton*

'3F' and '4F' locos, Fowler 0—8—0s and eventually '8F' 2—8—0s. A pair of BR 2—10—0s arrived in 1957, moving on to Tyne Dock, but succeeded by new engines Nos. 92113-92120.

No developments of any note, mechanical or structural occurred at the depot and very little was done even when it was finally given over to diesel servicing in 1966. Its last '4F' 0—6—0s, Nos. 44113, 44203, 44218 and 44278 were out of use early that year and by September 1966 the

only steam locos still at the shed were four '3F' tanks manned by NCB crews and used in the nearby William-thorpe Colliery. Westhouses was finally closed to steam on 3rd October 1966 and subsequently found use as a diesel stabling point. The tank engines for the NCB's use were in fact dealt with for a further year, until 7th October 1967. Westhouses had been 18B from 1935, but obtained its final code, 16G, when the district was disbanded in September 1963.

A drizzling afternoon at Westhouses, 4th July 1954.   *W. Potter*

0—6—0 tank No. 1347 outside
Barnoldswick shed in MR days.
Courtesy R. Higgins

Sheds Closed Prior to 1947

'ANCOATS, HYDE'

Despite being coded 21e, an outstation of Belle Vue in Symes' 1911 list, there was never a shed building here. The name in fact is a corruption of Ancoats, Hydc, referring to the *hydraulic* station and not to a shed at all. The actual district of Hyde is several miles from Ancoats and this instance illustrates the fallibility of 'lists', official or otherwise, when one is dealing with engine sheds!

APPLEBY

Appleby was included in the 1911 list, coded 33a, but the single road shed, on the 'up' side south of the station had been demolished in the early 1900s. There was, however, a turntable with siding, ashpit and an office/mess, situated by the spur north of the station connecting the Midland line with the NER Eden Valley branch. On Grouping it ceased to be regarded as a 'locomotive station'.

ASHCHURCH

Foundations for a turntable were laid at Ashchurch in 1863 and it was ordered 'that a temporary shed for one engine be erected' at the same time. In 1863 'a corrugated iron locomotive shed' was ordered to be provided, at a cost of £35 and in 1914, an indication that rising prices are by no means a modern phenomenon, the coal stage received a new roof, 'estimated cost, £50'. The shed itself may have gone out of use by this time and in any case did not survive the Grouping.

AVONMOUTH

There was a small one road shed and coal stage here, with access direct from a 60 ft turntable. The Midland operated the line jointly with the GWR and decisions taken by the joint committee of the 'Clifton Extension Railway' were

separately approved by the two owners. The Midland provided a new water column in 1902 and erected the turntable but the shed appears to have been used mainly by the Great Western. It went out of use in 1924.

BARNOLDSWICK

Coded 30c under Skipton, there was a tiny one road shed here by 1880, when an 0—4—2WT was allocated. The shed presumably opened with the line and was still operational on 21st June 1923. By July 1926 it had gone out of use.

BARNSLEY

On 18th April 1871 the Way and Works Committee heard that the construction of a loco shed at Barnsley had been delayed because of difficulties in purchasing the necessary land. No subsequent reference has been discovered, and it is probable that the shed never materialised.

BATH

The Midland had its own separate building here, a two road stone structure close by the Somerset and Dorset shed. It operated more or less independently under Bristol (coded 8a) until 1928, being afterwards used mainly for storage. A detailed history of both buildings will follow in a subsequent volume detailing, among other companies, the S & DJR.

BOURNE

This small two road building was regarded as a sub-shed of Peterborough, coded 9a, but was in fact Midland and Great Northern Joint Railway property. It had originally been owned by the Great Northern, evidenced by the following minute, of 20th May 1897 — 'Agreed to Engine Shed at Bourne, owned by the Great Northern Company

Brecon in the 1930s. It was never a 'Joint' shed, in terms of the MR/LMS jointly owning the land or facilities. Rent was paid for a single road, a practice continued by the LMS even after the disappearance of many of the workings in the early 1930s. The actual building originally belonged to the Brecon & Merthyr Railway, a second building alongside but offset and built for the Cambrian, being demolished around 1934.

Collection R. J. Essery

but situated on Joint Property, transferring to the M & GN Committee, accountants to settle later'. Four engines were allocated in 1926 but the shed closed as far as the LMS was concerned on 31st December 1932.

BRECON

The Midland shared the establishment here where two small sheds, of Cambrian Railway and Brecon & Merthyr Railway origin, dating from the 1860s, stood side by side. It was coded number 5 by the Midland, who provided a set of shear-legs to aid the maintenance of their locomotives, allotted only a single road in the shed. 0–6–0s Nos. 700-706 (2592-2598 in 1907) were stationed there for many years prior to 1900, forwarding freights from Swansea onwards to Worcester and Birmingham. It was a sub-shed of Swansea ex-LNW, coded A33 (W33 from 1930) by July 1926 when thirteen engines were on its

allocation, but it declined steadily in importance. The LMS ceased running passenger trains below Brecon from January 1931 and the through service to Swansea (St. Thomas') from Hereford, Hay and Brecon was discontinued. The company had little use for the accommodation after this, removing the shear-legs in 1933 and regularly stabling only two or three locos. It was really by now a GWR shed although the practice of stabling engines there survived until at least 1946, Brecon becoming officially 4C under Upper Bank in 1935.

BUXTON

Buxton shed appears to have opened around 1862/63, and was extended in 1884. The shed, in stone, was considerably lengthened and William Brown's tender of £1,433. 10s. 0d. was accepted on 15th May that year. Additional shear-legs were provided outside in 1903 and in 1899 proposals had

Buxton in 1935.

W. A. Camwell

An unfortunately flawed but nevertheless interesting view of Buxton (MR) in August 1934.   *W. Potter*

been afoot to construct an entirely new shed. Its two roads were inadequate for the number of engines in use and purchase of the necessary land was recommended in November 1899. Nothing came of all this, but a new engine pit and breakdown van siding had appeared by 1915.

Buxton had an importance that belied its small size and it was coded number 20, with Rowsley as a sub-shed. The much larger ex-LNWR establishment was the natural preference when the LMS got around to rationalising arrangements in the town, but the old MR shed was sufficiently important to be retained until the mid-1930s. In July 1926 the shed had thirty-seven engines, together with lifting and other facilities not enjoyed by the larger LNW establishment, with its fifty-four locos. New sidings had to be installed at the larger depot, which was also equipped with mechanical coal and ash plants and the remaining ex-Midland locos were finally transferred in 1935. The shed closed on 19th August and was afterwards demolished.

CAMBRIDGE

Midland locomotives, for many years 2–4–0 No. 239, working into Cambridge, stabled at the Great Eastern shed, but in the period 1892-1894 the minutes contain a number of references to a separate shed for the Midland's use. A proposal for a new shed 'in wood, with water tank, for two engines' costing £1565 was referred to the General Purposes Committee who 'deemed it more sensible to construct (the shed) in brick, total cost £1715'. If built, (which is still not clear!) it was presumably the building still intact on the east side of the line south of the station and reported in 1934 as 'closed a few years ago'. Its MR code was 12a under Kettering.

CARLISLE

The shed at Durran Hill, Carlisle, a standard roundhouse unit, opened in 1875 and housed the locos working over the Settle and Carlisle line from Leeds. The Glasgow and South Western Railway also stabled locos there, until its

MR days, when prosperity reigned at Durran Hill.   *Lens of Sutton*

Durran Hill in the summer of 1935. Two straight roads were added on the north side (to the left in this photograph). This has usually been attributed to the LMS, in order to house the 'Claughton' 4–6–0s used on the Carlisle turns from 1928-35, but in fact orders for the work date from 1912. Speculation has provided a number of possible reasons for the alterations, from snow plough accommodation to special stabling room for Glasgow & South Western 4–6–0s.

W. A. Camwell

own depot opened at Currock Junction in 1894. Two fitting shops, served by five turntables were also built, at the rear, and in 1901 a 60 ft turntable was provided in the yard. A second roundhouse had been proposed in 1907, but its construction was never implemented. The shed was coded 33 by the Midland and became 12C in the 1935 recoding, only to close in February of the following year.

Carlisle's final MR allocation had totalled over sixty locomotives and on 31st December 1922 included 2–4–0s Nos. 49 and 182, fourteen class '2' 4–4–0s and larger 4–4–0s Nos. 990-999, 1010 and 1023. There were seven '1F' tanks, Nos. 1650-1654, 1768 and 1769 and a variety of 0–6–0s, including '4F's Nos. 3997-3999 and 4000-4016.

Although officially closed, servicing facilities remained intact and it reopened for wartime use (after a spell as an army petrol dump) in 1943. The yard and facilities remained in use following the close of hostilities and the building continued as an engine store until November 1959, 'dead' ex-LTS 'Tilbury Tanks' Nos. 41971-41974 rusting outside from 1948 until at least 1955. By 1966 the building had been demolished.

CARNFORTH

Carnforth, a roundhouse of the square variety, opened in 1874, replacing a smaller building afterwards converted by the Traffic Department for wagon repairs. It stood on the north side of the Wennington line and although described as 'joint' in contemporary Midland minutes, it is not thought that Furness Railway engines were serviced there.

Coded number 31, the shed's engines, mainly 0–6–0s, worked freights from the Furness district along the 'Little North Western' towards Leeds. 2–4–0s were available for passenger traffic. Along with the ex-FR shed it came under Western Division control following the Grouping and eventually went out of use when the new Carnforth depot opened in 1944. (It was sited more conveniently near the station and was described in full in Volume One). The shed was sold to a private user and is still intact today.

Carnforth in May 1934. *W. Potter*

CHELTENHAM

The MR had a road reserved for its own use at the Midland and South Western Junction Railway shed here.

LMS '3F' tank No. 16548 stabled at Cheltenham M & SWJ shed. Outstationed from Gloucester the single LMS loco kept here, with an outside road reserved for its use, shunted the MR/LMS sidings.

Collection R. Carpenter

The long-closed MR shed at Coventry in December 1936.   *W. A. Camwell*

COLNE

Coded 30b, a sub-shed of Skipton, Colne was a small two road stone building, having replaced an original shed dating from the 1840s. It stood to the north of the station and when in May 1891 a new 50 ft turntable was provided it was noted: 'The Lancashire and Yorkshire Railway Company agree to contribute to the annual cost of maintaining the buildings and works under which arrangement they will pay about £193 per annum instead of £100 per year as hitherto paid by them in the shape of rent'. The East Lancashire had been making use of the Midland shed since at least 1849 and its successor, the L & YR, did not finally vacate the premises until it erected its own, much larger shed to the south in 1900. Interestingly, both sheds at Colne, although on opposite sides of the line, were on the 'up' side, the 'down' line from Accrington becoming the 'up' line from Colne to Skipton!

Both sheds were made redundant by the LMS and were closed in September 1936, the ex-MR shed suffering demolition almost immediately. In happier times rebuilt '50' class 2—4—0s, dating originally from 1863, had been regular inmates at Colne and for many years Nos. 14 and 20 worked the Skipton trains, subsequently running through to Otley over the new Skipton and Ilkley line, opened in 1889. Nos. 122A and 145A, nearing the end of their careers, formed the allocation in 1892.

COVENTRY

There was a small one road shed here, at the Birmingham end of the 'down' platform, built by the Midland in the 1860s when the company began working its own goods trains from Nuneaton. It provided a home for a single Kirtley 0—6—0 for many years, outstationed from Leicester, but it closed in 1904. The building was not finally demolished until 1959.

Another view of Coventry.   *L & GRP*

DONCASTER

Coded 25c under Sheffield, the 'Engine Station' of the 1911 list is presumed to have been the Great Northern establishment. A solitary 0—6—0, No. 440, was allocated in 1880.

EVESHAM

The small shed at Evesham, later coded 7b under Gloucester, was erected in 1870/71. Water pipes 'to the new shed' were laid in 1870 at a cost of £49, as well as a tank with water crane and gas fittings, costing £47, installed the following year. Ten years later a single 2—4—0, No. 182, was shown allocated, but by the early 1890s no regular engine was assigned here. Consideration was given to a replacement shed and in 1899, on 21st September, the matter arose at a meeting of the Way and Works Committee. A new shed was proposed, but this idea was

The closed shed at Malvern, intact on 27th May 1937, with No. 3078 alongside.

W. A. Camwell

rejected, 'postponed, so that an alternative plan and estimate can be prepared'. The shed (two roads with a 42 ft turntable) closed on 14th September 1931, but as late as 1954 engines were still stabled there (fires were cleaned, crews signed on and off etc.).

GREAT MALVERN

On 16th January 1866 the members of the Way and Works Committee listened to the sombre news: 'the recent gales have carried away the roof of the Engine Shed at Malvern Wells Junction', and that a local builder had been employed to replace it. The building was less than two years old and some twenty years later, in 1883, 'the present engine shed' was 'renewed in wood' by Messrs. S. Robertson at a cost of £126. In June 1898 gas fittings were supplied to 'the extension of the engine shed, authorised in September 1897. The shed, coded 4b, was administered by Worcester and stabled the branch engine, normally an 0–4–4T, finally closing on 14th September 1931. The turntable and water tank remained in use, until at least 1939, but the shed itself was dismantled. It had been more generally known as Malvern and at the time of its 'renewal in wood' had housed 2–4–0 No. 184. Twenty years later this had been replaced by an 0–4–4T, No. 1832.

HARROGATE

The Midland stabled two engines at the North Eastern Railway shed at Starbeck, Harrogate, a practice which continued until September 1928. It had begun in the late 1880s and the company at first paid £25 per annum for the privilege. It was regarded as part of the Bradford district and in the early years of this century the 2–4–0 No. 156, the first of a famous class, was housed there, working MR trains between Harrogate and Bradford.

HENDON *See Cricklewood.*

HEMEL HEMPSTEAD

This was a tiny one road shed, built in timber with entry direct from a turntable sited immediately outside. In February 1877 the cost of a water tank, pipes, sand

The site of the shed at Hemel, long demolished. *W. A. Camwell*

The old shed at Hendon in 1964, steadily falling further into ruin. *W. T. Stubbs*

furnace and washing out apparatus was estimated at £162 and the shed itself was more or less complete by July. Visited by officers of the company during the period 11th–14th September 1877, it was noted that: 'The new engine shed at Hemel Hempstead was inspected. The cost of this wood building to be obtained showing separately the cost of the water tank. The building met the approval

Hereford on 20th July 1935.
W. A. Camwell

of the Committee as being suitable for similar locations'. A surprisingly large allocation of six 0—6—0Ts is shown for 1880, Nos. 1121-1125 and 1128, while by 1905 Midland & Great Northern Joint Railway 4—4—0T No. 8, plus a Pullman car, was to be found working the branch. The shed went out of use at an unknown date prior to 1911 and has since been demolished.

HEREFORD

The Midland shed at Hereford, known as Moorfields to distinguish it from its LNWR and GWR neighbours, was coded 5a, a sub-shed of the Brecon district. It was of relatively modern design and replaced an older, smaller structure. In 1892 this had housed an old Little North Western 0—4—2T and a Kirtley goods engine. Provided with a Cowans Sheldon 50 ft turntable, the new shed opened in 1894 and serviced locos working off the South Wales line, particularly Upper Bank '1F' and '3F' 0—6—0Ts on freights from Brecon and Swansea. It closed shortly after Grouping, on 10th December 1924, and its locos and men were afterwards accommodated at the town's ex-LNWR shed, Barrs Court.

HITCHIN *photo on page 19*

Until the opening of the London Extension, of course, Hitchin was the point where the Midland forwarded its traffic for the capital. Its trains were worked to Kings Cross over Great Northern metals and thus in the 1860s Hitchin was of considerable importance. After 1868 it rapidly took on the air of a country branch, but nevertheless the shed continued in use and indeed was subsequently rebuilt. On 2nd January 1861 a Mr. Hutchinson had reported that he 'had let the Engine Shed at Hitchin (now not used) to Messrs. Lucas & Franklin, at £26 p.a.' A new shed had been erected but thirty years later was itself replaced. On 17th December 1891 it was ordered: 'that a new engine shed be erected at Hitchin 70' long to replace one 115' long blown down on the 11th ultimo'. Messrs. J. Hicks' tender of £760. 13s. 2½d. was duly accepted the following year, on 5th February and on 5th May 1894 orders were issued from Derby to remove the redundant 42 ft turntable from Bedford and install it at Hitchin. The shed became 14a under Bedford and for many years stabled Johnson 0—4—4Ts and 2—4—0s on passenger work and 0—6—0s off the branch goods. The turntable was reported

still in use as late as 1960, but the shed itself apparently went out of use prior to the Grouping. It is still standing, in excellent condition.

HULL

When the Midland introduced a passenger service to Hull from Milford Junction in 1883, according to Ahrons, 2—4—0s Nos. 53, 54 and 55 (190-192 in 1907) 'were sent to Hull'. The shed involved was presumably the old North Eastern Railway building, by Paragon station, but the MR locos, latterly 2—2—2s, were withdrawn on the termination of the service in 1889.

KINGS CROSS

The roundhouse at Kings Cross 'Top Shed' was for the exclusive use of Midland engines working in from Hitchin and remained under the supervision of a Midland foreman until the opening of St. Pancras in 1868. After this the 'Derby Shed', as it was known, was given over to the Great Northern, who used it for tanks and goods engines.

LIVERPOOL

A three road wooden building of Manchester Sheffield and Lincolnshire Railway origin, the shed opened about 1872. It was actually at Brunswick near the city's docks and MR engines began making use of it from 1873, additional sidings being provided to accommodate them. The shed rapidly became overcrowded and the MSL constructed a new brick shed for its own use on the opposite side of the line, bequeathing the original building to the Midland. 'Liverpool', coded 19 by the MR, was concerned principally with passenger engines, goods types being dealt with mainly at the sub-shed, Walton. For many years the ten original 6' 6" 4—4—0s of 1876 were based there and Nos. 1318-1321 (306-309 in 1907) were at the shed in the 1890s. The surviving engines were transferred away during the Great War and several Johnson singles were resident, Nos. 620-623, for Liverpool portions of St. Pancras expresses (to and from Cheadle Heath or Chinley) until the early 1920s. The shed closed in February 1929 when the complement comprised only five locos, 4—4—0s Nos. 350, 351, 353 and 443 and 0—6—0 No. 4247. LMS engines subsequently made use of a single road in the 'new shed' opposite, a practice which did not finally cease until June 1945. The passenger locos in 1929

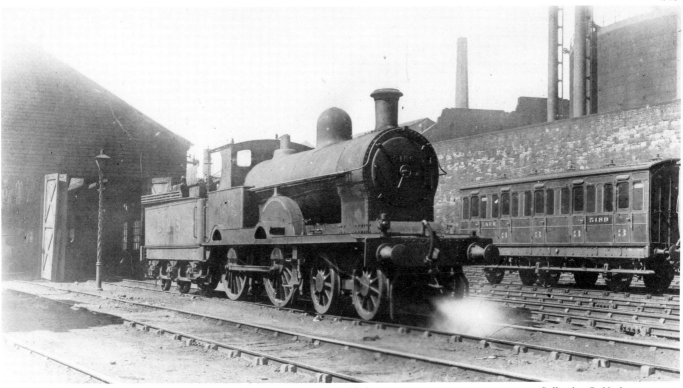

Ex-LNWR 'Renown: 4—4—0 No. 5155 *Irresistible* at Brunswick around 1928.   *Collection B. Mathews*

had still worked the Liverpool Central-Chinley trains (with a through coach to London) and the previous year had included three ex-LNW 'Renown' 4—4—0s, Nos. 5155 *Irresistible*, 5157 *Black Prince* and one other.

LOWER DARWEN

The Lancashire and Yorkshire Railway's Blackburn shed was yet another of this company's buildings to stable Midland engines, a couple of them residing here for a while for the Marple workings. 'Over Darwen', as it was known in its early years, also serviced Midland locos off the Liverpool Exchange—Hellifield trains, which were joined to the Manchester portions at Blackburn. This shed will be fully covered in a future volume of this series.

MARKET HARBOROUGH

In March 1869 plans and estimates were received for a shed here to house two locos, costing £1720, but in May it was decided merely to erect a 'Temporary Engine Shed (in wood)' Neither of these proposals appears to have been carried out but in November 1870 it was at least decided to provide an engine pit.

NAILSWORTH

The Nailsworth branch opened in 1867, the small wooden engine shed being erected in the same year. By 1873 the coal stage required replacement and the shed also was in poor condition. By November 1895, it was disused and the Locomotive Committee recommended removal of the water tank and coal stage, for use elsewhere.

NEWARK

There was reportedly a shed here, 'closed 14th September 1931' but examination of various maps back to the 1880s have failed to produce evidence of an actual shed building. It does not appear on the MR list of 1911 (not conclusive in itself), but there were certainly engine facilities prov-

ided. These comprised turntable, water tank, ashpit, office/mess, etc., sited by the connecting line to the Great Northern Railway.

NEWTON HEATH

Under arrangements made with the L & YR for Midland engines to work trains between the two main cities of Lancashire and Hellifield (connecting with Scotland) new 4—4—0s Nos. 1808-1813 (378-383 in 1907) were stationed at Newton Heath, the L & Y's largest depot. The idea was to avoid engines running light the 4½ miles between the L & YR station at Manchester Victoria and the MR shed at Belle Vue, but after a few years the locos were removed to their 'home ground'. The development of Newton Heath will be fully described in a subsequent volume covering sheds of Lancashire and Yorkshire origin.

NORTHAMPTON

This was one of the early series of 'standard' buildings, a two road brick built shed similar to St. Albans. As early as 6th September 1864 a tender for £683. 18s. 3d. had been accepted for the construction of the first shed at Northampton and by 1871 a further tender of £3500 for a shed to hold four locos was being discussed. The estimates were later raised to £6000 and a second shed eventually opened in 1873. The original building, which stood nearby, was subsequently demolished. Coded 13a, a sub-shed of Wellingborough throughout its existence, it housed a handful of 2—4—0s (six in both 1880 and 1892) engaged on branch workings from there or Bedford. With the much larger LNWR shed only a short distance away it closed shortly after the Grouping, on 1st October 1924.

NORTHWICH

Engines were outstationed at the CLC shed here (coded 21a by the Midland) from Belle Vue throughout MR and LMS days but the shed was not operated 'jointly' in the

Stockingford after closure, a standard straight shed constructed, unusually, in wood.

W. A. Camwell

same sense as Trafford Park or Heaton Mersey. On Nationalisation it was merged, of course, with other LMS sheds in the area and was amongst the last operational steam depots in the north-west.

OLNEY

A small one road shed with 50 ft turntable and 9000 gallon water tank was erected here in the early 1890s for the MR loco working the short lived passenger service to Towcester, over what was to become the SMJR. The shed officially closed in 1928 but locos were serviced on the site for many years, until the mid-1950s.

OVERSEAL

A two road shed built and operated jointly with the LNWR, the latter company made the greater use of the facilities. The official MR code was 2a, under Burton. This shed's history has been chronicled in detail in Volume 1 of this series.

POPLAR

There was a small shed here, coded 16a in 1911, for a single 0—6—0T and two sets of men. A plan had been examined in March 1889 for a small wooden 'engine house' for one engine, 'estimated cost £394' and its construction was approved on 18th July. By February 1890 the 'new engine shed at Poplar' was ready to receive gas lighting. There was also a battery locomotive at Poplar, No. 1550, housed in a separate establishment at West India Dock.

RUGBY

The origin of Rugby shed lay in the days when the Midland's London traffic was forwarded from this point, the Midland Counties Railway establishing a depot in the earliest days (probably 1840 and certainly by 1844). After Hitchin had partly inherited this role, Rugby declined steadily and indeed closed prior to the Grouping. Standing at the west end of the LNWR station it comprised two separate buildings, of four and two roads respectively, the tracks of the smaller shed leading onto a turntable (supplied in 1876) at the eastern extremity of the yard. Rugby was for long the home of the little Kirtley 2—2—2 engines dating from the 1860s. The allocation included five of them in the 1890s together with ten 0—6—0s. By

1936 demolition of all but the offices and water tank was complete.

SANDHILLS

Better known as Bank Hall, Nos. 1814-1818 (384-388 in 1907) of the series of 4—4—0s specially constructed for the Manchester/Liverpool-Hellifield traffic, were stationed at this L & YR shed for a number of years at the end of the nineteenth century. These were soon replaced by some of the earlier 6' 6" Kitson built engines dating from 1876, Nos. 1312-1317 (later 300-305) which remained at 'Sandhills' until the First World War. The full history of Bank Hall shed will be found in a subsequent volume in this series.

SHEEPBRIDGE and STAVELEY WORKS

The use of the MR engines at the various works dated from the well known 1866 Agreement, when the Midland agreed to supply locomotives for one hundred years, taking over the stock of the then Staveley Company. Sheepbridge was coded 24a under Staveley in MR days but, as with the small shed inside Staveley Works, its precise status is uncertain. The depots were on works property and regarded as sub-sheds really only for operating purposes. Staveley Works acquired fame through the prolonged survival of Johnson '1F' tanks on shunting work, due in part to the 1866 agreements. By 1961 a pair of 350 hp diesels were in use at Sheepbridge Works, manned by BR crews (unlike the steam locos in Staveley Works) and were stabled overnight on a pair of ashpits, all that remained of the old shed. In 1880 0—6—0s Nos 360-362 had been allocated and the parent shed had four 0—4—0STs, three 0—6—0WTs and an 0—6—0ST available for duty in the Works. The final steam allocation at Staveley Works comprised '1F' 0—6—0Ts Nos. 41708, 41734, 41763, 41804, 41835; ex-MR 0—4—0Ts Nos. 41528 and 41533; and Kitson 0—4—0Ts Nos. 47001 and 47005. By July 1966 these were in store at the rear of Canklow coaling stage, awaiting disposal instructions.

SPALDING

A lengthy correspondence, increasingly acrimonious, occupied the Midland and the Great Northern companies from 1893 to 1895. The GNR had stabled engines at the small shed here since 1868, paying rent to the Midland, but in 1893 the MR proposed stabling two of its own locos, as well as increasing the annual sum required of the Great Northern. This posed quite a problem for the latter company, the shed housing only four locos, 'two; with two outside'. After protracted altercation the problem was solved by altering the proposed workings, so that they could be taken over by the Midland and Great Northern Joint Committee.

STOCKINGFORD

The Midland's Nuneaton depot was a standard building in wood. A boiler, pump, water tank and columns etc. had been supplied as early as 1866, with a turntable installed in 1873, but the later shed had its origin in the present century. It had three roads, a coal stage and a 60 ft turntable, the original estimates having been obtained in 1901. Including land and new sidings these had amounted to over £18,000 with the successful tender for the building itself totalling £4754. 5s. 10d. Brick had been considered but the company finally decided on timber, being slightly cheaper, and the shed opened in 1903. Leicester was the parent depot and Stockingford was coded 10a. The shed closed on 7th November 1932 but the yard remained open for servicing and indeed with wartime congestion at the ex-LNWR Nuneaton shed, consideration was given to its reopening. This was never enacted, but locos were still making use of the yard as late as 1954, and crews working beyond Abbey Street still signed on and off at Stockingford. By 1960, however, the facilities were out of use and a 'to let' sign adorned the shed building.

STOKE

Engines were outstationed from Burton at the North Staffordshire Railway shed here, a practice rendered unnecessary following the formation of the LMS. It was given a code by the Midland, 2b.

Thornbury shed, in use as a garage, 25th August 1956.
T. J. Edgington

STROUD

There was a shed listed here in 1892, sub to Gloucester. It was not mentioned in 1880, or in 1911 and no further details are known.

THORNBURY

Coded 8b, Thornbury was a sub-shed of Bristol and appears to date from 1872, when a temporary engine shed was ordered to be erected 'as cheaply as possible'. A tank and water supply costing £400 were arranged at the same time, the shed housing the branch passenger engine. Twenty years after opening this had been Johnson 0—4—4T No. 1825. The shed closed with cessation of passenger services on 19th June 1944.

WAKEFIELD

The MR stationed engines here in the years up until Grouping, the depot being coded 26a under Normanton. The shed concerned was a small building in Westgate goods

Thornbury in 1935.

B. Mathews

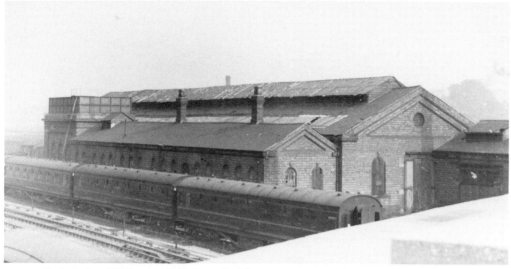

Pleck shed on 7th October 1962. It survived for many years, used for stock storage purposes.

W. T. Stubbs

yard, owned jointly with the Great Central. It was also known as Barn Lane, the MR stabling a single 0—6—0T and an 0—6—0.

WALSALL

Plans of the 'new metal shed' at Walsall, Pleck East Junction, were completed on 29th September 1879, the shed opening the following year. It was provided with a 50 ft turntable and measured 220 ft by 48 ft, with one of its three roads originally designed to pass right through the building. It was intended to accommodate twelve engines and eventually housed a collection of 0—6—0s and tanks amounting to rather more than this figure. The initial complement was made up of six 0—4—4Ts, an 0—6—0T No. 1417, and a pair of 2—4—0s, Nos. 86 and 120, and by 1892 the total had still not exceeded the accommodation available, with only four 0—6—0s allocated in addition to the six passenger tanks. The former LNW depot was dominant in the area and Walsall's duties passed to the old rivals' shed at Ryecroft on 2nd September 1925. The shed's code in Midland days had been 3b, with Saltley the parent shed.

WALTON

Walton-on-the-Hill was a four road shed, in northlight pattern style, sited alongside the small station on the outskirts of the city near Aintree. A CLC establishment, the Midland stabled their goods engines employed in the Liver-

pool district at the depot, five, Nos. 1778-1781 and 1794 being there in 1892. A couple of 0—4—0STs were allocated for work at Sandon Dock in 1897 and three or four remained until shortly after Grouping, when ex-L & Y 'pugs' replaced them. It was coded 19a under Liverpool (Brunswick) shed and though 'official closure' came as early as 1926, the *Railway Observer* of 1930 reported that over thirty LMS locos still made use of the shed, mainly 0—6—0s. The shed was coded 23F in 1935 and the LMS engines were removed shortly afterwards, in September 1936.

WEST BRIDGE

West Bridge was the Leicester terminus of the Leicester and Swannington Railway, opened in 1832 and there was a small shed here from the first, the doors requiring renewal in 1853, 'having been broken by an engine'. A few 0—6—0s were housed there for many years, No. 638 in 1880 and a few engines in the 1626-1631 series in the early 1890s. The shed was apparently rebuilt on a different site by the Midland, but closed in its turn on 26th June 1926. It had been coded 10c, a sub-shed of Leicester, throughout its existence and latterly housed the West Bridge shunting engine.

WIDNES

The Midland kept one or two engines at the two road CLC Tanhouse Lane shed for many years, the loco in 1880 being 0—6—0ST No. 1326. The practice continued with standard '3F' tanks well into LMS days. No. 7464 for instance was at Widnes (coded 19c by the MR) from March 1935 to December 1941.

WIGSTON *photos on pages 13 and 15*

This was a standard 'square shed' erected in 1873, along with a number of cottages, to provide much needed extra accommodation in the Leicester area. It relieved Leicester shed of a number of goods turns and later had a separate code, number 11. In 1880, apart from thirty-six 0—6—0s, a couple of small tanks were kept here, one of which, an old 2—4—0T built by Stephensons and numbered 203, worked the St. Pancras—Birmingham through carriage round the south curve between Wigston station and Glen Parva Junction. It was replaced by No. 201, an old

The 'new metal shed' at Walsall, Pleck, after closure.

W. H. Whitworth

Leicester West Bridge on 23rd September 1937. It officially went out of use in 1926 but engines continued to take water, etc. Shunting the adjacent yard on this day was ex-MR '2F' 0—6—0 No. 3190.

W. A. Camwell

0—4—2WT in 1885. By 1892 several 0—6—0Ts had arrived, including four of the '1377' class. Thus 0—6—0s and tanks comprised the bulk of the allocation, transferred to Leicester on the closure of Wigston on Guy Fawkes Day, 1934. It remained standing, however, and on the rebuilding of Leicester in the closing years of the war, was examined with a view to re-opening. It was partially opened to relieve the pressure on the main shed and was found to be in excellent condition, apart from broken windows. The major hindrance to servicing work was the lack of washout hydrants, thoughtlessly concreted over during

the shed's spell of inactivity! Leicester was more or less complete by 1946, but Wigston remained in use for engine storage and the stabling of return workings. It seems finally to have gone out of use in April 1955.

WIRKSWORTH

This was a two road shed, partly detailed in the introductory notes to this volume. It stabled the locomotives required for the branch passenger turns as well as the (still substantial) local stone traffic. It appears to have gone out of use around the turn of the century.

The shed at Wirksworth, closed for engine purposes but still in use for goods in 1956.

J. Shelbourn

The timber shed at Worcester on 27th May 1937.

W. A. Camwell

WORCESTER

Coded number 4 by the Midland, the first shed here came into use in 1870 and was rebuilt in 1894. 2—4—0s Nos. 189-192, dating originally from 1867, were at Worcester in the 1890s and except for No. 192, remained there for many years, the type generally giving way to older 4—4—0 engines following the Grouping. Only two 2—4—0s, Nos. 80 and 81, had been provided in 1880, the rest of the allocation comprising 0—6—0s Nos. 707-714. It closed on 12th December 1932, Saltley taking over responsibility for its sub-shed at Bromsgrove. Malvern, a second sub-shed, had closed the previous year. The building was demolished in 1939.

YORK

2—4—0s Nos. 55, 56, 57, 58 and 59 (193-196 in 1907) were sent to York in May 1879 on the opening of the Swinton and Knottingley Joint line to passengers and the North Eastern Railway allowed them to be stabled in a circular roundhouse next to their own, similar, building at the south end of the station. They were joined by five 0—6—0s, increasing to eight by 1892. Midland engines continued to make use of this building until after the Grouping, after which they were transferred across the line to share quarters with the former Lancashire and Yorkshire engines at Queen Street shed. As late as 1926 the two had still been separate, with seventeen engines at the MR roundhouse and four at the L & Y depot. In 1930 the allocation included Compounds Nos. 1198 and 1199 mainly for express work to Liverpool Exchange and Manchester Victoria and in 1931 the first two LMS '2P' 4—4—0s were there, Nos. 563 and 564. In 1933 these latter two were accompanied by MR '3P' locos Nos. 728 and 729. In 1932 the LMS engines were again transferred, across to the former Great North of England straight shed adjoining the 'South' roundhouses, the allocation being officially withdrawn on the outbreak of war, a solitary class '5' having been allocated the previous year. The MR code was 27, changed to 19F in 1935. The building was latterly used for the storage of redundant locos and was finally demolished in 1963.

'York LMS' shed.

Collection W. A. Camwell

1945 ALLOCATION LIST

Power classifications did not remain static throughout the LMS period and further alterations came about in BR days. For continuity and clarity the final and most familiar BR codes have been employed in the following 1945 allocation.

4C UPPER BANK

MR '1F' 0—6—0T	1769, 1824, 1852, 1860, 1864, 1893
MR '3F' 0—6—0T	7230, 7232, 7256, 7258, 7259
LMS '3F' 0—6—0T	7477, 7478, 7479, 7480, 7481

14A CRICKLEWOOD

LMS (Fowler) '3MT' 2—6—2T	21, 22, 23, 24, 25, 26, 27, 28, 31, 32, 34, 35, 39
MR '1P' 0—4—4T	1294, 1385
MR '1F' 0—6—0T	1712, 1724, 1805, 1811, 1829
'Crab' 2—6—0	2839, 2855
MR '2F' 0—6—0	2987, 3049, 3150, 3366, 3508
MR '3F' 0—6—0	3246, 3261, 3313, 3400, 3408, 3440, 3565, 3800, 3806
MR '4F' 0—6—0	3858, 3934, 3947, 3965, 3992, 3995
LMS '4F' 0—6—0	4028, 4029, 4043, 4228, 4425, 4457, 4581, 4582, 4590
MR '3F' 0—6—0T	7200, 7201, 7203, 7204, 7205, 7206, 7207, 7208, 7209, 7210, 7211, 7212, 7213, 7214, 7215, 7216, 7217, 7218, 7219, 7220, 7221, 7222, 7223, 7224, 7225, 7226, 7227, 7244, 7251, 7252
LMS '3F' 0—6—0T	7433, 7434, 7435, 7621

14B KENTISH TOWN

LMS (Fowler) '3MT' 2—6—2T	29, 30, 33, 36, 37, 38, 40, 64
LMS (Stanier) '3MT' 2—6—2T	92, 100, 114, 148, 149, 166, 167
MR '2P' 4—4—0	477, 547
LMS '4P' 4—4—0	1051, 1054, 1074
MR '1P' 0—4—4T	1374, 1377, 1379, 1380
MR '1F' 0—6—0T	1660, 1661, 1664, 1668, 1671, 1672, 1674, 1713, 1850
LMS (Fowler) '4MT' 2—6—4T	2333, 2335, 2383
LMS (Stanier) '4MT' 2—6—4T	2479, 2550, 2556, 2558
MR '2F' 0—6—0	2990, 3016, 3021, 3149, 3764
MR '4F' 0—6—0	3887
LMS '4F' 0—6—0	4176, 4229, 4235, 4470, 4529, 4531, 4532, 4563, 4584, 4601, 4602
Stanier '5MT' 4—6—0	4806, 4810, 4816, 4817, 4822, 4829, 4830, 4846, 4855, 5041, 5065, 5068, 5267, 5277, 5279, 5285, 5288, 5342
'Jubilee' 4—6—0	5610, 5614, 5615, 5616, 5639, 5650, 5654, 5662, 5663, 5667, 5682, 5685
MR '3F' 0—6—0T	7229, 7240, 7241, 7242, 7245, 7246
LMS '3F' 0—6—0T	7260, 7262, 7263, 7282, 7283, 7427, 7428, 7429, 7432, 7640, 7644, 7645

14C ST. ALBANS

LMS (Stanier) '3MT' 2—6—2T	91, 161
MR '1F' 0—6—0T	1854
LMS (Fowler) '4MT' 2—6—4T	2300, 2302, 2325, 2328, 2329, 2374, 2377, 2380
MR '3F' 0—6—0	3245, 3801
LMS '3F' 0—6—0T	7261

15A WELLINGBOROUGH

LMS (Stanier) '3MT' 2—6—2T	116
MR '1P' 0—4—4T	1239, 1246, 1340
MR '1F' 0—6—0T	1781
MR '3F' 0—6—0	3796, 3797, 3808, 3830
MR '4F' 0—6—0	3870, 3876, 3909, 3977, 3982
LMS '4F' 0—6—0	4033, 4134, 4160, 4242, 4287, 4332, 4403, 4574, 4575
MR '3F' 0—6—0T	7238
LMS '3F' 0—6—0T	7264, 7265, 7279, 7333, 7446, 7543, 7554, 7636, 7642
Stanier '8F' 2—8—0	8024, 8050, 8082, 8141, 8167, 8180, 8181, 8198, 8222, 8264, 8278, 8281, 8305, 8334, 8338, 8359, 8360, 8363, 8364, 8365, 8492, 8617, 8644, 8645, 8646, 8651, 8671, 8678, 8692, 8694, 8695, 8699
LNW 0—8—0	9438, 9443
LMS '7F' 0—8—0	9536, 9544, 9563, 9596, 9599

15B KETTERING

MR '2P' 4—4—0	454, 537, 550
MR '1F' 0—6—0T	1889
MR '2F' 0—6—0	2999, 3011, 3038, 3042, 3095, 3195, 3416, 3525, 3551, 3561, 3566, 3601, 22930
MR '3F' 0—6—0	3782
MR '4F' 0—6—0	3888, 3889, 3896
LMS '4F' 0—6—0	4232, 4278, 4465
LMS '3F' 0—6—0T	7437
Stanier '8F' 2—8—0	8285, 8355, 8356, 8491, 8704
LMS '7F' 0—8—0	9501, 9572, 9580, 9583
MR '1P' 2—4—0	20216

15C LEICESTER

LMS (Stanier) '3MT' 2—6—2T	75, 145, 171, 182
MR '2P' 4—4—0	536, 538, 542, 543, 549
LMS '2P' 4—4—0	563
MR '3P' 4—4—0	707, 738, 740, 763
MR '4P' 4—4—0	1008, 1010, 1011, 1020, 1023, 1031, 1039, 1041, 1042
LMS '4P' 4—4—0	1061, 1071, 1088, 1089
MR '1P' 0—4—4T	1402, 1407
LTSR '3P' 4—4—2T	2119, 2120, 2121
LMS (Fowler) '4MT' 2—6—4T	2331, 2334
'Crab' 2—6—0	2791, 2792, 2795
MR '2F' 0—6—0	3081, 3166, 3190, 3423, 3430, 3648, 3688, 22954
MR '3F' 0—6—0	3183, 3205, 3232, 3326, 3333, 3411, 3467, 3653, 3676, 3710, 3728, 3748, 3790, 3807, 3829
MR '4F' 0—6—0	3937
LMS '4F' 0—6—0	4031, 4034, 4231, 4423
MR '3F' 0—6—0	7248
LMS '3F' 0—6—0T	7441, 7442, 7533, 7534
Stanier '8F' 2—8—0	8006, 8132, 8211, 8309, 8397, 8398, 8399, 8619, 8668

15D BEDFORD

LMS (Stanier) '3MT' 2—6—2T	141, 162, 165
MR '2P' 4—4—0	510, 548, 551
MR '3P' 4—4—0	755, 762
MR '4P' 4—4—0	1007, 1009, 1013, 1017, 1034, 1038

LMS '4P' 4—4—0	1070, 1091
MR '1P' 0—4—4T	1260, 1272, 1273, 1302, 1401
MR '1F' 0—6—0T	1793, 1810
MR '2F' 0—6—0	3157, 3164, 3707, 22933, 22968
MR '3F' 0—6—0	3222, 3402, 3428, 3474, 3721, 3766, 3768, 3777, 3785
MR '4F' 0—6—0	3910, 3926, 3967, 3971
LMS '4F' 0—6—0	4362

16A NOTTINGHAM

LMS (Stanier) '3MT' 2—6—2T	99, 147, 160, 163, 164, 172, 178, 193
MR '2P' 4—4—0	394, 404, 411, 415, 416, 417, 419, 427, 478, 496, 498, 502, 504, 535, 540, 559, 560
MR '3P' 4—4—0	719, 739, 747, 757
MR '4P' 4—4—0	1002, 1012, 1032
LMS '4P' 4—4—0	926, 929, 1050, 1094, 1096
MR '1P' 0—4—4T	1230, 1249, 1344, 1382, 1409, 1423, 1425
MR '1F' 0—6—0T	1666, 1727, 1762, 1826, 1895
LTSR '2P' 4—4—2T	2096, 2099, 2101, 2103, 2104, 2109
LMS (Fowler) '4MT' 2—6—4T	2338, 2339, 2361
LMS (Stanier) '4MT' 2—6—4T	2555
'Crab' 2—6—0	2794, 2823, 2899
MR '2F' 0—6—0	3051, 3054, 3073, 3177, 3262, 3377, 3511, 3602, 3696, 22941, 22944
MR '3F' 0—6—0	3185, 3192, 3249, 3324, 3367, 3369, 3378, 3399, 3458, 3538, 3564, 3637, 3711, 3724, 3729
MR '4F' 0—6—0	3869, 3933, 3948, 3954, 3956, 3958, 3962, 3969, 3994
LMS '4F' 0—6—0	4030, 4039, 4047, 4055, 4095, 4107, 4108, 4131, 4132, 4158, 4164, 4180, 4215, 4223, 4230, 4247, 4264, 4266, 4267, 4275, 4313, 4401, 4408, 4412, 4414, 4416, 4480, 4533, 4546, 4577, 4578
LMS '5MT' 4—6—0	4825, 4827, 4861
LMS '3F' 0—6—0T	7277, 7422, 7438, 7485, 7539, 7549, 7552, 7629, 7631, 7632, 7637
Stanier '8F' 2—8—0	8003, 8070, 8134, 8170, 8206, 8207, 8217, 8218, 8275, 8279, 8282, 8293, 8380, 8381, 8614, 8635, 8639, 8666, 8675
L & Y '2F' 0—6—0	12121, 12123, 12135
MR (Kirtley) double framed '1P' 2—4—0	20002
LNW 'Cauliflower' '2F' 0—6—0	28507, 28508

16B PETERBOROUGH

LMS (Stanier) '3MT' 2—6—2T	180
MR '2P' 4—4—0	408, 410, 520, 532, 533, 546, 552, 558
LMS '2P' 4—4—0	569
MR '3P' 4—4—0	756, 767
MR '1F' 0—6—0T	1846, 1884
'Crab' 2—6—0	2754, 2764
MR '3F' 0—6—0	3253, 3317, 3319, 3371, 3651, 3652
MR '4F' 0—6—0	3854, 3859, 3861, 3864, 3898, 3920, 3921, 3957, 3980, 3981
LMS '4F' 0—6—0	4097, 4152, 4155, 4172, 4174, 4218, 4238, 4239, 4273, 4293, 4296, 4458, 4476, 4509, 4518, 4519, 4521, 4522
MR '3F' 0—6—0T	7202
LMS '3F' 0—6—0T	7269, 7270, 7566, 7622

16C KIRKBY IN ASHFIELD

MR '2P' 4–4–0	409, 458, 482
LMS '2P' 4–4–0	568, 630
MR '2F' 0–6–0	3023, 3139, 3424
MR '3F' 0–6–0	3494, 3572, 3578, 3759, 3773
MR '4F' 0–6–0	3894, 3895, 3907, 3918, 4005, 4021
LMS '4F' 0–6–0	4082, 4113, 4140, 4202, 4205, 4206, 4268, 4415, 4463, 4472, 4589
Stanier '8F' 2–8–0	8000, 8007, 8009, 8027, 8029, 8092, 8096, 8097, 8098, 8100, 8104, 8108, 8109, 8114, 8166, 8191, 8192, 8193, 8214, 8215, 8223, 8224, 8225, 8267, 8268, 8269, 8270, 8272, 8378, 8379, 8382, 8383, 8392, 8393, 8608, 8616, 8641

16D MANSFIELD

MR '2P' 4–4–0	424, 503
MR '1P' 0–4–4T	1297, 1341, 1350
MR '1F' 0–6–0T	1771, 1885
LTSR '2P' 4–4–2T	2093, 2098
LTSR '3P' 4–4–2T	2122, 2125, 2129, 2140, 2143, 2144
MR '2F' 0–6–0	22935
MR '3F' 0–6–0	3193, 3239, 3381, 3431, 3587, 3634, 3762, 3765, 3802
MR '4F' 0–6–0	3874, 3983, 3997, 4004
LMS '4F' 0–6–0	4394
Stanier '8F' 2–8–0	8622, 8643

17A DERBY

LMS (Stanier) '3MT' 2–6–2T	90, 98, 111, 118
MR '2P' 4–4–0	378, 407, 418, 513, 516
LMS '2P' 4–4–0	632
MR '3P' 4–4–0	734, 735, 743, 760, 775
MR '4P' 4–4–0	1000, 1003, 1033
LMS '4P' 4–4–0	930, 1057, 1059, 1060, 1083
MR '1P' 0–4–4T	1252, 1337, 1361, 1370, 1373, 1404, 1408, 1426, 1429
MR '0F' 0–4–0T	1535
MR '1F' 0–6–0T	1695, 1708, 1726, 1754, 1773, 1779, 1788, 1795, 1833, 1847
LMS (Stanier) '4MT' 2–6–4T	2547
'Crab' 2–6–0	2758, 2774, 2847, 2870
MR '2F' 0–6–0	3083, 3121, 3123, 3141, 3175, 3196, 3230, 3264, 3353, 3526, 3536, 3545, 3725, 22934, 22943, 22958, 22959, 22982
MR '3F' 0–6–0	3191, 3200, 3312, 3315, 3323, 3364, 3368, 3370, 3459, 3496, 3548, 3550, 3584, 3598, 3735, 3745, 3763, 3776
MR '4F' 0–6–0	3838, 3839, 3840, 3881, 4024
LMS '4F' 0–6–0	4195, 4214, 4409, 4419, 4420, 4432, 4542, 4565, 4566
Stanier '5MT' 4–6–0	4809, 4815, 4818, 4819, 4839, 4851, 5088, 5261, 5407
'Jubilee' 4–6–0	5602, 5609, 5636, 5640, 5649, 5656, 5679, 5696, 5699
Stanier '8F' 2–8–0	8008, 8074, 8265, 8390, 8647, 8654
MR double framed '2F' 0–6–0	22849

17B BURTON

LMS (Stanier) '3MT' 2–6–2T	142, 146
MR '2P' 4–4–0	364, 395, 426, 436, 456, 500, 525
LMS '2P' 4–4–0	631
MR '1P' 0–4–4T	1357, 1424
MR '0F' 0–4–0ST	1516, 1523
MR '0F' 0–4–0T	1536
MR '1F' 0–6–0T	1718, 1749, 1770, 1839, 1859, 1865
LTSR '2P' 4–4–2T	2094, 2095
'Crab' 2–6–0	2757, 2763, 2767, 2768, 2846, 2898
MR '2F' 0–6–0	3055, 3360, 3537, 3632, 3646, 3703, 3744, 22924, 22979, 22984
MR '3F' 0–6–0	3214, 3244, 3247, 3256, 3286, 3306, 3340, 3388, 3395, 3582, 3608, 3619, 3623, 3646, 3709, 3744, 3815

MR '4F' 0–6–0	3837, 3847, 3916, 3930, 3938, 3976, 4002
LMS '4F' 0–6–0	4035, 4046, 4048, 4087, 4100, 4124, 4166, 4170, 4171, 4226, 4265, 4270, 4295, 4316, 4428, 4429, 4433, 4434, 4435, 4436, 4482, 4526, 4527, 4528, 4551, 4585, 4597, 4598, 4599, 4600
Kitson '0F' 0–4–0ST	7000
MR '3F' 0–6–0T	7233, 7253, 7257
LMS '3F' 0–6–0T	7464, 7641, 7643, 7646
L & YR '0F' 0–4–0ST	11217, 11235
CR '0F' 0–4–0ST	16020
MR double framed '2F' 0–6–0	22822

17C COALVILLE

LMS (Stanier) '3MT' 2–6–2T	79
MR '2P' 4–4–0	541
MR '1F' 0–6–0T	1815
MR '2F' 0–6–0	2989, 3001, 3176, 3229, 3434, 3437, 3445
MR '3F' 0–6–0	3429, 3682, 3779, 3780
MR '4F' 0–6–0	3835, 3865, 3872, 3905
LMS '4F' 0–6–0	4085, 4103, 4109, 4123, 4148, 4227, 4252, 4260, 4279, 4539
Stanier '8F' 2–8–0	8106, 8107, 8273

17D ROWSLEY

LMS (Stanier) '3MT' 2–6–2T	119, 169
MR '3P' 4–4–0	711, 741
LMS '4P' 4–4–0	1049
MR '1F' 0–6–0T	1700, 1875
'Crab' 2–6–0	2756, 2760, 2845, 2872, 2873, 2874, 2902
MR '2F' 0–6–0	3027, 3045, 3109, 3113, 3116, 3119, 3127, 3131, 3153, 3270, 3372, 3485, 3492, 3543, 3603, 3616
MR '3F' 0–6–0	3290, 3338, 3342, 3778
MR '4F' 0–6–0	3925, 3955, 4017, 4018
LMS '4F' 0–6–0	4050, 4101, 4163, 4168, 4209, 4246, 4249, 4262, 4263, 4430, 4540, 4588
LMS '3F' 0–6–0T	7274, 7457, 7459, 7460, 7461, 7679
NLR '1F' 0–6–0T	27505, 27515, 27527, 27530

18A TOTON

SDJR '2P' 4–4–0	325
MR '2P' 4–4–0	383, 400, 406, 422, 526
MR '2F' 0–6–0	2993, 3000, 3003, 3050, 3071, 3079, 3108, 3134, 3154, 3420, 3617, 22921, 22932, 22963, 22974, 22983
MR '3F' 0–6–0	3188, 3211, 3212, 3259, 3287, 3305, 3327, 3405, 3453, 3469, 3482, 3499, 3583, 3599, 3629, 3631, 3633, 3650, 3668, 3753, 3787, 3793, 3794, 3795, 3798, 3799, 3803, 3804, 3805, 3810, 3816, 3817, 3818, 3819, 3820, 3821, 3823, 3824, 3825, 3826, 3827, 3828, 3831, 3832, 3833, 3834
MR '4F' 0–6–0	3885, 3891, 3892, 3901, 3914, 3917, 3923, 3929, 3939, 3961, 3970, 3972, 3974, 3975, 3979, 3988, 3990, 4011, 4012
LMS '4F' 0–6–0	4051, 4052, 4089, 4091, 4106, 4133, 4136, 4150, 4156, 4157, 4196, 4233, 4241, 4250, 4317, 4376, 4475, 4547, 4583
Diesel Electric 0–6–0	7083, 7084, 7085, 7089, 7091
MR '3F' 0–6–0T	7243
LMS '3F' 0–6–0T	7447, 7449, 7454, 7551, 7555, 7623, 7630
Beyer-Garratt 2–6–0/0–6–2	7967, 7969, 7970, 7972, 7974, 7975, 7976, 7977, 7978, 7979, 7981, 7982, 7985, 7986, 7987, 7988, 7989, 7991, 7994, 7995, 7996, 7998, 7999
Stanier '8F' 2–8–0	8002, 8004, 8033, 8037, 8075, 8112, 8117, 8119, 8133, 8142, 8144, 8168, 8178, 8182, 8194, 8196, 8197, 8199, 8200, 8201, 8202, 8203, 8204, 8205, 8221, 8304, 8330, 8348, 8349, 8350, 8361, 8362, 8384, 8385, 8386, 8387, 8388, 8490, 8606, 8607, 8615, 8618,

	8636, 8637, 8638, 8662, 8672, 8681, 8683, 8684, 8685, 8696, 8703
LNW 'Cauliflower' '2F' 0–6–0	28512, 28619

18B WESTHOUSES

MR '2P' 4–4–0	414
MR '2F' 0–6–0	2995, 2996, 3044, 3227
MR '3F' 0–6–0	3235, 3254, 3266, 3331, 3379, 3580
MR '4F' 0–6–0	3850, 3860, 3866, 3867, 3880, 3882, 3966, 4014
LMS '4F' 0–6–0	4130, 4188, 4191, 4243, 4321
LMS '3F' 0–6–0T	7466
Stanier '8F' 2–8–0	8011, 8056, 8057. 8060, 8063, 8076, 8083, 8102, 8115, 8118, 8125, 8136, 8212, 8280, 8333, 8342, 8353, 8358, 8391, 8494, 8495, 8620, 8621, 8623, 8650, 8661

18C HASLAND

MR '2P' 4–4–0	337, 370, 466, 490, 491, 506, 555, 556, 557
MR '0F' 0–4–0ST	1518
MR '0F' 0–4–0T	1531, 1532
MR '1F' 0–6–0T	1871, 1873
LTSR '2P' 4–4–2T	2102, 2108
MR '3F' 0–6–0	3219, 3318, 3454, 3510, 3622, 3769, 3771, 3774
MR '4F' 0–6–0	3856, 3890, 3936, 3959, 3968
LMS '4F' 0–6–0	4053, 4054, 4162, 4244, 4274, 4288, 4294, 4410
Kitson '0F' 0–4–0ST	7003, 7004
LMS '3F' 0–6–0T	7272, 7278, 7423, 7426, 7535
Beyer Garratt 2–6–0/0–6–2	7968, 7971, 7973, 7980, 7983, 7984, 7990, 7992, 7993, 7997

18D STAVELEY

MR '0F' 0–4–0T	1528, 1529, 1533, 1534
MR '1F' 0–6–0T	1710, 1711, 1747, 1752, 1753, 1755, 1763, 1802, 1803, 1804
MR '2F' 0–6–0	3114, 22967
MR '3F' 0–6–0	3224, 3234, 3240, 3242, 3252, 3292, 3294, 3297, 3298, 3299, 3308, 3309, 3310, 3386, 3406, 3515, 3524, 3546, 3575, 3751, 3809
MR '4F' 0–6–0	3857, 3862, 3863, 3993
LMS '4F' 0–6–0	4066, 4070, 4104, 4122, 4129, 4147, 4154, 4182, 4210
LMS '3F' 0–6–0T	7424, 7455, 7625, 7626, 7627, 7628
Stanier '8F' 2–8–0	8010, 8053, 8054, 8064, 8111, 8120, 8122, 8179, 8195, 8210, 8213, 8332, 8341, 8493, 8609, 8652, 8653, 8663, 8686

19A SHEFFIELD

SDJR '2P' 4–4–0	324
MR '2P' 4–4–0	362, 401, 468
MR '3P' 4–4–0	716, 728, 729, 731, 765
MR '4P' 4–4–0	1016
LMS '4P' 4–4–0	1084, 1181
MR '1F' 0–6–0T	1768, 1855, 1857, 1891
'Crab' 2–6–0	2761, 2769, 2797, 2904
MR '2F' 0–6–0	2992, 3031, 3048, 3066, 3096, 3101, 3118, 3126, 3140, 3343, 3425, 3470, 3512, 3689, 22950, 22951, 22970
MR '3F' 0–6–0	3241, 3334, 3468, 3595, 3596, 3605, 3607, 3661, 3662, 3683, 3715, 3749, 3755, 3772, 3775
MR '4F' 0–6–0	3844, 4006
LMS '4F' 0–6–0	4165, 4211, 4212, 4284, 4285, 4334, 4355, 4418, 4426, 4437, 4550, 4568, 4572, 4573
Stanier '5MT' 4–6–0	4858, 4859, 5262
MR '3F' 0–6–0T	7236
LMS '3F' 0–6–0T	7328, 7513, 7545, 7548, 7624
Stanier '8F' 2–8–0	8017, 8105, 8219, 8284, 8314, 8315, 8316, 8642

19B MILLHOUSES

LMS (Stanier) '3MT' 2-6-2T	82, 113, 139
MR '2P' 4-4-0	487, 545
LMS '2P' 4-4-0	564
MR '4P' 4-4-0	1019, 1026, 1037
LMS '4P' 4-4-0	1047, 1062, 1063, 1072, 1075, 1078, 1079
MR '1P' 0-4-4T	1286, 1295, 1342, 1396, 1403
MR '2F' 0-6-0	3666, 3746
Stanier '5MT' 4-6-0	4860, 5263
'Jubilee' 4-6-0	5554, 5573, 5585, 5596, 5607, 5621, 5626, 5664

19C CANKLOW

MR '2P' 4-4-0	485
MR '3P' 4-4-0	726, 727
MR '1F' 0-6-0T	1797, 1813, 1835, 1869
LTSR '2P' 4-4-2T	2092
MR '2F' 0-6-0	3002, 3047, 3056, 3057, 3058, 3144, 3167, 3171, 3220, 3382, 3391, 3466, 3493, 3533, 3577, 3635, 3642, 3739, 22900, 22926, 22965, 22969, 22975
MR '3F' 0-6-0	3174, 3208, 3243, 3265, 3300, 3325, 3660, 3664, 3669, 3747, 3813, 3814
MR '4F' 0-6-0	3843, 3906, 3927, 3946, 3950, 4013, 4015, 4026
LMS '4F' 0-6-0	4036, 4071, 4127, 4128, 4173, 4477, 4537, 4569
LMS '3F' 0-6-0T	7546, 7547
Stanier '8F' 2-8-0	8026, 8065, 8067, 8209, 8317, 8682
LMS 0-8-0	9631

19D HEATON MERSEY

LMS (Stanier) '3MT' 2-6-2T	94, 95
MR '2P' 4-4-0	453, 544
MR '2F' 0-6-0	3027, 3078, 22929
MR '3F' 0-6-0	3811
MR '4F' 0-6-0	3908, 3945, 4010
LMS '4F' 0-6-0	4090, 4110, 4111, 4117, 4142, 4144, 4177, 4178, 4237, 4271, 4286, 4407, 4421
Stanier '8F' 2-8-0	8089, 8099, 8116, 8135, 8190, 8208, 8216, 8220, 8329, 8667, 8676, 8697

19E BELLE VUE

MR '1F' 0-6-0T	1690, 1702, 1748, 1756, 1814
'Crab' 2-6-0	2765, 2896
MR '3F' 0-6-0	3361, 3574, 3612, 3630, 3638, 3723, 3756
MR '4F' 0-6-0	3836, 3900, 3943, 3952, 3985, 4022, 4023, 4025
LMS '4F' 0-6-0	4040, 4114, 4261, 4371, 4459, 4552
Stanier '5MT' 4-6-0	4802, 4803, 4845, 5031, 5284
LMS '3F' 0-6-0T	7336, 7440, 7512

19G TRAFFORD PARK

LMS (Stanier) '3MT' 2-6-2T	88, 89, 93, 168
MR '4P' 4-4-0	1014, 1021, 1024
LMS '4P' 4-4-0	1052, 1066, 1076
LMS '4F' 0-6-0	4236
Stanier '5MT' 4-6-0	4826
'Jubilee' 4-6-0	5570, 5572, 5628, 5655
Stanier '8F' 2-8-0	8680, 8698

20A LEEDS (HOLBECK)

MR '2P' 4-4-0	432, 455, 489, 519, 562
LMS '2P' 4-4-0	567, 633
MR '3P' 4-4-0	720, 725, 736, 748, 758, 759
MR '4P' 4-4-0	1018, 1040
LMS '4P' 4-4-0	910, 927, 928, 1069, 1087, 1117, 1137, 1144
MR '1P' 0-4-4T	1247, 1315, 1422
MR '1F' 0-6-0T	1745
'Crab' 2-6-0	2850
MR '3F' 0-6-0	3401, 3665
MR '4F' 0-6-0	3878, 4020
LMS '4F' 0-6-0	4044, 4151, 4431, 4501
Stanier '5MT' 4-6-0	4820, 4821, 4823, 4824, 4828, 4847, 4848, 4849, 4850, 4853, 4854, 4856, 4857, 5040, 5043, 5092, 5093, 5187, 5260, 5276, 5280, 5289
'Patriot' 4-6-0	5534, 5535, 5538
'Jubilee' 4-6-0	5558, 5562, 5565, 5568, 5569, 5587, 5589, 5594, 5597, 5598, 5604, 5605, 5608, 5611, 5619, 5620, 5648, 5651, 5658, 5659, 5660, 5694
'Royal Scot' 4-6-0	6103, 6108, 6109, 6117
MR '3F' 0-6-0T	7254
LMS '3F' 0-6-0T	7418
Stanier '8F' 2-8-0	8001, 8073, 8090, 8110, 8121, 8124, 8126, 8127, 8128, 8129, 8137, 8138, 8143, 8176, 8177, 8306
L & YR '2P' 2-4-2T	10622, 10630, 10634, 10689, 10880

20B STOURTON

MR '1F' 0-6-0T	1738, 1739, 1759, 1794, 1816, 1838, 1842, 1890
'Crab' 2-6-0	2759, 2771, 2798, 2816, 2897
MR '2F' 0-6-0	2998, 3039, 3384, 3519, 3539, 3590
MR '3F' 0-6-0	3137, 3267, 3392, 3449, 3456, 3476, 3579, 3636, 3678, 3681, 3705, 3731, 3737, 22945, 22976, 22977
MR '4F' 0-6-0	3851, 3852, 3855, 3931, 3987, 3989, 3998
LMS '4F' 0-6-0	4037, 4094, 4245, 4400, 4467, 4564, 4605
MR '3F' 0-6-0T	7228
LMS '3F' 0-6-0T	7271, 7420, 7463, 7538
Stanier '8F' 2-8-0	8140, 8276, 8277, 8283, 8354, 8640
LMS '7F' 0-8-0	9537, 9540

20C ROYSTON

This shed was detailed in the Introduction of Volume One of this series as the only entirely new shed on the LMS having a post-Grouping origin. For completeness, its 1945 allocation was also listed in Volume One. It was, of course, part of the Midland Division of the LMS and, once again for the sake of completeness, the 1945 complement is also listed here, with the sheds of Midland origin.

Stanier '3MT' 2-6-2T	96, 112, 120
MR '2P' 4-4-0	444, 514
LMS '4P' 4-4-0	1045, 1081
MR '1P' 0-4-4T	1368, 1395, 1428
Fowler '4MT' 2-6-4T	2326, 2336
Stanier '4MT' 2-6-4T	2551
'Crab' 2-6-0	2770, 2784, 2827, 2857
MR '2F' 0-6-0	2988, 3064, 3451, 3732, 22927, 22940
MR '3F' 0-6-0	3233, 3250, 3332, 3341, 3446, 3448, 3509, 3553, 3789
MR '4F' 0-6-0	3919, 3942, 3991, 4003
LMS '4F' 0-6-0	4141, 4143, 4161, 4446
LMS '3F' 0-6-0T	7421, 7448, 7462, 7581, 7634
Stanier '8F' 2-8-0	8035, 8062, 8095, 8103, 8113, 8161, 8162, 8169, 8376, 8377, 8677, 8700, 8701
L & Y '2P' 2-4-2T	10633

20D NORMANTON

LMS (Stanier) '3MT' 2-6-2T	140, 183
MR '2P' 4-4-0	480, 521
LMS '4P' 4-4-0	1067, 1068
MR '1F' 0-6-0T	1686, 1778, 1844
'Crab' 2-6-0	2747, 2895
MR '3F' 0-6-0	3156, 3301, 3497, 3514, 3639, 3656, 3714, 3742, 3770
MR '4F' 0-6-0	3871, 3903, 3913, 3963
LMS '4F' 0-6-0	4098, 4099, 4153, 4179, 4216, 4217, 4290, 4335, 4336, 4337, 4338, 4404, 4562, 4570, 4586, 4603, 4604

20E MANNINGHAM

LMS '3F' 0-6-0T	7334, 7335, 7405
Stanier '8F' 2-8-0	8036, 8084, 8101, 8123, 8130, 8131, 8139, 8146, 8160, 8266, 8271, 8274, 8352, 8357, 8394, 8395, 8396, 8670, 8702
L & YR '2P' 2-4-2T	10621, 10625, 10686, 10901, 10903
L & YR '2F' 0-6-0	12089, 12095, 12108, 12114, 12252, 12258
L & YR '4F' 0-6-0	12559

LMS (Stanier) '3MT' 2-6-2T	184
MR '2P' 4-4-0	391
MR '4P' 4-4-0	1004, 1043
LMS '4P' 4-4-0	1048
MR '1P' 0-4-4T	1255, 1413
LMS (Fowler) '4MT' 2-6-4T	2340
LMS (Stanier) '4MT' 2-6-4T	2545, 2548, 2549
'Crab' 2-6-0	2762
MR '2F' 0-6-0	3677
MR '3F' 0-6-0	3351, 3783
LMS '2P' 0-4-4T	6400, 6401, 6402, 6403, 6404
MR '3F' 0-6-0T	7255
LMS '3F' 0-6-0T	7417, 7419
L & YR '2P' 2-4-2T	10631, 10636, 10681, 10714

20F SKIPTON

SDJR '2P' 4-4-0	323
MR '2P' 4-4-0	351, 359, 452, 484
MR '1P' 0-4-4T	1253, 1275, 1277, 1366
MR '1F' 0-6-0T	1681, 1751, 1767, 1820
MR '2F' 0-6-0	3037, 3052, 3477, 3554
MR '3F' 0-6-0	3251, 3295, 3337, 3558, 3784
MR '4F' 0-6-0	3893, 3960, 3984, 3999, 4000, 4007
LMS '4F' 0-6-0	4041, 4197, 4222, 4276, 4277, 4282, 4299, 4579
Stanier '8F' 2-8-0	8081
L & YR '2P' 2-4-2T	10623, 10671, 10795

20G HELLIFIELD

LMS (Stanier) '3MT' 2-6-2T	155
MR '2P' 4-4-0	459, 470, 472
MR '4P' 4-4-0	1006
LMS '4P' 4-4-0	932, 1056, 1080
MR '1P' 0-4-4T	1430
'Crab' 2-6-0	2893
MR '2F' 0-6-0	3352
MR '3F' 0-6-0	3173, 3186, 3226, 3231, 3335, 3585, 3586, 3781
MR '4F' 0-6-0	3904, 3944
LMS '4F' 0-6-0	4149, 4555, 4571
Stanier '8F' 2-8-0	8005, 8145, 8189
L & YR '2P' 2-4-2T	10842, 10896, 10899

20H LANCASTER

MR '2P' 4-4-0	353, 488
LMS '2P' 4-4-0	565
MR '4P' 4-4-0	1005, 1022, 1044
LMS '4P' 4-4-0	931, 1065, 1095
MR '1P' 0-4-4T	1358
MR '3F' 0-6-0	3187, 3293, 3307, 3330
LMS '4F' 0-6-0	4032, 4201, 4280, 4405, 4468, 4554, 4556
LMS '3F' 0-6-0T	7381, 7468, 7469, 7470, 7471, 7532
Stanier '8F' 2-8-0	8055

21A SALTLEY

LMS (Stanier) '3MT' 2-6-2T	74, 97, 117, 175
SDJR '2P' 4-4-0	326
MR '2P' 4-4-0	385, 463, 486, 493, 505, 509, 511, 512

MR '3P' 4—4—0	715, 745
MR '4P' 4—4—0	1015, 1029, 1035
LMS '4P' 4—4—0	1055, 1064
MR '1P' 0—4—4T	1338, 1367, 1411
MR '1F' 0—6—0T	1682, 1777, 1856, 1879
LMS (Fowler) '4MT' 2—6—4T	2327
LMS (Stanier) '4MT' 2—6—4T	2546, 2554
'Crab' 2—6—0	2790, 2793, 2799, 2818, 2822, 2824, 2825, 2826, 2829, 2900, 2903
MR '2F' 0—6—0	2994, 3085, 3103, 3110, 3138, 3311, 3432, 3473, 3516, 3527, 3535, 3592, 3699, 3758, 22946, 22947, 22953, 22955
MR '3F' 0—6—0	3201, 3203, 3223, 3225, 3277, 3284, 3321, 3336, 3339, 3359, 3374, 3433, 3435, 3441, 3443, 3484, 3490, 3491, 3522, 3523, 3529, 3531, 3540, 3568, 3621, 3624, 3644, 3667, 3674, 3680, 3684, 3686, 3690, 3698, 3767, 3812
MR '4F' 0—6—0	3845, 3879, 3911, 3912, 3940, 3941, 3949, 3951, 3986
LMS '4F' 0—6—0	4049, 4084, 4088, 4092, 4137, 4139, 4145, 4184, 4185, 4186, 4190, 4200, 4203, 4207, 4213, 4224, 4248, 4304, 4327, 4333, 4406, 4413, 4427, 4515, 4516, 4520, 4524, 4525, 4538, 4545, 4567, 4591
Stanier '5MT' 4—6—0	4811, 4813, 4814, 4840, 4841, 4842, 4852, 5186, 5265, 5268, 5269, 5273, 5274, 5447
'Jubilee' 4—6—0	5641, 5709
MR '3F' 0—6—0T	7239, 7249
LMS '3F' 0—6—0T	7273, 7276, 7425, 7436, 7443, 7638, 7639
Stanier '8F' 2—8—0	8351, 8389, 8669

LMS '7F' 0—8—0	9672, 9673, 9674
MR double framed '2F' 0—6—0	22846

21B BOURNVILLE

LMS (Stanier) '3MT' 2—6—2T	105, 173, 179
MR '2P' 4—4—0	439, 517
LMS '4P' 4—4—0	917, 934, 1073, 1077
MR '1F' 0—6—0T	1699
LMS (Fowler) '4MT' 2—6—4T	2337, 2342, 2373
LMS (Stanier) '4MT' 2—6—4T	2559
MR '3F' 0—6—0	3316, 3355, 3463, 3562, 3675, 3687
LMS '4F' 0—6—0	4138, 4289
MR double framed '2F' 0—6—0	22579, 22630, 22818, 22834, 22853, 22863

21C BROMSGROVE

MR 0—10—0 Banker	2290
MR '2F' 0—6—0	3099, 3130
MR '3F' 0—6—0T	7234
LMS '3F' 0—6—0T	7301, 7303, 7305, 7308, 7313, 7565

22A BRISTOL

LMS (Stanier) '3MT' 2—6—2T	174
MR '2P' 4—4—0	499, 553
LMS '2P' 4—4—0	601
MR '4P' 4—4—0	1025, 1028, 1030

LMS '4P' 4—4—0	935, 1046, 1053, 1058
MR '1P' 0—4—4T	1389, 1397
MR '1F' 0—6—0T	1706, 1874, 1876
MR '2F' 0—6—0	3090, 3094, 3517, 3593, 3712, 3727
MR '3F' 0—6—0	3178, 3180, 3181, 3204, 3228, 3419, 3436, 3439, 3444, 3464
MR '4F' 0—6—0	3853, 3928, 3953
LMS '4F' 0—6—0	4112, 4135, 4169, 4411, 4422, 4424, 4466, 4534, 4535, 4536
Stanier '5MT' 4—6—0	4804, 4805, 4812, 4843, 5272
'Jubilee' 4—6—0	5557, 5590, 5612, 5618, 5622, 5627, 5629, 5652, 5657, 5665
LMS Sentinel 0—4—0	7190
LMS '3F' 0—6—0T	7544, 7550, 7678
L & YR '0F' 0—4—0ST	11212

22B GLOUCESTER

MR '2P' 4—4—0	423, 437, 523, 530
MR '4P' 4—4—0	1001, 1027, 1036
LMS '4P' 4—4—0	1097
MR '1P' 0—4—4T	1303, 1330, 1353, 1365, 1375, 1390
MR '0F' 0—4—0T	1530, 1537
MR '1F' 0—6—0T	1720, 1742, 1870, 1878
'Crab' 2—6—0	2812
MR '2F' 0—6—0	3062, 3695
MR '3F' 0—6—0	3213, 3527, 3258, 3263, 3273, 3344, 3373, 3427, 3462, 3506, 3507, 3604, 3645, 3658, 3754, 3788, 3791
MR '4F' 0—6—0	3846, 3924, 3932, 3935, 3964, 3978
LMS '4F' 0—6—0	4045, 4167, 4175, 4269, 4279, 4553, 4576
MR '3F' 0—6—0T	7237
LMS '3F' 0—6—0T	7619, 7620, 7635

— M.R. 1920 ALLOCATION LIST —

1 DERBY

2—4—0	4, 5, 74, 77, 201, 203, 205, 236, 237, 238, 239
4—4—0	328, 488, 490, 491, 492, 493, 494, 495, 496, 497, 498, 499, 500, 501, 502, 503, 504
4—2—2	600, 644
Cl.3 4—4—0	751, 754, 756, 757, 759, 760, 761, 763, 765, 766, 767, 768, 769, 770, 773, 776, 777, 778, 779
0—4—4T	1428, 1429
0—4—0T	1501, 1512, 1515, 1526, 1527
0—6—0T	1644, 1645, 1646, 1795, 1797, 1834, 1839, 1865
0—6—4T	2016, 2020
0—6—0	2401, 2660, 2737, 2738, 2739, 2740, 2741, 2844, 2845, 2847, 2849, 2850, 2852, 2853, 2854, 2855, 2856, 2858, 2859, 2865, 2867
0—6—0	3056, 3068, 3088, 3193, 3196, 3218, 3219, 3227, 3229, 3230, 3312, 3315, 3395, 3396, 3397, 3399, 3401, 3488, 3489, 3600, 3603, 3613, 3770, 3816, 3817, 3818, 3878, 3879
C.M.E. 0—4—4T	1210, 1215

2 BURTON

2—4—0	7, 8, 9, 13, 200, 241
0—4—4T	1248, 1249, 1332, 1333
0—4—0T	1500, 1504, 1516, 1519
0—6—0T	1600, 1601, 1602, 1604, 1625, 1758, 1770, 1771, 1772, 1774, 1833, 1880, 1881
0—6—0	2395, 2398, 2466, 2469, 2479, 2544, 2567, 2581, 2688, 2701, 2742, 2743, 2744, 2801, 2802, 2803, 2824, 2825, 2832, 2833
0—6—0	2953, 3051, 3052, 3053, 3055, 3057, 3061, 3067, 3069, 3335, 3360, 3362, 3472, 3478, 3537, 3539, 3596, 3623, 3641, 3642, 3643, 3646, 3647, 3654, 3655, 3657, 3658, 3685

3 BIRMINGHAM

2—4—0	1, 18, 19, 23, 24, 25, 39, 80, 93, 96, 120, 121, 126, 173, 174, 175, 176, 177, 198, 281
4—4—0	375, 395, 405, 429, 430, 431, 435, 439, 505, 507, 508, 509, 510, 511, 512, 514, 515

0—4—4T	1226, 1247, 1251, 1253, 1323, 1324, 1327, 1328, 1386, 1387, 1391
0—6—0T	1643, 1647, 1649, 1740, 1741, 1742, 1756, 1757, 1759, 1773, 1879
0—6—4T	2014, 2015, 2023, 2027, 2028, 2031, 2032, 2033, 2035, 3036, 3037, 3038, 3039
0—6—0	2302, 2314, 2320, 2327, 2334, 2335, 2336, 2337, 2340, 2347, 2349, 2353, 2356, 2357, 2359, 2360, 2363, 2402, 2413, 2416, 2457, 2467, 2470, 2474, 2559, 2582, 2593, 2600, 2625, 2627, 2629, 2674, 2675, 2676, 2677, 2678, 2680, 2686, 2697, 2702, 2745, 2746, 2747, 2748, 2749, 2813
0—6—0	2934, 2956, 2957, 3063, 3065, 3066, 3070, 3074, 3077, 3084, 3104, 3154, 3156, 3171, 3173, 3223, 3277, 3352, 3373, 3392, 3425, 3431, 3432, 3433, 3520, 3521, 3522, 3523, 3524, 3525, 3526, 3527, 3529, 3530, 3531, 3532, 3533, 3534, 3535, 3536, 3541, 3542, 3543, 3544, 3551, 3595, 3624, 3640, 3644, 3653, 3671, 3672, 3673, 3674, 3675, 3677, 3678, 3679, 3683, 3686, 3687, 3688, 3689, 3690, 3691, 3692, 3693, 3694, 3695, 3696, 3697, 3698, 3699, 3700, 3703, 3704, 3726, 3728, 3785, 3786, 3787, 3822, 3823, 3827, 3828

4 WORCESTER

2—4—0	95, 97, 204, 206, 244, 279
4—4—0	371, 397
0—4—4T	1322, 1330
0—6—0T	1720, 1933, 1934, 1935, 1936, 1937, 1938, 1954, 1955
0—10—0	2290
0—6—0	2307, 2403, 2414, 2608, 2614, 2615, 2616, 2628, 2630, 2750, 2751, 2752, 2753, 2754, 2755
0—6—0	2905, 3010, 3174, 3185, 3263, 3264, 3462, 3757

5 BRECON

0—4—4T	1331, 1421, 1422, 1423
0—4—0T	1508
0—6—0T	1620, 1621, 1932, 1950, 1953, 1956, 1958, 1959
0—6—0	2465, 2599, 2848

6 UPPER BANK

0—4—4T	1424
0—4—0T	1523, 1524
0—6—0T	1629, 1632, 1633, 1634, 1635, 1636, 1637, 1638, 1648, 1676, 1677, 1775, 1776, 1777, 1778, 1779, 1816, 1817, 1818, 1819, 1824, 1832, 1850, 1851, 1852, 1853, 1860, 1864, 1930, 1931
0—6—0	3207

7 GLOUCESTER

2—4—0	2, 158, 164, 165, 166, 167, 168
4—4—0	368, 414, 420, 459, 466
4—2—2	604, 668
0—4—4T	1206, 1230, 1231, 1361, 1362, 1363, 1364
0—4—0T	1525, 1531
0—6—0T	1606, 1608, 1690, 1691, 1875, 1876, 1877, 1878
0—6—0	2411, 2412, 2415, 2471, 2505, 2541, 2570, 2571, 2572, 2578, 2594, 2595, 2596, 2672, 2681, 2683, 2692, 2792, 2860
0—6—0	3194, 3388, 3400, 3424, 3460, 3461, 3464, 3561, 3611, 3638, 3756, 3776, 3815

8 BRISTOL

2—4—0	90, 92, 104, 155, 157, 159
4—4—0	426, 506, 513, 516, 517, 518, 519, 520, 521, 522, 523, 524, 525, 526, 527, 531
4—2—2	607, 614, 635, 636, 639, 648, 661, 662, 664, 665, 670
0—4—4T	1228, 1334, 1335, 1336, 1337, 1339, 1388, 1389, 1390
0—6—0T	1870, 1871, 1872, 1873, 1874
0—6—0	2490, 2576, 2609, 2610, 2632, 2634, 2665, 2829
0—6—0	2951, 2952, 2988, 3034, 3062, 3071, 3072, 3076, 3079, 3087, 3155, 3159, 3181, 3326, 3593, 3594, 3604, 3615, 3621, 3712, 3713, 3829

9 PETERBOROUGH

2—4—0	129, 131, 132
4—2—2	602, 619, 621, 622, 637, 663
0—4—4T	1257, 1304
0—6—0T	1630, 1883, 1884, 1885
0—6—0	2423, 2424, 2425, 2426, 2427, 2428, 2431, 2434, 2435, 2436, 2438, 2440, 2441, 2442, 2443, 2445, 2526, 2700, 2705, 2789, 2828
0—6—0	2983, 2984, 2985, 3013, 3014, 3054, 3064, 3083, 3129, 3201, 3203, 3220, 3316, 3473, 3474, 3625, 3627, 3628, 3629, 3650, 3651, 3652

10 LEICESTER

2—4—0	10, 31, 32, 33, 34, 105, 107, 272, 274, 275, 276, 277, 278, 280
4—4—0	333, 529, 530, 532, 536, 537, 538, 539, 540, 541, 542, 543, 544, 545, 546, 547, 549, 550, 561
4—2—2	628, 629, 651, 652, 653, 654, 655, 656, 657, 659, 671, 673, 674
Cl.3 4—4—0	700, 701, 702, 703, 704, 707, 710, 711, 713, 749, 750, 764
0—4—4T	1365, 1366, 1367, 1368, 1369, 1370, 1743, 1744, 1825, 1826, 1827, 1828, 1829, 1830, 1831
0—6—4T	2024
0—6—0	2310, 2315, 2333, 2407, 2527, 2528, 2530, 2531, 2545, 2546, 2590, 2591, 2696, 2699, 2703, 2768, 2769, 2770, 2771, 2772, 2790, 2791, 2804, 2809, 2863
0—6—0	2947, 2948, 2949, 2954, 2955, 3049, 3050, 3081, 3089, 3105, 3106, 3107, 3108, 3109, 3110, 3111, 3113, 3114, 3115, 3116, 3117, 3120, 3121, 3122, 3123, 3124, 3125, 3126, 3127, 3128, 3160, 3161, 3162, 3163, 3164, 3165, 3166, 3167, 3190, 3192, 3200, 3202, 3204, 3205, 3206, 3208, 3209, 3210, 3211, 3213, 3255, 3355, 3407, 3409, 3411, 3412, 3413, 3414, 3415, 3416, 3417, 3418, 3419, 3420, 3421, 3422, 3423, 3434, 3463, 3558, 3648, 3649, 3804, 3805, 3824, 3825, 3826, 3839, 3930, 3931, 3932, 3933, 3934

11 WIGSTON

2—4—0	76, 94, 194, 195, 197
0—4—4T	1229, 1259
0—6—0T	1631, 1733
0—6—0	2548, 2549, 2550, 2551, 2552, 2553, 2554, 2555, 2556, 2557, 2558, 2560, 2561, 2562, 2563, 2564, 2565, 2566, 2583, 2584, 2585, 2586, 2587, 2588, 2657, 2773, 2774, 2775, 2776
0—6—0	2938, 2939, 2940, 2941, 2942, 2943, 2944, 2945, 3403, 3404, 3437, 3467, 3563, 3682

12 KETTERING

2—4—0	30, 64, 108, 109, 130, 133, 135, 138, 212, 227, 231, 233, 234, 235, 240
4—2—2	627, 642, 666, 683, 693, 694
0—4—4T	1242
0—6—0T	1780, 1889
0—6—0	2779, 2780, 2781, 2782, 2783, 2784, 2785, 2786
0—6—0	2937, 2962, 3011, 3040, 3041, 3042, 3043, 3080, 3139, 3177, 3199, 3240, 3262, 3291, 3481, 3545, 3547, 3670

13 WELLINGBOROUGH

2—4—0	222, 223, 224, 225, 226
4—2—2	603, 640, 658, 672
0—4—4T	1241, 1252, 1260, 1329, 1372
0—6—0T	1642, 1683, 1886, 1887, 1888
0—6—0	2916, 2930, 2958, 2960, 2963, 2966, 2967, 2968, 2969, 2976, 2980, 2981, 2982, 2986, 3012, 3175, 3176, 3222, 3239, 3241, 3257, 3259, 3313, 3344, 3375, 3381, 3405, 3428, 3441, 3450, 3459, 3483, 3484, 3496, 3580, 3601, 3635, 3769, 3772, 3779, 3790, 3800, 3809, 3885, 3886, 3887, 3888, 3889, 3890, 3891, 3892, 3893, 3894, 3895, 3896, 3897, 3898, 3899, 3900, 3901, 3902, 3912, 3913, 3914, 3915, 3916, 3917, 3918, 3919, 3920, 3921, 3922, 3923, 3924, 3925, 3926, 3927, 3928, 3929

14 BEDFORD

2—4—0	53, 54, 55, 56, 57, 61, 62, 69, 89, 229, 230
4—4—0	461, 462, 533, 534, 535, 551, 552, 553, 554, 555, 556
4—2—2	618, 624, 625, 626, 634, 641, 660

15 CRICKLEWOOD

0—6—0T	1724, 1735
0—6—0	2497, 2645, 2787, 2788, 2795, 2796, 2799, 2800, 2821
0—6—0	3058, 3059, 3060, 3103, 3112, 3119, 3170, 3195, 3197, 3198, 3214, 3217, 3402, 3427, 3477, 3626, 3707, 3708

15 CRICKLEWOOD

2—4—0	35, 58, 59, 60, 115, 123, 169, 170
0—4—4T	1213, 1214, 1216, 1219, 1254, 1373, 1374, 1375, 1376, 1379, 1380, 1381, 1382, 1383, 1384, 1385
0—6—0T	1710, 1711, 1712, 1713, 1714, 1715, 1716, 1717, 1718, 1719, 1791, 1792, 1793, 1794, 1796, 1805, 1806, 1807, 1808, 1809, 1810, 1811, 1812, 1813, 1814, 1815, 1854, 1900, 1901, 1902, 1903, 1904, 1905, 1906, 1907, 1908, 1909, 1910, 1911, 1912, 1913, 1914, 1915, 1916, 1917, 1918, 1919, 1920, 1924, 1925, 1926, 1927, 1928, 1929, 1942, 1943
4—6—4T	2100, 2101, 2102, 2103, 2104, 2105, 2106, 1207
0—6—0	2931, 3150, 3256, 3260, 3261, 3289, 3508, 3554, 3555, 3559, 3560, 3564, 3565, 3566, 3567, 3605, 3606, 3607, 3608, 3609, 3659

16 KENTISH TOWN

2—4—0	15, 20, 110, 171
4—4—0	419, 528, 548, 557, 558, 559, 562
4—2—2	608, 610, 611, 612, 613, 615, 685, 687, 688, 689, 690, 691, 692
Cl.3 4—4—0	709, 712, 714, 715, 716, 717, 718, 719, 745, 746, 752, 753, 758, 762
Cpd 4—4—0	1029, 1030, 1031, 1032, 1033, 1034, 1035, 1036, 1037, 1038, 1039, 1040, 1041, 1042, 1043, 1044
0—4—4T	1200, 1201, 1202, 1203, 1204, 1205, 1207, 1208, 1209, 1211, 1212, 1217, 1218, 1220, 1221, 1222, 1223, 1224, 1225, 1234, 1283, 1284, 1285, 1294, 1311, 1312, 1313, 1314, 1315, 1316, 1317, 1318, 1319, 1320, 1321, 1371, 1377, 1378, 1426, 1427
0—6—0T	1610, 1611, 1612, 1613, 1614, 1615, 1616, 1617, 1618, 1619, 1660, 1661, 1662, 1663, 1664, 1665, 1666, 1668, 1669, 1670, 1671, 1672, 1673, 1674, 1675, 1721, 1722, 1787, 1788, 1789, 1790, 1921, 1922, 1923, 1940, 1941, 1944, 1945, 1946, 1947, 1948, 1949, 1951
0—6—0	3242, 3243, 3244, 3245, 3246, 3251, 3253, 3258, 3548, 3550, 3552, 3575, 3801, 3806, 3807, 3808

17 TOTON

2—4—0	68, 70, 72, 75, 202, 273
4—4—0	323
4—2—2	605, 630, 631, 632, 633, 646, 647, 649, 650, 681, 682, 684
0—6—0T	1624, 1640, 1641, 1700, 1701, 1702, 1703, 1704, 1705, 1706, 1707, 1708, 1709, 1856, 1858
0—6—4T	2004, 2005, 2011, 2012, 2013, 2017, 2029, 2034
0—6—0	2409, 2417, 2420, 2421, 2430, 2432, 2433, 2439, 2543, 2597, 2637, 2638, 2639, 2640, 2641, 2664, 2666, 2694, 2756, 2757, 2758, 2759, 2760, 2761, 2762, 2763, 2764, 2765, 2805, 2807, 2808, 2810, 2811, 2812, 2820, 2823
0—6—0	2908, 2917, 2987, 3178, 3212, 3225, 3231, 3236, 3300, 3301, 3303, 3304, 3306, 3317, 3318, 3321, 3322, 3323, 3327, 3328, 3330, 3331, 3332, 3334, 3336, 3339, 3340, 3341, 3342, 3379, 3390, 3408, 3426, 3435, 3436, 3439, 3440, 3443, 3444, 3446, 3449, 3557, 3573, 3719, 3753, 3771, 3774, 3775, 3831, 3835, 3836, 3837, 3838, 3839, 3840, 3841, 3842, 3843, 3844, 3845, 3846, 3847, 3848, 3849, 3850, 3851, 3852, 3853, 3854, 3855, 3856, 3857, 3858, 3859, 3860, 3861, 3862, 3863, 3864, 3865, 3866, 3867, 3868, 3869, 3870, 3871, 3872, 3873, 3874, 3875, 3876, 3877, 3880, 3881, 3882, 3883, 3884, 3903, 3904, 3905, 3906, 3907, 3908, 3909, 3910, 3911

18 NOTTINGHAM

2—4—0	16, 17, 26, 63, 67, 98, 102, 113, 147, 148, 149, 150, 160, 161, 162, 163, 172, 178, 179, 180, 181, 183, 184
4—4—0	403, 404, 406, 407, 408, 409, 410, 411, 415, 416, 417, 418, 421, 422, 423, 424, 425, 427, 428, 450, 457, 483, 484, 485, 486, 487, 560
4—2—2	675, 677, 678, 679
Cl.3 4—4—0	720, 721, 722, 723, 730, 733, 738, 774, 775
0—4—4T	1227, 1235, 1243, 1246, 1261, 1300, 1301, 1302, 1303, 1305, 1306, 1307, 1308, 1309, 1310, 1325, 1340, 1341, 1342, 1343, 1344, 1345, 1346, 1347, 1348, 1349, 1350, 1401, 1402, 1403, 1407, 1408, 1409, 1410, 1418, 1419

19 LIVERPOOL (continued, right column top)

0—4—0T	1502, 1505, 1511, 1517
0—6—0T	1626, 1627, 1682, 1684, 1685, 1686, 1687, 1688, 1689, 1845, 1846, 1847, 1848, 1849, 1895, 1896, 1897, 1898, 1899
0—6—4T	2018, 2019
0—6—0	2354, 2366, 2369, 2370, 2371, 2388, 2389, 2406, 2463, 2476, 2579, 2603, 2679, 2684, 2687, 2693, 2698, 2704, 2706, 2733, 2734, 2735, 2736, 2793, 2794, 2797, 2798, 2806, 2817, 2826, 2827, 2842, 2843
0—6—0	2959, 2964, 3073, 3075, 3096, 3187, 3228, 3235, 3248, 3249, 3319, 3320, 3363, 3364, 3365, 3366, 3367, 3368, 3369, 3370, 3371, 3372, 3374, 3376, 3377, 3378, 3380, 3382, 3383, 3384, 3385, 3458, 3494, 3510, 3511, 3514, 3515, 3517, 3518, 3571, 3572, 3574, 3577, 3578, 3582, 3583, 3584, 3585, 3586, 3587, 3588, 3589, 3590, 3591, 3592, 3597, 3598, 3599, 3729, 3759, 3760, 3761, 3762, 3763, 3764, 3767, 3768, 3810, 3811, 3812, 3813, 3814

19 LIVERPOOL

4—4—0	329, 330, 331, 332, 334, 335, 336, 337, 338
4—2—2	616, 620, 623
0—4—0T	1503, 1509, 1510
0—6—0T	1723, 1730, 1731, 1732, 1734, 1736
0—6—0	3168, 3169, 3224, 3233, 3247, 3250, 3252, 3254, 3356, 3391, 3500, 3501, 3503, 3504, 3506, 3507, 3509, 3516, 3519, 3546, 3556, 3576

20 BUXTON

2—4—0	128, 139, 140, 141, 142, 143, 144, 145, 146, 258, 260
0—4—4T	1263, 1272, 1273, 1397, 1404, 1420
0—6—0T	1695, 1696, 1697, 1957
0—6—0	2324, 2444, 2460, 2498, 2499, 2510, 2512, 2513, 2519, 2520, 2727, 2728, 2729, 2730, 2731
0—6—0	2912, 3044, 3045, 3090, 3118, 3267, 3268, 3269, 3270, 3271, 3274, 3275, 3276, 3278, 3279, 3280, 3281, 3282, 3283, 3284, 3310, 3349, 3394, 3445, 3479, 3493, 3512, 3538, 3645, 3717, 3750, 3780, 3781, 3782, 3783, 3784

21 MANCHESTER

4—4—0	339, 340, 341, 342, 343, 344, 345, 346, 347, 348, 349, 350, 351, 352, 353, 354, 355, 356, 357, 358, 398, 447
Cl.3 4—4—0	705, 706, 708, 725, 726, 727, 728, 742, 743, 747, 748
Cpd 4—4—0	1011, 1012, 1013, 1015, 1016, 1017, 1018, 1019, 1020, 1021, 1022
0—6—0T	1622, 1623, 1698, 1699, 1726, 1781, 1782, 1784, 1785
0—6—4T	2000, 2001, 2002, 2003, 2006, 2007, 2008, 2009, 2010, 2021, 2022
0—6—0	2900, 2904, 2932, 2933, 2974, 2991, 2992, 2993, 2994, 3046, 3047, 3048, 3078, 3172, 3179, 3180, 3182, 3183, 3184, 3186, 3191, 3221, 3226, 3265, 3266, 3272, 3273, 3302, 3305, 3307, 3308, 3309, 3324, 3329, 3361, 3498, 3616, 3684, 3701, 3702, 3710, 3711, 3714, 3715, 3716, 3718, 3720, 3721, 3722, 3723, 3724, 3725, 3727, 3765, 3766, 3777, 3796, 3797, 3802, 3803, 3832, 3833, 3834

22 WESTHOUSES

2—4—0	12, 99, 101, 263
0—6—0T	1798, 1836, 1837, 1838, 1839, 1840
0—6—0	2311, 2328, 2393, 2399, 2400, 2405, 2461, 2477, 2478, 2483, 2574, 2577, 2592, 2606, 2607, 2611, 2612, 2621, 2622, 2623, 2624, 2669, 2670, 2671, 2673, 2690, 2723, 2724, 2777, 2778
0—6—0	2902, 2903, 2906, 2907, 2910, 2911, 2913, 2915, 2918, 2919, 2961, 2971, 2977, 2978, 3216, 3311, 3442, 3610, 3614

23 HASLAND

2—4—0	71, 100, 103, 112, 116, 117, 118, 119, 122, 187, 188, 189, 190, 256, 257, 259, 261, 262, 266
0—4—0T	1518
0—6—0T	1799, 1800, 1801, 1802, 1803, 1804
0—6—0	2305, 2383, 2419, 2446, 2447, 2448, 2449, 2450, 2451, 2452, 2453, 2542, 2573, 2626, 2631, 2685, 2861, 2862
0—6—0	2925, 2935, 3130, 3131, 3132, 3133, 3134, 3136, 3137, 3138, 3285, 3287, 3288, 3620

24 STAVELEY

2-4-0	6
0-4-4T	1238, 1239, 1262, 1267, 1326
0-4-0T	1513, 1514, 1520, 1521, 1522, 1528, 1529, 1530, 1532
0-6-0T	1746, 1747, 1748, 1749, 1750, 1751, 1752, 1753, 1754, 1835
0-6-0	2300, 2481, 2568, 2569, 2580, 2604, 2605, 2613, 2661, 2663, 2668, 2722, 2725, 2726, 2766, 2767, 2819, 2864
0-6-0	3009, 3135, 3151, 3152, 3153, 3157, 3158, 3215, 3234, 3290, 3292, 3293, 3294, 3295, 3296, 3297, 3298, 3299, 3337, 3338, 3406, 3430, 3438, 3490, 3505, 3602, 3612, 3617, 3618, 3619, 3622, 3676, 3705, 3751

25 SHEFFIELD

2-4-0	81, 82, 83, 84, 85, 87, 185, 186, 193, 232, 264, 265, 268, 270, 271
4-4-0	300, 303, 304, 305, 306, 308, 317, 319, 320, 325, 326, 327, 369, 373, 374, 376, 377, 378, 379, 380, 381, 382, 383, 384, 385, 386, 387, 388, 389, 390, 391, 392, 393, 394, 396, 412, 413
0-4-4T	1232, 1250, 1255, 1256, 1258, 1392, 1393, 1394, 1395, 1396, 1398, 1399, 1400
0-6-0T	1639, 1694, 1755, 1796, 1855, 1857, 1861, 1862, 1863, 1866, 1867, 1868, 1869, 1890, 1891, 1892, 1893, 1894
0-6-0	2410, 2473, 2487, 2502, 2503, 2636, 2642, 2643, 2644, 2646, 2647, 2648, 2649, 2650, 2652, 2653, 2654, 2655, 2656, 2658, 2659, 2662, 2667, 2717, 2718, 2719, 2720, 2721, 2818, 2822, 2846
0-6-0	2946, 2950, 2965, 2970, 3082, 3085, 3086, 3093, 3094, 3095, 3097, 3098, 3100, 3101, 3140, 3141, 3142, 3143, 3144, 3145, 3146, 3147, 3148, 3149, 3325, 3343, 3471, 3475, 3476, 3480, 3482, 3485, 3486, 3487, 3499, 3568, 3631, 3632, 3633, 3634, 3636, 3637, 3639, 3660, 3661, 3662, 3663, 3664, 3665, 3666, 3667, 3668, 3669, 3705, 3749, 3752, 3754, 3755, 3758, 3798, 3819, 3820, 3821

26 NORMANTON

2-4-0	10, 21, 22, 36, 37, 38, 41, 153, 220
4-2-2	606, 676
0-6-0T	1678, 1729, 1737, 1738, 1739, 1761, 1844
0-6-4T	2025, 2026, 2030
0-6-0	2514, 2515, 2516, 2517, 2522, 2523, 2524, 2525, 2532, 2533, 2535, 2536, 2537, 2538, 2539, 2540, 2547, 2601, 2633, 2635, 2830, 2834, 2835, 2836, 2838, 2839, 2840, 2841, 2857, 2866
0-6-0	2926, 2936, 3015, 3020 3021, 3092, 3222, 3731, 3732, 3733, 3734, 3799

27 YORK

2-4-0	124, 191, 192, 196
4-4-0	399, 400, 401, 402

0-6-0	2617, 2618, 2619, 2620, 2715, 2716
0-6-0	3238, 3286, 3455, 3470, 3709

28 LEEDS

2-4-0	45, 46, 47, 50, 245, 246, 247, 248, 249, 250, 251, 252, 253
4-4-0	359, 360, 361, 362, 363, 364, 365, 366, 367, 370, 372, 440, 441, 473, 474, 475, 476, 477, 478, 479, 480, 481, 482
4-2-2	617, 638, 643, 645, 667, 669, 680
C13 4-4-0	724, 729, 731, 732, 734, 735, 736, 737, 739, 740, 741, 744, 755, 771, 772
Cpd 4-4-0	1000, 1001, 1002, 1003, 1004, 1005, 1006, 1007, 1008, 1009, 1014, 1027, 1028
0-4-4T	1274, 1275, 1276, 1277, 1278, 1279
0-6-0T	1655, 1657, 1692, 1728, 1745, 1760, 1762, 1763, 1764, 1765, 1766, 1783, 1841, 1842, 1843, 1882
0-6-0	2303, 2408, 2480, 2492, 2494, 2495, 2496, 2508, 2509, 2511, 2518, 2534, 2602, 2689, 2691, 2709, 2710, 2711, 2713, 2714, 2814, 2815, 2816, 2831, 2837, 2851
0-6-0	2909, 2920, 2921, 2922, 2923, 2924, 2928, 2929, 2973, 2975, 3016, 3017, 3018, 3019, 3026, 3028, 3091, 3099, 3348, 3447, 3448, 3449, 3451, 3452, 3453, 3454, 3456, 3457, 3469, 3579, 3581, 3730, 3735, 3737, 3739, 3740, 3741, 3742, 3743, 3744, 3745, 3746, 3747, 3748, 3773, 3778, 3789

29 BRADFORD

2-4-0	40, 152, 154, 217, 218, 219, 221
0-4-4T	1233, 1236, 1240, 1244, 1264, 1265, 1280, 1286, 1287, 1288, 1289, 1290, 1291, 1292, 1293, 1295, 1296, 1297, 1298, 1299, 1351, 1352, 1353, 1354, 1355, 1356, 1357, 1358, 1359, 1360
0-6-0T	1658, 1679, 1725, 1727, 1820, 1821, 1822, 1823, 1859, 1939, 1952
0-6-0	2309, 2472, 2488, 2489, 2491, 2501, 2682
0-6-0	3022, 3023, 3024, 3025, 3027, 3029, 3030, 3031, 3032, 3033, 3736, 3737, 3738

30 SKIPTON

2-4-0	11, 14, 78, 156, 207, 208, 214, 215, 216, 267, 269
4-4-0	310, 311, 314, 460, 464, 465, 467, 469, 470, 471, 472

31 CARNFORTH

2-4-0	209, 210, 211, 213
0-6-0T	1659
0-6-0	3189, 3314, 3357, 3358, 3359, 3389, 3390, 3410, 3502, 3680

0-4-4T	1266, 1268, 1269, 1270, 1271, 1411, 1412, 1413, 1414, 1415, 1417, 1430
0-6-0T	1680, 1681
0-6-0	2404, 2437, 2455, 2456, 2458, 2468, 2475, 2484, 2485, 2493, 2504, 2506, 2507, 2598, 2707
0-6-0	2914, 3036, 3037, 3038, 3039, 3188, 3237, 3333, 3345, 3346, 3347, 3350, 3351, 3353, 3354, 3387, 3429, 3453

32 LANCASTER

2-4-0	242, 243, 254, 255
4-4-0	448, 449, 451, 452, 453, 454, 455, 456
0-6-0T	1656, 1693, 1767
0-6-0	2486, 2500, 2651, 2695, 2708
0-6-0	2989, 2990, 3393

33 CARLISLE

2-4-0	49, 182, 228
4-4-0	432, 433, 434, 436, 437, 438, 442, 443, 444, 445, 446, 458, 463, 468
4-4-0	990, 991, 992, 993, 994, 995, 996, 997, 998, 999
Cpd 4-4-0	1010, 1026
0-6-0T	1650, 1651, 1652, 1653, 1654, 1768, 1769
0-6-0	2901, 2972, 2995, 2996, 2997, 2998, 2999, 3000, 3001, 3002, 3003, 3004, 3005, 3006, 3007, 3008, 3386, 3465, 3466, 3468, 3491, 3492, 3495, 3497, 3562, 3569, 3570, 3630, 3656, 3788, 3791, 3792, 3793, 3794, 3795, 3830

LT & SR

2-4-0	3, 44, 127, 134, 136, 137
0-4-4T	1405, 1406, 1416
0-6-0T	1667, 1786
4-4-2T	2110, 2111, 2112, 2113, 2114, 2115, 2116, 2117, 2118, 2119, 2120, 2121, 2122, 2123, 2124, 2125, 2126, 2127, 2128, 2129, 2130, 2131, 2132, 2133, 2134, 2135, 2136, 2137, 2138, 2139, 2140, 2141, 2142, 2143, 2144, 2145, 2146, 2147, 2148, 2149, 2150, 2151, 2152, 2153, 2154, 2155, 2156, 2157, 2158, 2159, 2160, 2161, 2162, 2163, 2164, 2165, 2166, 2167, 2168, 2169, 2170, 2171, 2172, 2173, 2174, 2175, 2176, 2177, 2178, 2179, 2180, 2181, 2182, 2183, 2184, 2185, 2186, 2187, 2188, 2189, 2190, 2191, 2192, 2193, 2194
0-6-0	2895, 2899
0-6-0	2454, 2589
0-6-0	3035, 3102, 3513, 3526

Carmarthen ex-LNWR shed, 1st June 1936. Ex-LNW locos include Nos. 6619, 6675 and, inside, 6757.   *W. A. Camwell*

Appendix and Errata to Volume One

When dealing with a subject as vast and complex as LMS engine sheds, errors will inevitably occur. We are indebted to those people who corresponded and to those colleagues who pointed out mistakes and helped 'iron out' obvious differences of opinion. We would also like to take the opportunity of apologising to those photographers who were incorrectly credited and hope the corrections listed in the following pages are of some consolation. We are particularly indebted to Mr. W. A. Camwell who brought to our attention a number of his photographs that were incorrectly credited. He not only supplied additional information and dates but was also kind enough to search out his original prints. Thus where certain views were reproduced from copy prints, we have taken the opportunity to repeat them here.

The list 'LMS sheds immediately after the Grouping' presented in Volume 1 has aroused a certain amount of interest and the authors acknowledge that its inclusion might have benefited from some additional explanation. The arrangement differs significantly from pre-Grouping listings particularly where the Midland is concerned and also from subsequent practice. The list is a 'first attempt' on the part of an anonymous officer at Derby to arrange the sheds sensibly for approval by his superiors, one obvious criteria being a proper geographic ordering. Thus Gloucester is included under Bristol etc., with apparent sub-shed status. The whole of the 1925 list was not adopted (although its old spelling mistakes are reproduced verbatim, for instance 'Blairatholl' should of course be 'Blair Atholl', Blackpool (22) should read (32) etc.) but the seeds of rearrangement are already visible. Gloucester had indeed acquired a certain dependence on Bristol in MR days, losing its repair work to the latter shed and was thus already 'sub' in this respect. Indeed it was incorporated into the Bristol district in 1935. The MR shed at Walsall Pleck had already been grouped with the Western Division, where it was to remain and Carnforth MR followed in 1926.

The unfortunate fact is that events were extremely fluid at this time, various 'power centres' were striving for dominance on the newborn LMS and in addition to shed closures (which in themselves were often protracted with 'official' closure bearing no relation to actual closure) we must add straightforward confusion and ignorance of 'foreign' systems! One can produce any number of 'lists' originating in the 1920s, and each one has its particular champions. It is rather like attempting to unravel the veritable circus of changes on BR in the last ten years or so of steam with the handicap of less documentation, virtually no first hand evidence and the burden of a 50 year time lapse. The exact status and inter-relationship of many of these sheds in the early LMS period will never be known and it is facile to imagine that they ever will.

Tebay, 14th May 1937. W. A. Camwell

Ingleton shed, 11th October 1936. In the distance is the Greta Viaduct and the Midland station. W. A. Camwell

Page 23. Bottom caption should read 'No. 45692 *Cyclops*'.

Page 28. Caption: 'Scot' should read 'Patriot'.

Page 61. Lower photo by R. Tourret not R. J. Essery.

Page 68. Top photo caption: 'Prince of Wales 4—6—0 No. 1351 (LMS 5714)' should read 'an unidentified 19″ goods 4—6—0'.

Page 107. Whilst it is correct to say Whitchurch serviced ex-works locomotives, this location only came to prominence in BR days. In LNW/LMS times Whitmore was the favoured destination.

Page 107. Bottom photo of Crewe stock shed by W. A. Camwell not B. Mathews. Date 13th October 1935. Visible are 5276, 5294, 5316, 5287 and 5380.

Page 119. Lower photo of Sheep Pasture shed by W. A. Camwell not B. Mathews. Date 29th August 1935 and showing 2—4—0T 6425 inside shed.

Page 120. Caption upper photograph: 'Box Tank' number should read '7859'.

Page 124/125. Track Plan: 'To London (Broad Street)' should read 'To South Bromley and Poplar'.

Page 144. Caption upper photograph: Date should read '1955'.

Page 146. Photo of Leighton Buzzard shed by W. A. Camwell. Date 29th November 1935. No. 9336 outside.

Page 157. Track Plan: 'To Rhyl' should read 'To Chester'.

Page 172. Photo of Oxford shed by W. A. Camwell not V. Forster. Date 4th November 1934. On shed are 6704, 7121, 8739 and 25552.

Page 189. Bottom photo of Seaton shed by W. A. Camwell not V. Forster. Date 19th May 1934. Inside shed was 2—4—2T 6739.

Page 200. Top photo of Stafford shed by W. A. Camwell not B. Mathews. Date 3rd November 1935 and visible (l. to r.) LNE 4141 *Colwick*, 8766, 28526, 5277, 25712, and right hand shed 25612, 5278 and 126.

Page 210. Centre photo of Tebay shed by W. A. Camwell not B. Mathews. Date 14th May 1937. On shed outside 6960; inside 4060, 4070, 6961, 6794, 7337/8 and 16422.

Page 219. Caption lower photograph: 'No. 54736' should read '5473'.

Page 234 and 237. 'Altringham' should read 'Altrincham'.

Page 238. Bottom photo of Carmarthen shed by W. A. Camwell not B. Mathews. Date 1st June 1936. On shed 6619, 6675 and inside 6757.

Page 240. The photograph of Doncaster is in effect of Netherfield and Colwick.

Page 241. Bottom photo of Ingleton by W. A. Camwell not B. Mathews. Date 11th October, 1936.

Page 244. 'Siddock' should read 'Siddick'.

Page 247. 1945 Allocation List: We would like to thank Mr. Vic Forster for advising us of the corrections listed below.

1C Watford: 'LNW 1F 0—4—2T' should read 'LMS Stanier 2P 0—4—4T'.
2C Northampton: 'MR 3F 0—6—0 3655' should read 'MR 2F 0—6—0'.

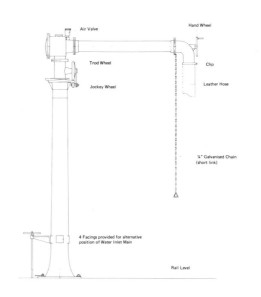

LMS WATER CRANE (from 1944 Horwich drawing).

Air Valve
Hand Wheel
Trod Wheel
Clip
Jockey Wheel
Leather Hose
¼″ Galvanised Chain (short link)
4 Facings provided for alternative position of Water Inlet Main
Rail Level

SCALE: 4 mm to 1 foot

2E Warwick: 'MR 3F 0—6—0 3738' should read 'MR 2F 0—6—0'.
2F Coventry: 'MR 3F 0—6—0 3489 and 3726' should read 'MR 2F 0—6—0'. 'MR 1F 0—6—0 22567' should read 'MR 2F 0—6—0'.
3B Bushbury: 'LNW 1P 2—6—2T 6933' and '6935' should read '0—6—2T'.
3C Walsall: 'LMS 4F 0—8—0' should read '0—6—0'.
3D Aston: '2963' and '2966' should read 'Stanier 2—6—0'.
4A Shrewsbury: 'MR 4F 0—6—0' should read 'MR 3F 0—6—0'.
9A Longsight: 'LMS 2P 4—4—0 539' should read 'MR 2P 4—4—0'.
9B Stockport: 'MR 2F 0—6—0 3218' should read 'MR 3F 0—6—0 No. 3281'.
11A Carnforth: 'LMS 3F 0—6—0T 7206-7210' should read 'LMS 3F 0—6—0T 7406, 7407, 7409, 7410, and 7605'.
20C Royston: 'MR 3F 0—6—0 3451' and '3732' should read 'MR 2F 0—6—0'.

SHEDS CLOSED BEFORE 1947.

Since Volume One went to press two sheds have come to our attention.

Birstall

In 1952 the 'old loco shed' at Birstall was reported sold to the 'local Gas Board'. Birstall was the terminus of a short branch off the LNW Leeds-Dewsbury line but no details are at present available regarding the shed and its facilities.

Cleator & Workington Railway

The Cleator & Workington Railway had a small shed and works to service a handful of locos used primarily on coal and passenger traffic. Absorbed by the LMS at grouping,

The two road shed, of the C & WR, lay west of the main line and south of Workington Central Station. The only apparent additions to the building were a small office, sited at the rear of the shed, and the extension of one of the shed roads to form a run round loop. The workshops are just visible to the left of the building in this 1930s photograph.

W. H. Whitworth

the Railway's shed accommodation was very modest, having two roads and being constructed in stone and brick.

In 1923, the railway had five locomotives, 11564 (C & W No. 6) *Brigham Hall*, 11565 (C & W No. 7) *Ponsonby Hall*, 11566 (C & W No. 8) *Hutton Hall*, 11567 (C & W No. 9) *Millgrove* and 11568 (C & W No. 10) *Skiddaw Lodge*, all 1F 0—6—0STs. It is quite probable that the shed closed on grouping, along with the joint shed at Siddick in May 1923, the locos transferring to Workington LNW a short distance away.

The engines saw little use under LMS auspices, the first being scrapped in 1926 and the last, *Skiddaw Lodge*, being sold to Hartley Main Collieries in 1932 where it remained until 1956.

The diminutive C & WR workshops.   *W. H. Whitworth*

ACKNOWLEDGEMENTS

We would like to express our thanks above all to Alan Wilson. His patience, enthusiasm, willing submission to our repeated enquiries and intimate knowledge of LMS engine sheds, has allowed us to include a wealth of detail that would otherwise have been denied us.

Our gratitude is also due to Stephen Summerson who spent innumerable hours painstakingly reading and correcting our proofs as well as contributing greatly to their content.

Bob Essery once again has figured prominently amongst our advisors. Not only did he spend much of his valuable time reading the manuscript, but was also kind enough to put his extensive photographic collection at our disposal.

John Edgington, Brian Radford, Bob Oliver and Oliver Carter also read the proofs and supplied valuable additional information.

Vic Forster spent some hours uncovering bogus loco numbers and allocation anomalies in both this and the previous volume. To him also must go our sincere thanks.

To the photographers who contributed to this volume we are particularly indebted. They are: Brian Hilton, Dick Riley, Bernard Mathews and his 'White Horse', Hugh Ballantyne, A. G. Ellis, H. C. Casserley, Ken Fairey, Tim Shuttleworth, W. Potter (who kindly loaned us his valuable negatives), Peter Winding, Bill Stubbs, N. S. Eagles, Frank Dean, Roger Griffiths, Phillip Kelley, Brian Morrison, David Banks, John Scrace, the National Railway Museum, York, the BBC Hulton Picture Library, British Railways, W. H. Whitworth, Gordon Coltas, L. Hanson, C. R. L. Coles, B. K. B. Green, L & GRP courtesy David & Charles, L. B. Lapper, Roger Carpenter (who also supplied

some of the drawings), Photomatic, Lens of Sutton, G. S. Lloyd, N. E. Preedy, R. J. Buckley, J. E. Kite, H. A. Gamble, A. Wainwright A. V. Fincham, N. R. Knight, Tony Wright, Terry Nicholls, and of course W. A. Camwell who is also mentioned elsewhere.

May we also extend our gratitude to the following people, establishments and societies for their contribution and help during the compilation of this book: Andy Hilton, photographer Birkbeck College; Kim for services rendered; R. E. Swainson, Birkbeck College; Dr. Peter Lewis, Birkbeck College, who we acknowledge for his help with certain dates; Ross Wollard who supplied the allocations; staff of Cambridge University Library, particularly Ken Winch and Roger Fairclough; Ordnance Survey, Southampton; the British Museum map room and library; Public Records Office, Kew; the LMS Society; the Midland Trust Ltd; Alec Swain; British Railways and their officials at Derby, Euston, Nottingham, Toton, Swansea, Liverpool, Preston, Manchester, Paddington and Glasgow; the staff of the Senate House Library, University of London; David Tee; Chris Turner who unselfishly supplied many references whilst pursuing his own research; Peter Webber who kindly supplied the company map and details of Tewkesbury; Robin Higgins the Reverend Awdry who kindly supplied track plan and additional information on Bromsgrove; Greg Fox; Roy Anderson; Paul Bolger; Robin Whittle; George Dow; Ron Dyer; June Judge and Paul Karau.

Last, but of course by no means least, Beverly and Wendy have again spent countless hours bashing away on the typewriter. To them both we owe a considerable debt and would like to extend our special appreciation.